Da

PLAYS ONE

AN AUDIENCE CALLED EDOUARD
LIVINGSTONE AND SECHELE
RICHARD III PART TWO
MOTOCAR

OBERON BOOKS
LONDON

An Audience Called Edouard, Richard III Part Two and *Motocar* first published in 1979 by Faber and Faber Ltd.

First published in this collection in 2000 by Oberon Books Ltd. (incorporating Absolute Classics)
521 Caledonian Road, London N7 9RH
Tel: 020 7607 3637 / Fax: 020 7607 3629
e-mail: oberon.books@btinternet.com

A catalogue record for this book is available from the British Library.

ISBN: 1 84002 076 8

Cover illustration: Andrzej Klimowski

Cover typography: Jeff Willis

Printed in Great Britain by Antony Rowe Ltd, Reading.

Contents

Introduction, 5

AN AUDIENCE CALLED EDOUARD, 9

LIVINGSTONE AND SECHELE, 71

RICHARD III PART TWO, 131

MOTOCAR, 215

INTRODUCTION

David Pownall

After seeing one of these plays (you have to guess which one), Bernard Levin, then critic for *The Times*, suggested in his review I should consider teaming up with another playwright in vogue in those days. One of us had the stagecraft and one the intelligence. (After reading these plays, you have to guess which one I lacked.) The other flawed author and I never got down to discussing this proposition. Although the contemporary appetite even then had a distinctly Jacobean flavour, his exhortation 'Beaumont and Fletcher weren't too proud' fell on deaf ears and we went our own conceited ways and have been properly damned for ignoring good advice. Twenty years later it's amusing to read Levin's off-the-cuff journalism and remember the time a furious man broke into a television studio during a live programme and knocked Bernard off his stool for destroying not his own play, but his wife's – *Savagery and Delight* it was called – with a vicious, wrecking review. What happened to her? And what happened to the unborn Beaumont and Fletcher? More to the point – what do we, who write plays for the stage, deserve? Bernard Levin or understanding spouses?

By far the most difficult thing to write, the stage play, never stops asking itself questions. The elements require a rare fusion of powers of mind and feeling. We fall short so often, changing the play to catch up with our own criticisms of it, then finding all the forces within the structure have shifted.

Yet it is the best, the sweetest, the most exciting of forms to write in when one of those performances occur – note I say <u>performances</u>, not productions, when the whole thing works. Not as you wanted it to when you wrote it – that's impossible once rehearsals begin – but when within its own existence and forces the play comes through, pushing through your fears and embarrassments.

Every departure can be at the wrong time. Missing something back home is the curse of the exile. Leaving England in April 1963 for Africa was my greatest adventure in life to date but, as if by some infernal cue, things started to happen the moment the ship left Southampton. The greyness and inertia was challenged. What I had been glad to leave I might have been glad to be part of. When I read the two plays set in Africa in this volume – *Motocar* and *Livingstone and Sechele* – the transfiguration of Britain's colonial power in the Sixties act as an ironical chorus. Wherever there is change theatre sits outside the door. My apprenticeship to the stage was spent in amateur playhouses on the Zambian Copperbelt, acting (Pinter, Beckett, Stoppard, Wesker, Arden, Osborne, we did them all), directing and writing. I could have a play written and on the stage in three months – a luxury I said goodbye to when I stopped working with Paines Plough in 1981. But I bet those old Jacobeans thrived on that luxury, not on watching natural impulses and energies shrivel on the vine because everything takes so <u>long</u>.

After five years of being resident playwright at the new Duke's Playhouse Lancaster, where my African fast track production was repeated – fortunate indeed – I emerged after countless folk epics, late-night reviews, touring shows and pantomimes, with a craving to write exactly what <u>I</u> wanted – not what a town needed. Publishing novels and short stories, writing for radio and television, had made the essential but suppressive ideal of writing for and with a community in mind bearable, but part of my ideal had been mined out. All four of these plays represent the overflow of that release – *Richard III Part Two* and *An Audience Called Edouard*, particularly so. In the ornateness of their conceits – a play pressed into a board-game in one, and into the painting of Manet's 'Déjeuner sur l'Herbe' on the other, is a heartfelt reaction to the regimens of subsidised theatre.

Touring plays of this nature all over Britain and Ireland was possible, however. In a way, one parish had been exchanged for another. When the National Theatre first opened it was seen as the axle of a great wheel. Plays off the rim would come into the Cottesloe. After all, we were all part of the true national theatre: theatre emerging out of the provinces as well as London. *Richard III Part Two* and *Motocar* shared in that early, now abandoned, idealism – performed at the Cottesloe by Paines Plough in 1977, the year before *Livingstone and Sechele* at the Traverse, Edinburgh, and *An Audience Called Edouard* at Greenwich. So, all four plays within this volume were written one after another in a twenty month period. Old habits die hard. One can almost smell the urgency.

Viewed from the hill of the twenty-first century, the plays cluster into a quartet linked by the theme of power playing on time. *Richard III Part Two* works off history trapped within relativity; *Motocar*, the loss of history; *An Audience Called Edouard*, creating future history; and *Livingstone and Sechele*, history made in a panic by the immediate need to survive. These were obviously concerns as the Seventies shunted identities around, socialism began to falter, capitalism sat back and waited for the worst to happen, and the defamation of ideas began to leak out of the universities into the streets.

I can honestly admit how this quartet structure was never there until now perceived. If an outsider had drawn it to my attention I'd have brushed it aside as a fallacy, claiming all four plays were simply stories which had intrigued me to the point where they had to be made into drama. But why does a man in his late thirties embrace history so hard? To stop it being taken away? To imprint its patterns indelibly on the memory before the market – that most timeless of teachers – proved beyond doubt civilisation had to be for sale or die? Enough to say that within three years of the first of these plays hitting the boards we all knew the theatre's future had changed. The revenge of the Tories for twenty years of relentless leftism by subsidised theatre was unleashed on us. (Where are you, Beaumont and Fletcher, to write that one?) It was simple. It was brutal. It was coming. Overnight it felt as though the world I had re-entered on my return to England ten years previously had been out on notice. You've had your time, the Maid of Cheapside said.

These remarks have sufficient sweep to arouse suspicion of the brush. Everything did not stop. Only hope was modified. The interpretation is provided merely to provide the backing up of these plays against a dam which was sure to break. But when explaining to a young actor what happened during that exchange of power from left to right, I don't feel uncertain about the way I present it. We still live in the aftermath of that revenge.

Gall, curiosity, appetite, astonishment at the lives of others, driving on past the ancient rules of the stage into wilderness, all these can tangle the typewriter ribbon. Re-reading work doesn't age me, nor do I feel a great distance between who I am now and the new playwright on the national scene eying every bush in case it burst into flames. Most of all I remember the actors as they dug their trenches in the lines, not for war but to grow something.

Theatre is, for me, theatrical – not a pejorative word in my lexicon. The priest-conjuror is always in the wings whether you want him or not. The challenges to credulity's need to be brave and absolute, not watery and lame. Terror is the starting-point of all four plays here, hand-shielded flickers of my incomplete questioning. What are we? Can we live within what we do? What do we make here on earth?

When it succeeds (those miracle hours) theatre enthrals because it confesses its faults and fights for redemption in front of our eyes. There is an obscure side-myth from Greece about the day atlas dropped the world, and the first playwright (who he?) picked it up.

David Pownall
Guildford, 2000

AN AUDIENCE CALLED EDOUARD

For Andrew Hewson
in friendship

Characters

FERDINAND
aged 25

VICTORINE
aged 25

GUSTAVE
aged 25

BERTHE
aged 28

HUGO
aged 45

ERIQUE
aged 25

An Audience Called Edouard was first performed at the Greenwich Theatre, London on 19 October 1978, with the following cast:

FERDINAND, David Robb

VICTORINE, Susan Hampshire

GUSTAVE, Jeremy Irons

BERTHE, Stephanie Beacham

HUGO, David Burke

ERIQUE, James Taylor

Director, Alan Strachan

Set in France.

October 1862.

ACT ONE

A glade with small conifers, yew and holly on an island in the Seine. One shore, and the opposite bank of the river at Argenteuil, are seen as background.

A rowing-boat is drawn up under the trees up-stage left, its oars parked across the well of the craft.

A young woman of Junoesque build, her dark hair up in a classical style, is paddling. She is dressed in a white, semi-transparent, roomy shift which has slid off her right (down-stage) shoulder as she dips her hand in the water. This is BERTHE.

Front-stage right is a heap of discarded clothes – a long blue dress, a straw bonnet with a black band and blue bow, a shift – and an overturned wicker basket from which apples, plums, green melons and cherries have tumbled on to the grass. A small, knobbly golden loaf lies beside the fruit. There has been a picnic.

Front-stage centre three fungi are growing.

Centre-stage sits VICTORINE, naked. She has a young, well-fleshed, ivory-hued body. Her chestnut hair is drawn back from her face and braided in a thick ring round her head. She looks at the audience with a bold, collected stare: her right elbow resting on her raised right knee, her right hand cupping her chin. Her left leg lies bent and flat against the grass, the sole of her foot flat on to the audience. She is sitting on a light blue cloak which is also wrapped round her left (up-stage) leg.

Close to her, slighty up-stage and to the up-stage left, sits GUSTAVE, a young man in a brown frock-coat, cream trousers, shirt and tie. He has a short brown beard and a moustache. GUSTAVE is looking to the left of VICTORINE's gaze, his expression sad and thoughtful.

FERDINAND reclines to the left of GUSTAVE and VICTORINE, his legs spread to either side of VICTORINE's bare right foot. He is wearing a dark green frock-coat and light grey trousers, a light pink cravat and a round peakless cap with a hanging tassle. In his left hand (down-stage) he holds a short cane with a hooked handle, his elbow (left) propped upon a bank beneath a prominent tree. FERDINAND has a full black beard and moustache and is facing VICTORINE, his right hand raised towards her as if illustrating a conversational point with a gesture.

The characters remain perfectly still in these positions for ten seconds.

FERDINAND: (*Completing the gesture*) And where will the Suez
  Canal get us?
VICTORINE: Suez.
GUSTAVE: That's where you're wrong.
FERDINAND: It means France is getting deeper and deeper
  into debt.
GUSTAVE: The Egyptians have stopped working on it. The
  whole thing has come to a dead stop right in the middle of
  the desert. They'll never finish it.
BERTHE: The government says they will...
FERDINAND: The Emperor says they will. Let's be precise
  about who is saying what. It's the Emperor who supports
  the canal...
VICTORINE: But what use is it?
BERTHE: To get the navy out to Vietnam in double-quick
  time.
GUSTAVE: The Egyptians don't trust the French. That's why
  they've downed tools.
VICTORINE: Well, it's not their canal, is it?
FERDINAND: It will be in ninety-nine years' time. We've
  promised them that.
VICTORINE: The men digging it aren't bothered about that.
  Do you work for your great-grandchildren or yourself?
FERDINAND: A bit of both.
GUSTAVE: It's stuck at Ismailia. Can you imagine what it
  must be like our there now? All the supervisors are going
  mad...I don't want to think about it. (*Pause.*) Why do we
  have a navy anyway? So Edouard can paint it, of course.
BERTHE: I'd like a break now, Edouard. It's getting chilly
  in here...
FERDINAND: Give him a little while longer. He's working
  well today.
BERTHE: Swap places then. My back is breaking.
GUSTAVE: Edouard disliked the navy. He found the sea and
  sky tedious all the way to Rio de Janeiro. But not the
  carnival, eh, Edouard? What a young devil he was...
BERTHE: (*Moving.*) I'm getting out. Too late if you haven't got
  all you want. You must work faster.
FERDINAND: Give him another minute...

BERTHE: Sorry, I'm getting out. (*BERTHE gets out of the water.*)

VICTORINE: We're moving, Edouard.

BERTHE: You must have most of what you want by now.

FERDINAND: Hold on, let's see. Do you mind if we break the pose Edouard? We can go on if you want us to.

BERTHE: Oh no we can't. The bottom half of my legs have turned blue.

VICTORINE: (*Wrapping herself in the blue cloak she is sitting on.*) October's getting a bit late for this lark.

FERDINAND: Come on, it's warm.

VICTORINE: You're warm, Ferdy.

BERTHE: Are you sitting on the towel, Victorine? Don't get up, I can get it. (*She pulls a towel from under VICTORINE, who edges off it.*) I don't like the feel of that mud. It's slimy and I keep expecting worms and things crawling over my toes…

FERDINAND: You find crocodiles in the Seine you know.

GUSTAVE: They're in the Nile, and the Suez Canal, thousands of crocodiles, waiting. They've eaten half the labour force.

VICTORINE: Will you open that wine, Ferdy? I need something to warm me up inside.

BERTHE: Me too. Mind if I get close, Victorine? I'm frozen. (*BERTHE dries her legs and leans back against VICTORINE, rubbing against her.*)

VICTORINE: Come and have some wine, Edouard. Wash the taste of paint away.

GUSTAVE: Victorine, I have just been thinking – do you know what your best feature is?

VICTORINE: What d'you mean? The one that looks best or the one that works best?

FERDINAND: A good distinction from one who knows.

GUSTAVE: Both.

VICTORINE: Both?

GUSTAVE: Yes, both.

(*Pause.*)

VICTORINE: Gustave, you have not got much imagination.

GUSTAVE: It's your ears.

VICTORINE: Well, thank you, Gustave.

GUSTAVE: They're superb.

VICTORINE: I don't think so.

GUSTAVE: Ferdy, I appeal to you.

FERDINAND: No, I agree with Victorine. Her ears are a little large for my taste.

GUSTAVE: I'm not asking you to eat them.

VICTORINE: They are too big. They used to call me 'Elephant Ears' at school.

GUSTAVE: Edouard loves your ears. (*Pause.*) He always insists that you show them. See, today…every time he uses you, it's the ears he's after. Victorine, I am in desperate need of your ears.

BERTHE: What about the rest of her?

GUSTAVE: Not indifferent but…I don't feel the same way about that. Just those beautiful, luscious, classical ears.

VICTORINE: Gustave, if you'll give me a regular allowance, an apartment, a bank account…you can have an affair with my ears.

FERDINAND: One at a time or simultaneously?

VICTORINE: We'll have to work that out.

BERTHE: I wouldn't trust Gustave to behave like a gentleman. Don't sell anything to him, not even your ears. Keep your ears pure, love.

GUSTAVE: At least you'll be able to listen like a virgin even though you look like a tart. (*Pause.*) That bloody canal!

VICTORINE: You're going to lose every bloody franc you've got, I hope.

GUSTAVE: Everything.

FERDINAND: I bought some shares as well, not as many as Gustave, but enough.

BERTHE: Why?

FERDINAND: It was sold to us. We were persuaded.

GUSTAVE: I tell you – and don't pass this on – but most of the cash I'll get from father's will, when it's proved, is already in Suez shares. I borrowed up to the hilt on the strength of that money…

VICTORINE: All that thrown in a ditch? You're mad.

GUSTAVE: Of course I'm mad.

FERDINAND: It's difficult to get at the truth. The papers can't be trusted because they're holding stock as well and they don't want to start a scare that will drive the price down. But we know that the labour, the Egyptians, don't want to carry on working on it. Why? You'd think with the way things are out there they'd be glad of the chance to earn some decent wages.

BERTHE: What kind of wages are they getting?

GUSTAVE: Not enough, if they've stopped work.

FERDINAND: That doesn't necessarily follow.

VICTORINE: Gustave, you put all that money into that company with your old man only dead a few weeks ago?

GUSTAVE: Well it's mine, isn't it? I know it's there.

BERTHE: But sensible people don't take big decisions like that with the house in mourning…

GUSTAVE: House in mourning, me? You know how I feel…

BERTHE: You are not normal when there's been a death, no one is. It alters things for a while…

VICTORINE: You threw it away, Gustave, because it was burning a hole in your pocket…

GUSTAVE: Nonsense…

VICTORINE: Stupid tit. You should have given it to me.

GUSTAVE: They're not treating the native labour properly, that's obvious. Now they can do something about that. Make the work easier, pay better wages – I bet they get paid feathers – there is a way round the problem. But they won't do that, they must exploit them to the hilt, and destroy the whole scheme. That's what I can't understand.

FERDINAND: Well, we're shareholders, let's write to the company…

GUSTAVE: A lot of notice they'd take of us.

FERDINAND: It's our democratic right. We can go to the annual meeting…

GUSTAVE: The whole thing will be in ruins by then.

BERTHE: So what can you do?

FERDINAND: We have to trust in de Lesseps. We can't do anything.

BERTHE: It was a gamble, and you're losing. You've put nothing into it but money. Gustave, if you cared about that canal, then…well, it would be different. If you were de Lesseps, or even the bloody Emperor, old fool that he is, then I might sympathise…but you're not. You bet on a horse and it's stopped running. You're a mug to yourself.

GUSTAVE: Who was asking for sympathy?

BERTHE: You were. We've had this for days. I don't spend my time whining to you about my financial problems, do I? And I'm poor, Gustave, poor, really poor. Nothing is my own…

GUSTAVE: Alright, alright…

BERTHE: When my father died there was nothing. Nothing. Except debts.

VICTORINE: Don't try and tell Gustave that he was lucky with his old man. He'll start screaming.

BERTHE: Look at all the things he did for you; good, solid things. You had a beautiful house in the country, apartments in Paris, holidays, respect at school from the grovelling teachers…all this land, more houses with other people paying rent for you, for your legacy…ooh, Gustave, don't make me cry. His father was a saint, wasn't he, Victorine?

VICTORINE: Oh yes. When I saw him up there in the Palace of Justice looking down at me, I thought, there is a man who is close to God and all his holy angels. (*Pause.*) On the way out I was picked up by Edouard who gave me twenty francs, took me to a friend's apartment and spent the afternoon teaching me the difference between the Old Testament and the New Testament.

FERDINAND: How is your mother, Gustave?

GUSTAVE: Underneath, happy I think. She puts on a face.

BERTHE: After all those years? Your mother feels right now as if her leg had been cut off.

GUSTAVE: I don't believe that.

BERTHE: She does. You be careful with her.

GUSTAVE: She won't stay in the house here. I think she'll sell it.

BERTHE: And give the money to you, you hope?

GUSTAVE: Edouard needs it as much as me.

VICTORINE: If I owned this island, I couldn't sell it.
I thought you said it had been in the family for six hundred years? And you'd let her sell it?

GUSTAVE: I'd let her sell everything.

VICTORINE: That's stupid.

GUSTAVE: Why? I would make her free, and me free, and Edouard free. You want to try being chained to houses and fields and tenants. You can't cut yourself off from them. Why? Money. It's religious. Money is holy. It is the thing you pray to. Don't move. Don't think. Rest here, here's where the family money is. Sit on it. You can't escape.

VICTORINE: You don't want to anyway.

GUSTAVE: Oh yes I do.

VICTORINE: Then you can give me your share. I'll go and live with your mother. That would suit me fine.

GUSTAVE: I don't think it would fit in with her plans. Widowhood is supposed to be a tranquil time, sweetheart.

BERTHE: How much was the old man worth?

FERDINAND: Tut, tut. Watch your manners.

BERTHE: Why shouldn't I know? It's only a sum. Was he very well off when he died? Had he saved a lot?

GUSTAVE: Father was prudent. He was thinking of making it another hundred years that we'll be here, you see. We have to hold on, no matter what happens, we must have all this.

FERDINAND: And why not?

VICTORINE: Edouard, why not set me up here? Build a little house, put up a sign 'Private'. It's just what I need. I'd do some gardening, make my own clothes, bake bread. You promised me my own place. (*Pause.*) See the crab smile? He's tighter than his old man was, the mean git!

FERDINAND: Victorine, if this was given to you, in a year it would be a jungle. You would neglect it, abuse it, the cattle would die. Land has to be loved and cared for…that's not your strong point.

VICTORINE: Cretin, I am a part of the landscape.
Ask Edouard.

FERDINAND: Fun, that's you. For as long as you feel like.
You're too wilful to be a farmer, or a lawyer. The old man
was both, and good at it.

VICTORINE: You don't know that. If Edouard's father had
been a woman from a poor family he might have ended up
like me. We do what we have to. Now, if I had the chance, I
could be very dependable, very solid and respectable. You
don't believe me? I have friends who lived the same kind of
life as me and Berthe do, then they married, settled down,
and now they are so good and decent, children everywhere
– children! And cooks? You've never tasted food like it.
Their houses shine. You could eat your dinner off the floor.
The same could be true of me.

GUSTAVE: I hope not.

VICTORINE: I could do it if I wanted to. It's not hard.

BERTHE: There's a housewife in every nymph, and in every
lecher, Gustave, there's a little boy playing with himself
under the bedclothes.

VICTORINE: Every tart I know would settle down if she
could find a big-hearted, decent man…

BERTHE: This one wouldn't. What happens after five years?
He goes off you.

VICTORINE: Then you can go off him and do as you like –
and you've got security, the priest will help you out if he
starts talking about divorce – that's right out, my son, till
death do you part – and you've got a couple of kids you've
brought up on your side of the argument – a woman can't
lose. You've got him! He has to give you money, you take
what liberties you like and to hell with him. Let him get a
tart of his own, leave you in peace.

GUSTAVE: Sounds wonderful, Victorine. Is this your plan?

VICTORINE: Yes. By the time I'm forty I've got to have it all
set up. I'm just looking for the right man.

FERDINAND: I don't think Edouard would like to be
considered…

VICTORINE: I agree. He's not the type. I said he'd have to
be big-hearted and decent before I could even think about
exploiting him.

GUSTAVE: Yes, you did specify. Edouard, it seems you're out!

BERTHE: Not with me he isn't. Why do you keep me in the background Edouard? How you can fancy Victorine above me is...perplexing. Who admires you most? You are the sanest, most beautiful man I know. Ask me to share your life. I'll accept like a shot. We'll live quietly, intelligently, separated, together, married, unmarried. Do I mean it? (*Laughs.*) NO!

GUSTAVE: He's cross. I can tell. You're not taking him seriously.

FERDINAND: You're wasting his money. Come on, let's start again...

VICTORINE: Ferdy, shut up, will you? I've been in and out of Edouard's studio all week, posing for him, working half the night. This is supposed to be my day off, if he doesn't know what I look like now, he never will.

FERDINAND: You are getting paid, Victorine...

VICTORINE: Not much.

(*Pause.*)

FERDINAND: It's what he can afford.

VICTORINE: Cha!

FERDINAND: He doesn't sell much at the moment...

VICTORINE: And all that in the bank? Look Ferdy, he'll sell this. And why? Because I'm on it and I look good. Some old goat will buy it and stick it in his bedroom to get him going. Nobody's going to buy it because Edouard painted it.

FERDINAND: You better hadn't say that when he's listening...

VICTORINE: He's always listening, and I've said it to him myself. I said it over coffee this morning and I'll say it over dinner tonight. I'm the one who's known, and I'm the stupid bitch who's poor.

(*VICTORINE stands up, wraps the cloak round her and walks down-stage.*)

GUSTAVE: Going to apologise?

VICTORINE: If I feel like it.

GUSTAVE: I know he beats you in private.

VICTORINE: You mean you hope he does. (*Pause.*) Edouard, it feels odd. Are you sure it's the way you saw it? I mean, does it feel right to you? You're the one that matters. If you could only let me in on the secret – I did ask you last night but you didn't take any notice – what is the effect? (*Pause.*) I'll be honest with you, I don't feel right...no, that's not the way I wanted to say that...I don't feel at ease. You're trying something out I know, but I'm the one people will be looking at and I'll be sitting there next to Gustave and Ferdy and they won't even be able to guess what we are supposed to be doing. It can't be just new. I could be saying to Gustave, pass me my dress...Or Ferdy could be saying to me, did you cut my walking-stick in half? Or Berthe could be saying that she'd dropped her spectacles in the Seine. (*Pause.*) Yes, I know you must experiment and we are all trying our hardest to understand, my love...couldn't you help us? Explain? Gustave and Ferdy will just look like...

FERDINAND: (*Going across to VICTORINE.*) Victorine you should know better...leave him alone.

VICTORINE: ...themselves, in their own clothes! And me? What about me?

FERDINAND: Edouard has given strict instructions. This is not going to be a bunfight, it is work. It has to be done properly. Leave him alone.

VICTORINE: I don't think he knows what he's doing.

FERDINAND: Nonsense! He's already given you a very definite form.

VICTORINE: The very definite form has been mine for years. He's making me look like a tart.

GUSTAVE: Angel, you are a tart.

VICTORINE: Not today I'm not. Today I'm a model. There's a difference. Edouard should know that. (*Pause.*)

FERDINAND: Victorine, he is after your essence.

VICTORINE: Drink is it now?

FERDINAND: Edouard isn't interested in the false ideas you've got about yourself, or any pretensions. He's trying to find you, the real original you...the divine animal in its own time.

VICTORINE: Mooooooo! Ticktockticktockticktock. Mooooooo!

22

FERDINAND: We are what we are, Victorine. You're not
ashamed of it, are you? What do you want to see in
the painting?

VICTORINE: Not what I can see in any mirror. He should be
improving me.

FERDINAND: You mean telling lies?

VICTORINE: Alright, yes. What I might be, what I could be
– but what's the point of doing me as I am? I'm here, there
it is. Who needs two of me? I don't, you don't.

FERDINAND: Look, all I'm trying to do is keep the
conditions right so he can make his experiment…

BERTHE: Ferdy, you don't let on, do you? You keep
everything to yourself. Why the hell didn't you tell us that
Edouard had changed his job, given up painting altogether
and decided to be a scientist? It would have helped us
divine little white mice no end if we'd known. We'd have
behaved ourselves much better, wouldn't we? Of course we
would, quite naturally. Me, now I'd stay in my cage, tearing
round my treadmill, making eyes at Ferdinand, the
handsome, manly laboratory cat.

FERDINAND: You're very unfair.

BERTHE: Pusspusspusspuss.

FERDINAND: Try and understand, will you?

BERTHE: Perhaps we do, too well. We do have minds of our
own, you know.

FERDINAND: There must be a period when everything is in
place for him, when he can have order to work from.

GUSTAVE: What's the matter with disorder, Ferdy? A good
disorder is just as useful any day, and much more
interesting. (*To BERTHE.*) You see, Berthe, my love, you've
got it all wrong. Edouard is a painter and a scientist. He will
shortly paint a cure for cholera, wave it in front of Egypt's
diseased millions and they will be well again, well enough
to return to the diggings and the excavation of my
investment. So, for Doctor Edouard we must keep the
laboratory conditions stable on both counts. Oh God, the
river is rising! We have prior warning of an earthquake.
The test-tubes are trembling! The pipettes are positively
pixillating!

BERTHE: The germs are escaping! Come back, you
  bad bastards!

VICTORINE: They're getting in the paint! They're crawling
  on the canvas! I can hear them screaming – we're stuck!
  We're stuck!

GUSTAVE: Still life of typhus. Side view of smallpox. The
  plague, reclining nude with a background of Paris.

VICTORINE: And this gallery isn't big enough for Edouard's
  scientific pictures, is it? He's got to work on a large scale to
  say all he's got to say, hasn't he? Knock down that wall.
  Take off the roof. Ferdy, don't let the public get closer than
  ten paces or the picture will melt away into dots and
  numbers. Oh, and the light must be right. What time
  should we ask them to come round for the viewing?

BERTHE: Oh, dawn, dawn, definitely dawn. They can bring
  their breakfasts.

VICTORINE: What's this? You've been boozing! Smoking
  what? Opium! If you come in here, mate, the only
  inspiration you're supposed to get is from me! And
  you…you've just walked from Rheims? Had sex, a heavy
  dinner, come off the night shift? Get out of here. You're in
  no fit state to see what Edouard Manet makes of the world
  as it is today! What are you missing? What's the mystery?
  Well, it's a picture of an unadorned tart whose ears stick
  out. You'll give it a miss after all? Pity. You seem the perfect
  man to see this masterpiece – you're so normal, sir, which
  should give you a taste for abnormality. Five francs. Oh no,
  that's not the entry fee, that's the cost of this canvas – it's
  one of the new photographs! CHARLATAN!
  (*Pause.*)

GUSTAVE: Edouard, I warned you about using a model who
  can draw herself. She expects some element of flattering
  transformation. Now, you should be able to manage that.
  You were trained for a naval career so telling lies to women
  should come easy to you.

VICTORINE: I don't want a lie, you ape – I just want
  something of the best part of me…I'm leaving. That's it!

FERDINAND: You can't!

VICTORINE: Try and stop me!

FERDINAND: Please, Victorine…I implore you.

VICTORINE: I feel better now you're begging. You are doing it for Edouard, aren't you? Even at one step removed, it's sweet. There. I'll stay for you, you old groveller.

GUSTAVE: He's done it again. Without saying a word he has changed another mind. He did the same with Father. He had Edouard marked down for a naval career. It's true, it's true. Off he went in his uniform, looking very bright and blue, and was shipped off in a training vessel to South America. He hated it. Why? Now, Edouard, what is the difference between a line here – we'll say this one, from Victorine's divine coccyx, the stump of the monkey's tail…to the nape of her exquisite neck…beneath the shadow of her ears…and a line of latitude from Le Havre to Rio de Janeiro? Cannot a sailor paint? Or a painter sail? From that time in his tormented adolescence Edouard has been on eternal shore-leave.

VICTORINE: Boozing. Whoring.

BERTHE: Having a gay old time before his next voyage of discovery.

VICTORINE: The man who can only look in the mirror. The black box with the pin-hole in it. The man on the tripod who must remain still while the image registers. Before long we'll have no need for painters. They'll all be out of business.

FERDINAND: That could be caused by their models moving about so often they can't get any work done.

GUSTAVE: Father bought him out of his apprenticeship, allowed Edouard to talk him into sending him to old Couture's studio…a tremendous act of adolescent persuasion! How did you do it? It could have been blackmail. What did you threaten? Suicide?

FERDINAND: Edouard could not stop himself being a painter.

GUSTAVE: Could I stop myself becoming a doctor?

FERDINAND: You seem to be managing so far.

GUSTAVE: I was told I would be a doctor, Edouard chose…

FERDINAND: No. He was chosen.

GUSTAVE: Ferdy, what a slave you are.

FERDINAND: Perhaps.

(*Pause.*)

BERTHE: I'm getting hungry.

VICTORINE: How about some food, Ferdy? Are we allowed to eat now?

GUSTAVE: Edouard, you should have had some success as a painter before the old man died. He needed to know that he'd done the right thing, like a judge who gets a confession from the prisoner after the sentence. That would have been nice for him. As it is, Edouard, you haven't made it yet.

FERDINAND: He will.

BERTHE: I hope so.

GUSTAVE: I don't doubt it. I'm just thinking of our father, poor man, dying in doubt. That, for a gentleman of the Second Empire, must be like hanging over hell on a bar of butter.

VICTORINE: You'll get a rotten face put on you in this one, Gustave.

BERTHE: No, not Edouard. There's no vindictiveness there. (*Nestles up to FERDINAND.*) Warm me up, Ferdy.

VICTORINE: Edouard, we're going to have something to eat now. Come on over.

BERTHE: I bet he's put a backside on me like a carthorse. Now, Edouard, this lunch here – (*Touches the overturned basket right.*) we don't eat this lunch.

GUSTAVE: That lunch is not a real lunch. That lunch is Edouard's lunch.

BERTHE: Ferdy, be a good lad and get the genuine lunch out of the boat...

GUSTAVE: The authentic boat!

BERTHE: Which is floating...

GUSTAVE: Real trees! Real sky! Real autumn! Real water! Real ripples!

BERTHE: On the sincere Seine!

(*FERDINAND gets up and goes to the boat for the lunch-basket.*)

GUSTAVE: Victorine, give Edouard a smile.

VICTORINE: (*Smiling.*) There. (*Pause.*) He ignores it.

GUSTAVE: You know why?

VICTORINE: I'm not trying hard enough. (*Smiles.*) Ah, a flicker. Look, he's showing me his eye-teeth.

GUSTAVE: He loves you.

VICTORINE: He loves us all. Ferdy's sister, me on Mondays, Wednesdays and weekends. Mimi-the-Breton on Tuesday, Eggs-on-a-Plate on Thursday…

FERDINAND: Shut up, Victorine.

(*Pause. FERDINAND starts unpacking the basket.*)

BERTHE: You're talking yourself out of a job.

VICTORINE: I'll manage.

GUSTAVE: My girl, to Edouard you are a pot of pink paint.

BERTHE: That's not true. He's very fond of Victorine.

(*Pause. They lay out the picnic.*)

VICTORINE: Edouard, come and have something to eat.

GUSTAVE: Don't bother…

VICTORINE: (*Sharply.*) No! He must have something! He can't go on like this…Edouard, you must eat!

GUSTAVE: You sound like Mother. Victorine, Edouard is not eating these days. You know why. So why not leave him alone?

(*Pause.*)

VICTORINE: I notice that you still have a healthy appetite, Gustave.

GUSTAVE: My stomach has not gone into mourning. And you notice his insistence that it was a picnic he is painting. He will paint the idea of eating, but will not eat himself. Further, there have to be two lunch-baskets…don't you find that tantalising? (*Kisses VICTORINE.*)

VICTORINE: He's watching.

BERTHE: What a bore you are, Gustave. You try so hard.

GUSTAVE: There's no harm. It is not a real kiss. It is one ghost kissing another. (*Kisses VICTORINE again.*) And that was a reflection, a ripple effect. (*Kisses her again.*) And that was an echo, Narcissus.

VICTORINE: Edouard, I can never trust your eyes. They say everything I don't want them to say. You've got an animal's eyes.

GUSTAVE: She's mine. (*Kisses VICTORINE again.*) I'm the
one who's sitting next to her in the pose. You put me there.
(*Kisses her again.*) This is the potential, what could happen.
Now put that in as well. (*To FERDINAND, harshly.*) How old
is Leon now?

FERDINAND: Oh...er...about ten I should think. Yes,
about ten.

VICTORINE: See if I care. Why should I? Great ponce,
he is.

GUSTAVE: And his mother, Suzanne? Still playing the piano?

FERDINAND: Be quiet, Gustave.

GUSTAVE: If I had a son I would own him.

BERTHE: If you had a son you would die of fright.

FERDINAND: It is their business, Gustave. Suzanne has
made no complaint.

GUSTAVE: Of course not. She feels privileged. Now I would
like a son but there's no one who'll bear me one. God,
I would own him, be proud of him. Edouard, I will take
him from you and raise him. Tell your sister, Ferdy, that
you have found a home for the boy. We will go out to the
Suez Canal and dig it together. We will save the economy
of France, Uncle and natural Nephew. (*Waves.*) Yes, I'll get
married, Edouard, do it all myself and it will be nothing to
do with you. I am jealous that you can have a bastard and
no one minds, no one. It's wonderful!

VICTORINE: Your mother managed it with little fuss.

GUSTAVE: Oh, cruel!

BERTHE: One day you will push Edouard too far, then God
help you.

GUSTAVE: No, he would help Edouard.

FERDINAND: I'll get the rest of the wine. It should be nice
and cool by now.
(*FERDINAND goes over to the boat and takes two bottles
of white wine from under a stone in the water, then brings
them back. BERTHE takes out a newspaper and opens it.
FERDINAND wipes the bottles.*)
Will we drink them both fairly quickly?

BERTHE: Is that an invitation?

FERDINAND: If we're not going to then I'll put one of them back.

GUSTAVE: He worked that all out for himself, you know. (*FERDINAND goes back to the boat and puts one bottle back under the stone in the water. GUSTAVE opens the other.*)

BERTHE: Mexico, Mexico, Mexico, Mexico…(*Shuts the paper suddenly.*) Where is Mexico? What are we doing in Mexico?

GUSTAVE: In Mexico there is a snow-capped mountain, a volcano called Popocatepetl, which is shaped like a warrior kneeling at the feet of his sleeping sweetheart. That is all I know about Mexico.

FERDINAND: (*Returning.*) Mexico owes us money. She owes England money. If we don't do something to recover the debts…Mexico will renege…

BERTHE: Mexico is America. The Emperor is saying Mexico is in France. He is a terrible old fool and I would cut his balls off with an axe. After all we've been through we are still sending French soldiers to America, still. Shit! (*She crumples the paper up into a ball and pounds it together.*) It makes me ashamed! And you do as well! (*She hurls the paper ball at FERDINAND who hurls it back.*) What's happened to us? We're going backwards.

FERDINAND: America? There is no America! They're tearing each other to pieces. The continent is completely unstable. The civil war is killing it.

BERTHE: Over slavery, you fool! Mexico is not in France! Where is it? It is in Mexico! And Louis Napoleon expects us to care…

GUSTAVE: (*Pouring out the wine.*) Now, I have a solution to the problem of slavery. If the two sides in the United States would pause for a breather, put all their black people in boats and send them over to dig the Suez Canal, we would have peace on one hand, and prosperity on the other. Will anyone drink to that?

BERTHE: Edouard, if you ever paint the Emperor, or his stooge Maximilian, I'll pour all your paints down your throat and poison you! Well, don't you think it's vile,

Victorine? Trying to put a congenital cretin like that old Habsburg Maximilian on the throne in a new country?

GUSTAVE: Don't ask her. She doesn't understand. There, there. Drink your wine, my child. Now, Berthe, you have the wrong attitude. Maximilian will pay debts to France and introduce the drinking of schnapps to replace tequila, street-rioting to replace bull-fighting – infinitely more fun – and the Folies Bergère to oust the fandango. I mean, do we need another civilisation when we have this one? They won't be able to do anything better than we can. Let them use our expertise, our experience.

BERTHE: We will pay for it, like we paid for betraying our own revolution, not once but twice! Look at us…it makes you want to cry.

GUSTAVE: But we're very good at making emperors. The ones we make are nothing but the best. I mean, look at the Dutch…I know you'll forgive me Ferdy…how much better they would be for some really royal encrustations. Now Ferdy, I am prepared to sell you Louis Napoleon in exchange for a waggon-load of tulip bulbs. Don't hesitate. The next time your country is in any danger of flooding you will only have to send him up on the top of the dykes and the water will calm. It's a knack he has. What do you say?

FERDINAND: Of course. I'll arrange it immediately. (*Walks down-stage.*)

VICTORINE: I don't know why you let yourself get so upset, Berthe…

BERTHE: It is me who is being made a fool! Me! You stick an old goat like the Emperor on me! I'm disgusted! France is finished!

FERDINAND: Edouard, I hope you've been able to get some work done. Things have not been exactly perfect. Yes, I try. You're patient. I wish I were like you but I feel like beating him about the head sometimes…

VICTORINE: Berthe, he will die…the old goat will die.

BERTHE: When? I'll tell you, innocent, when I'm an old tart and you're an old tart and we won't give a damn who is in the government!

FERDINAND: Although Suzanne doesn't object to Victorine, and never will…whether it's her or…someone else…it has to be said before the wedding, that she doesn't want you to expect her to come to the studio or on jaunts like this. This will be your province. She will never interfere, or ask for explanations. Suzanne knows what kind of life you must lead in order to find what you want…but there are risks, you know.

VICTORINE: Who says I'm going to be an old tart?

BERTHE: Of course you are. It can't be helped. We all are. All I'm saying is that I don't want France making me a ridiculous old tart before my time!

FERDINAND: And Edouard, I'd like us to find time to talk about Leon. He knows you're his father but unless you do something about it soon he's not going to respect that relationship. His attitude is this – if you won't accept him, and only accept his mother…well, then he's an orphan. Those are his own words. He's a bright boy but I feel that hollowness, you know, that brittleness growing. He's just surface glitter.

BERTHE: I'll prove to you that you're going to be an old tart. Gustave, would you marry her?

GUSTAVE: Certainly not.

BERTHE: You know why?

GUSTAVE: Because I'm hopelessly in love with her.

BERTHE: Ah, how sad.

GUSTAVE: You understand?

BERTHE: Perfectly.

GUSTAVE: The Emperor is the man who started this fashion. He loves France, so he abuses her. Edouard loves Suzanne, Leon, Victorine, etcetera…so he is cruel to them. I worship Victorine but will not share my life with her…though we have things in common, don't we?

VICTORINE: Unfortunately.

GUSTAVE: Thus we get along. We can share a cup without wiping the rim.
(*Pause.*)

FERDINAND: Getting back to your material interests Gustave, what is really upsetting you; the Emperor is the

31

only person who will get the Suez Canal completed. He'll send the Foreign Legion in to finish it off before he'll let the Egyptians lose all your money for you.

GUSTAVE: That is very kind of the old fellow. However, my gratitude is mixed with resentment. Do you know who it was that made me buy fifty five-hundred-franc shares in a hole in the sand? The Emperor. He is the teacher who taught me to waste my resources, to spend dead men's money, and to be greedy. So, my feelings towards him are ambiguous. On the one hand I hate him and on the other I loathe his guts.

VICTORINE: Gustave, you're lazy. That is your fault, no one else's.

GUSTAVE: True.

VICTORINE: When did you last do any work on your studies?

GUSTAVE: Weeks ago.

VICTORINE: Was it the Emperor who kept dragging you into cafés and dance-halls and pouring drink down your throat?

GUSTAVE: I have been trying to forget that his name is Napoleon and that the only battle he has ever won has been against Frenchmen.
(*Pause.*)

VICTORINE: You are what you are. You don't really want to be a doctor.

GUSTAVE: No, get it right. I don't want to be a quack. (*Pause.*) Why did my father not buy any canal stock, not a solitary share? Did you know that? Rates went mad when they opened trading in those shares. You couldn't get near the Exchange I hear. But he wouldn't touch it.

FERDINAND: Which is why you did.

GUSTAVE: Talk sense, will you?

FERDINAND: Your father saved. You want to make money fast.

GUSTAVE: What's wrong with that? Do I want to die with it?

VICTORINE: Too damn right. Show me how.

FERDINAND: Only so you can be as rich as your father before Edouard. That's the key.

BERTHE: Ah-ha.

GUSTAVE: Well, what a revelation. Do I really?

FERDINAND: Rivalry is at the root of it.

GUSTAVE: For rivalry read revelry. I've never heard such rubbish. See, even Edouard is laughing.

FERDINAND: There is always a reason, and sometimes it's a dark one, deep inside yourself. You want to get there before Edouard. You compete with him in everything you do or say.

(*Pause.*)

VICTORINE: So there.

BERTHE: That's you fixed up.

FERDINAND: If you could, by some miracle, become an absolute replica of your father tomorrow, you'd do it.

GUSTAVE: And sleep with my mother, I suppose?

VICTORINE: I doubt if she'd notice the difference.

GUSTAVE: And I thought I was the one who always looked up to Edouard, who followed him around. Hear that, comrade? It wasn't that I wanted to be like you, I wanted to be better – cheaply. Well, Ferdy, my biography is yours. I give you full rights to print it. Christ in Heaven, you know it all!

(*Pause.*)

VICTORINE: How do you know all that about Gustave? Are you guessing?

FERDINAND: Oh no, I'm not that perceptive. Edouard told me.

(*Pause.*)

BERTHE: Hm. Anyone want to share a melon?

GUSTAVE: Edouard said that?

FERDINAND: Yes.

BERTHE: Did he tell it to you in confidence?

FERDINAND: No. He said everyone knew it anyway but he was just expressing it.

BERTHE: He's taken his brother to bits and seen what's wrong with him?

FERDINAND: No, how he is. That's his real gift. He can cut through. Edouard has a very clear vision of the truth. He knows Gustave's truth.

VICTORINE: Well, good old Edouard. God knows what he must think of me. What an opinion to have about yourself. It's not unlike the good God.

FERDINAND: It's not an opinion, it's a fact. He can get outside and look in…it's a mechanism, a quirk, the way his mind is built. Fascinating.

VICTORINE: I'll keep my eye on him in future. He never told me he was God.

(*Pause. GUSTAVE gets to his feet, walks down-stage.*)

GUSTAVE: Edouard…er…I have a suggestion to make…no, no, not about the work in hand…no, it's about a holiday we must take together. We have never been to the Dordogne you know, never. That is something we must remedy. We'll go to the Dordogne and we'll go to the prehistoric caves and we'll stand side by side and look at the paintings which men had to do in their brothers' blood because they had no better materials. And, you know, the world has yet to produce a painter to beat them. Go on, paint me an animal that lives, my Paris café caveman, let's see you wield your bison bristles at Tortini's tomorrow, real flesh, real animals. ME! What else have you been saying about me? ME? You are the one who wants success and you'll do anything for it, If I want to beat you to it, that's just a race between two men, but you? You want to lick the whole earth, have its neck in your claws, Mr Gentleman. You want genuine, sincere greed? There it is, looking exquisitely reasonable, poised, unconcerned; the human glacier rubbing the rocks down to make his going easier. I am not in competition with you. I can't paint. I can't sculpt like Ferdy, I can't even make a living out of friendship like the girls…so where's the challenge? You want to match me for losing money?

(*VICTORINE comes over to GUSTAVE and holds him.*)

VICTORINE: Gustave, you're drunk. Don't shout at Edouard.

GUSTAVE: He must stop being so critical of me! I didn't ask for it!

VICTORINE: He's not critical. He says that's the way you are, that's all…

GUSTAVE: And who is he to say so? A dauber? A dilettante? Let him go and suffer and then paint, smug sod…it's all rotten. He doesn't have to…

(*VICTORINE leads GUSTAVE back to the picnic.*)

…no, there's no necessity for him to paint. He's got his

private income, so he'll never be an honest painter.
He plays with it…God if I only had a job! And you, you
bloody know-all! You wait. I'll end up a better tart's doctor
than you'll be a painter. I'll cure them, you won't!
(*VICTORINE sits down and pillows GUSTAVE's head on her
lap, taps him.*)
VICTORINE: Shut up and I'll let you make love to my ears.
GUSTAVE: Yes, and you'll give Edouard the rest.
VICTORINE: Give? Never.
GUSTAVE: Go on, we know.
VICTORINE: Edouard always has his hand in his pocket for
me, don't you?
(*Pause.*)
FERDINAND: (*Swatting something on his cheek.*) Get off!
BERTHE: I thought all the flies should be dead by now.
Bastards!
(*An attack of flies. While VICTORINE, BERTHE and
FERDINAND are busy swatting them, driving them away
from the food, GUSTAVE lifts up his face and holds out his
hands.*)
GUSTAVE: Come on, come on, give me a kiss. Straight off the
dung. Come on.
FERDINAND: Bloody filthy things! Get away!
VICTORINE: They're after the meat. (*Covers it up.*)
GUSTAVE: Get them all in, Edouard. Don't forget the flies.
There's one, there's another. Now look at that, they won't
land on me. What's the matter with me? Come on, you
lads, free space here, plenty of room.
BERTHE: Leave them for a minute. Let them settle.
(*They stop moving, watching the flies.*)
GUSTAVE: Edouard, I have even been rejected by the flies.
How can I be a good doctor now? We all need friends,
Brother.
BERTHE: GO!
(*FERDINAND, VICTORINE and BERTHE swat flies
all round the picnic in a furious assault. Pause.*)
GUSTAVE: In the name of the Father, Son and Holy
Ghost, Amen.
FERDINAND: Well, I'm not eating that now…
VICTORINE: Don't be stupid. Flies never killed anybody.

FERDINAND: You please yourself. Just think what they've
    been walking in.

BERTHE: Ferdy, you've got to die sometime.

VICTORINE: In Africa they eat flies. (*Picking flies off the
    picnic.*) How about that?

GUSTAVE: As a fly-killer, I'm a failure. As a fly-lover, I'm a
    failure.

VICTORINE: Well, you can try to be a good doctor. That
    would be helpful.
    (*Pause.*)

GUSTAVE: Edouard will have seventy thousand francs,
    I repeat, seventy thousand francs! when the old man's
    affairs are all settled. Why do you bother to paint,
    Edouard? You don't need to earn a living…

FERDINAND: He could not stop if he wanted to. It's in
    his blood.

GUSTAVE: Then it should be in mine as well. But it isn't.
    Perhaps there isn't room in mine.

FERDINAND: You will feel a fool one day, Gustave. If
    Edouard is given the gold medal, if his work is hung in the
    Louvre in his own lifetime, if they make him a Chevalier
    d'Honneur, you will regret this attitude.

GUSTAVE: I am going to discontinue my studies.

VICTORINE: You are the only man I know who can stop
    what he never started.

GUSTAVE: Who needs a quack with my brother around? He
    can do a doctor's job. You've lost your nose? Whip round
    to his studio, sit still for a while, caramba! Hey presto! New
    nose! Not only a new nose, but a nose of genius.
    (*Distant shouts and whistles off, very faint.*)
    I…I could reconstruct the ancient face of Paris. You,
    Berthe, could have a pair of Victorine's ears…

BERTHE: I'll stick to my own if it's alright with you.

GUSTAVE: And Victorine could have a pair of Berthe's
    breasts for state occasions and funerals. It's a marvellous
    idea. Edouard, we should form a company and issue shares
    in your talent now!

FERDINAND: Gustave…

GUSTAVE: Edouard could paint over every defect he sees in
    us. It would be a new world. Girls, buy shares in Edouard
    at once!

FERDINAND: Will you please…

GUSTAVE: He is the canvas Christ. He can make us all entirely waterproof.

(*Pause.*)

FERDINAND: Apologise, quickly!

GUSTAVE: Sorry, Edouard. I got carried away with my own enthusiasm. Just one last request. When you re-paint the boulevards of the city, will you widen them a little so we can get your head along in the procession to the investiture ceremony.

BERTHE: (*Laughing.*) Edouard, give him at least a black look!

FERDINAND: You're being a disruptive influence, Gustave…

BERTHE: Oh don't be so solemn, Ferdy!

VICTORINE: Berthe is enjoying herself.

BERTHE: Oh dear.

VICTORINE: You want Edouard? Go and get him. He doesn't belong to me.

BERTHE: He can take a joke, I know that much. Gustave is always like this with him. Why be so sensitive?

VICTORINE: Because this picture is going to be…shit. I know it. You won't take him seriously, Gustave hates him…he gets thrown.

BERTHE: Nonsense. He knows every move he makes.

VICTORINE: You ask him now whether he can paint or not. He doubts himself. He doesn't know why he's put this picture together like this. He's groping…

GUSTAVE: Alright, we're groping with him, aren't we?

FERDINAND: You don't want him to succeed though, do you, Gustave?

(*Pause. GUSTAVE turns away, sinks down in VICTORINE's lap.*)

BERTHE: Ferdy, don't be so ham-fisted with Gustave again. It puts me off you for a long time.

FERDINAND: He knows what I'm talking about. He's perfectly aware of what's the matter with him.

(*GUSTAVE starts to snore loudly. VICTORINE strokes his head.*)

BERTHE: And what is that? I mean, that's different to the rest of us.

FERDINAND: He's jealous of Edouard.

(*GUSTAVE increases the volume of his snoring.*)

VICTORINE: The baby has dropped off. Now we can have some peace.

BERTHE: (*Touching VICTORINE.*) Sweetheart, I don't want him, honestly. Have I ever tried to take a man away from you? Besides, I don't think I'm that good…(*Kisses her.*) Alright? I tell you, Edouard will do a powerful job on this one, I know it…

VICTORINE: I shouldn't have snapped…but I am worried. I cannot bear to think of him being confused…

(*A bearded man – HUGO – suddenly erupts out of the river, spouting water, exhaling air.*)

FERDINAND: (*Jumping up.*) Hey, get out of here! Get out! This is private property!

BERTHE: (*Laughing.*) It's a river-god, Edouard! Just what you need!

VICTORINE: (*Pushing GUSTAVE off her lap.*) Come on out! Oh, look at him, he's out of breath…give him a hand.

FERDINAND: Go on, shove off, you've no right here…

VICTORINE: O shut up, Ferdy! Hey you, come and join us…

BERTHE: Don't send him away! Ask him over…

FERDINAND: Girls, you're ruining Edouard's afternoon…how is he going to paint with strangers here?

VICTORINE: Who cares? The picture's not going to work anyway.

FERDINAND: Get out, man! Go on! (*He raises his cane at HUGO as he wades out of the water.*) This is not a public bathing-place. You're trespassing…

(*HUGO, who is a swarthy, powerfully-built, shaggy character, grabs the cane and throws it away, still puffing and spitting water and wringing out his beard. He wears a tattered white pair of underpants.*)

HUGO: A hundred! I held my breath for a hundred.

FERDINAND: Edouard, for God's sake help me.

BERTHE: Welcome, river-god. Stop and recline a while. Edouard, got a pose for him? Can you handle a trident?

VICTORINE: Come and sit down. Here's a towel, dry yourself. (*She throws him a towel. Then she sees HUGO's boils for the first time. They are on his thighs.*)

HUGO: Sorry. I won't use your towel…

VICTIRINE: Go ahead. You're amongst friends.

FERDINAND: Look, let me explain…sir, we are having a picture painted…you are intruding…

VICTORINE: Give him some wine, Ferdy.

(*VICTORINE and BERTHE rub HUGO dry with the towel. FERDINAND unwillingly pours out a glass of wine, walks down-stage.*)

FERDINAND: Why don't you say something, Edouard? If you don't mind then I don't…the girls are just being awkward for the sake of it…they're bored I think. I'll let him stay for a couple of minutes then get rid of him…

HUGO: I would like to rest for a moment. I won't disturb you much longer. I ran out of breath and got frightened.

BERTHE: You swim late in the season.

HUGO: It is supposed to be good for me, the mineral salts in the water heal my boils…so my doctor says.

VICTORINE: Well, what is your name? Ferdy is too upset to introduce us.

FERDINAND: (*Giving the wine to HUGO.*) Not at all. Edouard does not seem to mind our visitor being here, so I can be as polite as naturally I would prefer to be. Forgive me, sir. I was protecting my friend's valuable working-time. I hope you will understand.

HUGO: Completely. Excuse my disrespect to your stick. (*He picks up the cane and returns it to FERDINAND with a smile.*)

FERDINAND: Now, we are composed again. At your feet, sir…is Monsieur Gustave Manet. He is not circulating in society today. So, an explanation of his presence rather than an introduction. This is Mademoiselle Victorine Meurent…

HUGO: Enchanted. My name is Moor.

VICTORINE: Moor? You have a first name?

BERTHE: It would be very difficult to call a river-god Moor.

HUGO: Hugo Moor.

FERDINAND: Then, Hugo, this is Madamoiselle Berthe Peudefrat.

HUGO: Enchanted.

BERTHE: Hello, Hugo Moor.

(*Pause.*)

HUGO: And your name, sir?

FERDINAND: Ferdinand Leenhoff.

BERTHE: Call him Ferdy like we do.

HUGO: Sir. (*Bows.*)

BERTHE: Have you had any lunch?

HUGO: Thank you, but I cannot join you. It is dangerous to swim on a full stomach and I must return to the other bank shortly. But I am enjoying this excellent wine. May I ask the name of the painter who is so busy?

VICTORINE: That is Edouard Manet, the brother of this thing here. It's alright, don't scratch your head, you've never heard of him.

HUGO: That is true, but then he has never heard of me. Neither of us need feel ashamed. What is this picture?

FERDINAND: I think he will call it 'The Bathers' or something like that. It's an idyllic, pastoral thing. You know what I mean. Victorine here is naked, Berthe is in the river, Gustave and I are just sitting around doing nothing in particular...talking, I suppose.

HUGO: You are models?

VICTORINE: Yes.

HUGO: Do you think he is a good painter?

VICTORINE: I don't know.

HUGO: Does he?

VICTORINE: Oh yes. He knows he's good.

HUGO: That is what matters. To me that sounds like a strong man.

BERTHE: But what if he isn't any good?

HUGO: Then it will be painful for him finding out. But as he is a strong man, he will survive it. I hope I'm not disturbing him too much.

VICTORINE: He's not batting an eyelid.

GUSTAVE: (*Still with his eyes closed.*) Now, I'm going to guess what the river-god looks like. I haven't seen him, only heard his voice. You're all a witness to that. I am going to give you a full, accurate description of this river-god purely

from his voice, the sounds he has made, and the thoughts
he has expressed. Would anyone care to make a bet that I
can't do it?

HUGO: Ah, the sleeper awakes.

GUSTAVE: Shamming, I'm afraid. I do a lot of shamming.
I sham all sorts of achievements, but my speciality is
breakdowns. I can break down at a moment's notice. Now,
no bets? Come on, this isn't easy, you know. Think of all
the possibilities. I don't know whether he's tall, or
short...anything, only the voice...ten francs anyone? Five?
(*He stands up, back to HUGO.*)

HUGO: I will pay you five francs for the entertainment, but
I will have to send it to you. Go on. It will be fun.

GUSTAVE: Are you all satisfied that I have not looked at this
river-god at all? That I am working only with my
imagination, and my intelligence...hear this Edouard? And
my sensitivity! And sixth sense!

VICTORINE: He must be talking about someone else.

GUSTAVE: The river-god has told me only two things about
himself: that he has boils – I apologise for raising that; and
that he likes to test himself – his underwater counting; ah,
three, he disarmed Ferdy with little effort; four, he
apologised; five, he did not give his first name; six, he likes
good wine...Hugo, you have told me so many things but
how does that help me make a real picture of you? What
do you look like? I'll tell you, river-god. (*Pause.*) You are a
golden myth, a dream with a disease. You are as much
a myth as Zeus, and Aphrodite – she's sitting next to you,
that pale, hairless thing like a Mexican dog, ears and all. It's
all a myth, except money. Fat and false and filthy and
French. And here we are in this beautiful world, talking to
men we have not seen.
(*Pause. GUSTAVE remains with his back to HUGO, then
puts out a hand. HUGO takes it. GUSTAVE smiles. They
hold the handclasp. Lights fade to blackout.*)

End of Act One.

ACT TWO

GUSTAVE and HUGO in the handclasp, GUSTAVE still with his eyes shut.

GUSTAVE: Good man.

HUGO: If you're going to look at me now, brace yourself. I'm a terrible sight.

GUSTAVE: Is it that bad?

BERTHE: Don't believe him, Gustave. He's a fine figure of a man.

GUSTAVE: Ssh! Don't demote him. He's a river-god, Berthe. (*Pause.*) When I open my eyes, however you look, I'm going to like you. Yes, I'm going to do that on trust. For as long as you are here, I'm going to like you, and have faith in you, river-god.

VICTORINE: Hugo, you are suddenly in a lot of trouble.

HUGO: It will be a risky business? Well, what else is life for? Sir, don't expect too much. I'm only a poor man.

GUSTAVE: Oh, stay a myth and make some money. (*Opens his eyes.*) There! You're just as I thought. You look the same as your voice sounds.

HUGO: I'll have to think about whether that is a compliment or not.

GUSTAVE: You are everything I expected. Edouard, look at this. Now here is a chance for me to be helpful. I know a secret. You have taken the positions in the picture from Gorgione, who took them from Raphael, who took them from some tombs in Rome. You don't deny it, you can't, I saw the sketches. Now, in the original, was a river-god, sitting like Ferdy is supposed to be, and naked. So, give Ferdy the elbow and substitute this splendid specimen who has just beached himself here by a stroke of great good luck! Ferdy is taking the whole thing far too seriously anyway. (*Pause.*) At least think about it. Go on, put him in the picture – Hugo, I regret to say that you have been rejected.

HUGO: How humiliating.

GUSTAVE: Now you have no function. You are useless.

HUGO: I am thoroughly ashamed of myself.

GUSTAVE: Would you like the loan of a razor?

> (*Pause. HUGO laughs and puts an arm round GUSTAVE's shoulder. GUSTAVE smiles then abruptly pushes HUGO away and points an accusing finger.*)

> What are you doing here?

HUGO: Pardon?

GUSTAVE: You should be back in Egypt, working on the canal.

HUGO: I should?

GUSTAVE: If you think you can desert your post, throw away your shovel and come to Paris to find more profitable employment, you are mistaken! You must return to the diggings at once, in chains! Swim back!

HUGO: I will have to think about it.

GUSTAVE: No time. What does the tribunal say?

BERTHE: Well, even if he doesn't go, his pants will have to. I'm not prepared to see the fashions altered to suit them. Victorine would look dreadful in those, wouldn't you, darling? What a sight.

VICTORINE: Have you got black blood in you?

HUGO: No.

GUSTAVE: Liar! Lowest of the lowest fellaheen! Do you eat flies?

VICTORINE: You're very dark. Berthe likes dark men.

HUGO: (*Bowing.*) Then I am content.

FERDINAND: Forgive them. We can't do anything about their manners when we hire them. This is all sport.

HUGO: I had seen that a long time ago. It is good to laugh so soon with new people.

> (*Pause.*)

GUSTAVE: Well, the kindest thing said today. For that he must be excused his pants.

> (*VICTORINE gives HUGO's pants a tug as if to pull them off. He sheers away.*)

FERDINAND: Victorine! Enough! Behave yourself.

VICTORINE: I just wanted to be sure he wasn't the Bearded Lady from the circus.

GUSTAVE: We are prepared to turn a blind eye to the fact
that you are an escaped labourer from the Suez Canal – no
doubt the company are scouring the desert for you right
now – providing, and you must swear to this, that you do
not own a single share of stock in that ridiculous enterprise.

HUGO: Not a one.

GUSTAVE: Promise?

HUGO: On my oath.

GUSTAVE: I would have to withdraw every kind word I've
said about you if I discovered that you were as big a fool as
I am. Now these people have not taken you into their
hearts like I have – but they will. These girls are trained to
take strangers into their bosoms with immense speed, and
this man will attack you with a chisel if you stand still long
enough. They are all of them mad. You're mad!

HUGO: Is he talking to me?

VICTORINE: It might seem that way, but he's actually
addressing every word to his brother.

GUSTAVE: Foiled again! More wine, Hugo? Now you mustn't
let me down. A river-god has got a job to do. Come on,
mystify! (*Pause.*) Mystify! Me!

HUGO: Er, abracadabra. It is not raining.

GUSTAVE: Brilliant! It's not!

HUGO: You are sober.

GUSTAVE: Completely true! The river-god works! Wind him
up and he works.

VICTORINE: You understand our problem with Gustave
now, Hugo. He is harmless enough. He gives his love as
easily as he pays for his drinks.

GUSTAVE: The gutter interests me most. I have asked
Edouard to paint me lying in the gutter covered in rubbish,
like this…(*Lies down.*) From here your boils look like
mountains. Berthe will squeeze them for you. She has long
nails and the icy spirit of a surgeon.

BERTHE: He should be in an asylum. We will get round
to it.

HUGO: Wine. It is very good wine. I could get that way
myself with very little encouragement.

VICTORINE: Edouard is sketching you, I think. No, don't keep still. It is over in a flash. There. I think he's finished. Painless, wasn't it?

HUGO: I must look terrible. Excuse these pants, but I had nothing else to wear. My decision to take a swim was rather spontaneous.

BERTHE: Ah, a man of impulse. They are decent, big-hearted garments. Victorine and I are students of such drawers, aren't we, love? We have a collection which we are going to donate to the National Museum when we die. It includes the Emperor's truss...

VICTORINE: The Emperor's liberty bodice.

BERTHE: His whalebone corsets – with diamonds.

VICTORINE: And his monocle, which he wears in his arse so he can watch the door for Republican spies.

GUSTAVE: Girls, you might be less vulgar with Hugo until you find out whether he's a priest or not. In his present state you can't tell whether he's religious or secular.

BERTHE: Are you a priest? Please say no.

HUGO: No, I am a sort of evangelical atheist.

VICTORINE: That will do. You're a good sport.

BERTHE: Are you married?

HUGO: Yes.

BERTHE: Do you love your wife?

HUGO: Yes.

VICTORINE: You don't! Look me in the eye and say that.

BERTHE: Are you sure? Victorine is hot for you.

HUGO: Absolutely certain.

VICTORINE: You never fancy a change?

FERDINAND: Don't answer them. They're playing with you.

BERTHE: Don't anticipate Ferdy, don't anticipate.

VICTORINE: Does your wife send you out in pants like that?

HUGO: I just grabbed a few things and put them in my case...

VICTORINE: You took them off the corpse of your wife's lover.

BERTHE: There's a twinkle in your eye. You don't love your wife.

HUGO: If you could meet my wife I know you would like her.

VICTORINE: That's nothing to do with it. What I'm saying is
    I bet she's worn you out. Admit it. Wives wear men out.
BERTHE: You can admit it to us. We understand.
VICTORINE: Give me ten minutes and I will make you
    forget your wife. It will be an experience from which you
    will never recover. Your whole life will change. Berthe,
    underneath all that I think he's blushing.
FERDINAND: Perhaps we should settle down now and let
    Edouard get on with his work…
HUGO: Yes, here is your towel, thank you. You have been
    kindness itself. I hope I will find an opportunity one day to
    pay you back.
GUSTAVE: No! Don't go…
FERDINAND: Sir, it would help…
GUSTAVE: We want him to stay. He's doing no harm.
    Edouard doesn't mind.
FERDINAND: You are imposing on his good-nature…
GUSTAVE: Edouard's got all the time in the world.
FERDINAND: My friend here doesn't want this picture
    completed. He has his own weird reasons which would
    take too long to explain. Without wishing to appear
    impolite, these reasons are nothing to do with wanting
    you here…
VICTORINE: Ferdy, what a slave-driver. Edouard isn't
    objecting. Let him stay for a while.
GUSTAVE: Why don't I want the picture completed, Ferdy?
    Enlighten me?
    (*Pause. HUGO listens, interested.*)
FERDINAND: Because you know it will get Edouard into
    the Salon.
    (*HUGO moves towards the river.*)
GUSTAVE: (*Abstractedly.*) Er…don't go, river-god, I need you.
    Can't you see why? You hear what this monster is saying?
FERDINAND: You are obstructing this painting, Gustave.
    You're frightened of it…
    (*GUSTAVE lunges after HUGO and grabs him by the foot.*)
GUSTAVE: No, don't go. Help me.
HUGO: I must get back…

GUSTAVE: Edouard, do this poor fish a favour, immortalise him. Why shouldn't we share…

HUGO: (*Laughing.*) Why don't you want this picture finished?

GUSTAVE: I might like it! That would ruin me!
(*Pause. HUGO prises GUSTAVE's fingers off his ankle.*)

HUGO: I could stay a while. (*Smiles.*) If the artist doesn't mind. Do you?

GUSTAVE: You're my only hope, river-god. If I could persuade you to transfer to being a canal-god it would be better, but I'll take you as you are, which is more than Edouard could. He would distort you, deliberately. (*Grabs HUGO's foot again, kisses it.*)

HUGO: (*Good-naturedly.*) Come on, you can let go now.
(*Struggles free.*)

GUSTAVE: My brother is mad. It has been creeping up on him for years. He will paint something, come back the next day, look at it and say – there! That is the truth. But it's in his head, not mine. It looks a mess to me. It looks unreal to me. But, Ferdy, even the girls when they're pleased with him, they say…yes, you've got it. That mess is the truth…

FERDINAND: You're blind, Gustave,…

GUSTAVE: No I'm not, I'm scared. You know why? Because I'm starting to be convinced. I look at what he's painting, then at the thing itself – which is completely different – and I swell the chorus! Yes, I mouth, that's real, that's the truth. And I know it's not! So what is happening to me…?
(*Whistle, shouts off. HUGO freezes.*)
…I'm being bullied by him…this picture's the last straw…

HUGO: Hush! Please…

BERTHE: What's the matter?

HUGO: Just a moment…

BERTHE: What is it? Are you in trouble? Is the filth after you?

GUSTAVE: A wanted man? You lucky fellow.

HUGO: I will explain later. If we could keep quiet for a moment.
(*Pause.*)

FERDINAND: You will understand if I ask for that explanation.

HUGO: Let me make sure. (*Pause.*) I think they've moved on.
Yes, of course. It is quite simple really. I am in France
illegally.

FERDINAND: You have not committed a crime?

HUGO: No.

VICTORINE: Why didn't you come in the proper way?

HUGO: They would not let me in.

VICTORINE: Why?

HUGO: They think I'm a nuisance.

VICTORINE: Why?

HUGO: Why don't you ask them?

VICTORINE: We don't talk to the filth. What have you done?

BERTHE: That's his business…

VICTORINE: Do you kill tarts?

HUGO: How good is your memory?

VICTORINE: Not bad.

HUGO: There was some trouble in Paris fourteen years ago. I
was involved. In all fairness I should add that France is not
the only country where I am not welcome. Belgium threw
me out, Prussia heaved me over the border…only England
will have me.

VICTORINE: Why will the English have you?

HUGO: Because they do not take me seriously.

FERDINAND: I thought the English took everything seriously.
(*Pause.*)

BERTHE: Hugo, there's no need to be afraid…

FERDINAND: I'll have to sort this out with Edouard.

BERTHE: What's it got to do with him?

FERDINAND: This is Manet land! If the police find him here,
with us, there could be a lot of trouble. It could affect
Edouard's chances with the Hanging Committee for
the Salon.
(*Pause. GUSTAVE hides his head, laughing.*)

BERTHE: Manet land? Does that make it holy? Ferdy, stop
making such a fool of yourself. The Salon is a room – just
that, a room. Edouard can survive without it. Stop being
such a shit. You're shaming him.

FERDINAND: Edouard! He must go. We can't have trouble
with the police.

VICTORINE: Ferdy, you're a disgrace. How do you think Hugo looks at us now, eh? Manet land. What a thing to say to anyone.

BERTHE: (*Walking off into the trees.*) Don't you talk to me again, Ferdy. I don't want to even look at you, you collaborator!

FERDINAND: As you like. (*Coming down-stage.*) Edouard, this is a serious matter…

HUGO: In a moment I will go the way I came. Monsieur Manet, I am sorry for the upset I have caused.

VICTORINE: Edouard is not asking you to go.

HUGO: I think the police have moved away.

FERDINAND: Edouard, the Emperor has complete control over the Hanging Committee. One whiff of scandal and you'll never have another painting accepted…

VICTORINE: For Christ's sake, Ferdy, don't make him worse than he is!

FERDINAND: You want him to end up like the others? Living out in the provinces on butchers' portraits, no medals, no one writing about him, no one taking notice… (*Returns.*) That's what can happen if you're not careful.

VICTORINE: Ferdy, Edouard can take care of himself. (*Pause.*) He's kept Suzanne quiet for long enough, and Leon.

FERDINAND: That doesn't involve the police. (*Turns to HUGO.*) Sir, I mean no personal offence, but I believe that man down there to be a great painter. I think he has some genius now, and will have more later. But he must have the time, the freedom, the right conditions. He is not the kind of artist who thrives on adversity.

VICTORINE: Stop poncing for him, Ferdy.

FERDINAND: No one has ever seen simple things the way he does. He will be recognised. People will come round to him. Now they are hostile, that is to be expected, but give them a few years and they will flock to him. He will be adored as he deserves to be.

HUGO: I respect your dedication. Does he?

FERDINAND: He does, but even if he didn't I would think the same. (*Pause.*)

HUGO: Sacrifices have to be made. I will go back the way I came. If the police catch me I will only be deported, not guillotined.

BERTHE: And you'd let him go, wouldn't you, Ferdy? The rest of us say no, Hugo, Edouard himself says no. We would never be so impolite as to help the filth.

HUGO: No, it is not important. I don't want to spoil your day…

(*HUGO walks towards the river. GUSTAVE bars his way, arms out-stretched.*)

GUSTAVE: I will not allow a river-god to go to his doom because of my brother. Edouard, that Manet mole-hill on Manet land is only a conventional, hypocritical pygmy who paints rebelliously for prizes.

FERDINAND: If there is a scandal, Gustave, your mother will hear of this! You're being stupid and irresponsible.

GUSTAVE: Ferdy, if you were a better sculptor you wouldn't be so concerned that Edouard should be a better painter.

BERTHE: And we never help the filth, Ferdy! Never! Let me ever catch you lifting a finger for them and I'll get someone to make mincemeat out of you. I mean it!

VICTORINE: Don't kid yourself about the filth, Hugo. They're bad.

BERTHE: Things have changed. These are the Emperor's police now.

VICTORINE: Once they get hold of you…finish.

HUGO: I don't think they'll go that far. I'm not a French citizen.

BERTHE: They'll just make you disappear. Ask the anarchists. They drop out of sight like peas off your plate.

HUGO: Really, I think it would be better if I went…

BERTHE: No you're not. You stay where you are. You can't be sure the filth have moved on. Have something to eat and a few drinks. Give them time to get miles away.

HUGO: They could come back.

VICTORINE: Then we'll let them have Gustave. He has been doing back-street abortions…

GUSTAVE: Purely for practice.

BERTHE: And Ferdy, well, he's got a record. He is the worst
sculptor to come out of Zalt-Bommel. It would be a wise
move to take away his mallet and lock him up for life.

HUGO: I must admit, that water looks colder every minute.

BERTHE: He's going to stay.

VICTORINE: Come on, Edouard, come and drink with us.
We're not doing any more work today. Take a rest, relax.
Leave it. (*Pause.*) Miserable louse. (*Angrily.*) Oh, give up on
it, will you. Who wants to look at us mixed up like that?
Come and get drunk...oh, suit yourself then...

BERTHE: I'll be very straight with you, Hugo. You're my kind
of man. I know there's a real chin under all that hair.
(*Pause.*) I fancy you.

GUSTAVE: When Berthe says that, most men either run up
the white flag or run up the street. What are you going
to do?

HUGO: Remind her that I am old enough to be her father.

BERTHE: You think that worries me? Hugo, I have to take
men who collapse when they take off their corsets, men
who have to pull themselves up with a chair...so you?
You're perfect. (*Pause.*) All my men have boils.
(*BERTHE swiftly kisses HUGO's leg. FERDINAND
leans back, adjusts his hat.*)

FERDINAND: (*Casually.*) What is it like in England now?

HUGO: They have the fastest machines you have ever seen,
and the worst poverty. It is an extreme country.

FERDINAND: Extreme? The English? Aren't they slow?

HUGO: Watch England. It is becoming very strong. May
I beg another glass of this wine? It is doing me a world
of good.

VICTORINE: I have never been to England.

HUGO: Go if you can. It is very interesting.

VICTORINE: Are people rich?

HUGO: Moving ahead, very quickly.

VICTORINE: Are you rich?

HUGO: No.

VICTORINE: Why do you live there?

HUGO: Who else will have me?

VICTORINE: Why do they keep chucking you out?

HUGO: You know what's the worst? I am Prussian! Yet I'm
thrown out of Prussia! What do you think of that?

GUSTAVE: I think that is very strange.

(*FERDINAND walks down-stage and sits on the edge of
the apron, sipping a glass of wine.*)

River-god, you haven't answered Victorine's question.

HUGO: Give me time. I'm thinking about it.

FERDINAND: Edouard, Leon. I'm afraid Suzanne is too
reticent. Much as I'd like to leave you free to concentrate
on your work, as the boy's uncle I must try and protect his
interests. I know the problem is the Salon. If you admit
paternity there may be a scandal and the Committee will
shut you out. So any public recognition of Leon is out, but I
think you should tell the boy you are his father in private.
He would appreciate that. I think he suspects the truth, but
he doesn't know, which puts him in a difficult position.
Edouard, he only wants to be real. Let him exist, let him
live in the full knowledge that he is a genuine Manet. Give
him the proof he needs. A signature on a piece of paper
which we will lodge with a lawyer. You are my son. I will
get him to agree not to publicise his authenticity until you
are dead. How about that as an idea? (*Pause.*) You are
unmoved. Then I must ask you to bring to mind another
boy, Alexandre, your little apprentice and brush-washer
from the old studio. He looked on you as his father. He
loved you, but you kept him at arm's length, didn't you?
You kept the poor child an orphan in spirit as well as fact.
You wouldn't join in his make-believe, which was cruel. Do
you remember the day you found him hanging in the
studio? Yes, next to your other pictures. Do you want Leon
to go the same way and kill himself because you will not
admit to his creation? (*Pause.*) Alright, forget it. I didn't
hope for much when I brought it up. Carry on with your
work and we'll sort something out...But I feel it, Edouard, I
feel it! You know, I never accepted the post-mortem verdict
on Alexandre, did you? The boy's brain can't have been
infected...no, no, not at that age, surely? You've got to be
sexually mature before you can contract it, and he wasn't,
was he?

HUGO: I think they threw me out because I am not a
    Prussian, I am an internationalist, a citizen of the world.

VICTORINE: Does it say that on your passport?

HUGO: No. Nor does it say under 'Profession' man of ideas.
    But that's what I am. You see these boils, blast them?! They
    are the physical consequences of finding ideas. I have to
    spend ten, twelve hours a day, reading. The benches are
    hard, my diet is not what it should be, my clothing is rough,
    my skin sensitive…so, boils. One bursts, another heals,
    another starts. See the scars all over my legs, and my
    backside too…

GUSTAVE: We'll take your word for it.

VICTORINE: Tell us some of your ideas, or will it give you
    mouth ulcers?

HUGO: My doctor recommends swimming. It is a circulation
    problem. (*Pause.*) First, that man has an economic destiny.
    Secondly, that though it is inevitable, being destined, it can
    be accelerated. Thirdly, it is governed by science.

GUSTAVE: Would your idea enable me to qualify earlier
    and obtain a profitable practice in a fashionable quarter of
    Paris?

HUGO: It would not, I'm afraid.

GUSTAVE: Then, as an instrument of change, you are as
    much use to me as my brother's masterpieces. You both
    just lie there and expect us to stagger back, blinded with
    amazement.

HUGO: That kind of reaction does help on the days when one
    is feeling insecure.

GUSTAVE: I think you are some kind of confused god like my
    brother. Do you keep yourself?

BERTHE: Gustave, why in hell do you always have to
    know that?

GUSTAVE: It matters. I love this man. I pledged myself to
    him. I have a right to know whether he is a parasite or not.
    Who keeps you?

HUGO: My friends, my mother, my colleagues.

GUSTAVE: You have no paid employment?

HUGO: No.

GUSTAVE: Brother! (*Hugs him.*) You are one of us.

HUGO: I have employment though. I am in the middle of writing a very long book. No, don't look hopeful. It is not a novel. My guess is that it would bore you to death. It does me, sometimes.

GUSTAVE: I knew you were my brother in spirit. You are as useless as I am. A book no one will want to read? How will you sell it, by weight? For a doorstop?

HUGO: Or propping up furniture. But not government furniture.

GUSTAVE: Ah!

HUGO: You are excited.

GUSTAVE: Edouard, paint this man's picture quickly and we can sell it to the police.

VICTORINE: Is that all you do? Scribble?

HUGO: Yes, nearly.

VICTORINE: You don't have to come to Paris in secret to scribble.

HUGO: No. I have come to meet some people. They invited me over.

VICTORINE: What's this book about?

HUGO: Economics.

VICTORINE: I don't know what that is.

HUGO: It's the science of money. I am a scientific writer.

VICTORINE: You come to Paris just to see some friends? You take a risk like that?

HUGO: They have asked me for some help.

VICTORINE: About money?

HUGO: Yes, in a way.

VICTORINE: Then you can give Berthe and me a hand while you're here. We're broke.

HUGO: (*Laughing.*) I have to work on a big scale.

VICTORINE: We can get you as many people as you can handle. If you are good with money why haven't you got any?

HUGO: I didn't say I was interested in making it, just studying it.

VICTORINE: Oh. Just looking at it? (*Pause.*) I think you must be crazy.

HUGO: There are others who agree with you.

VICTORINE: But I'll read your book. I wouldn't miss that.

FERDINAND: Hugo, I'm quite interested…er, casually you know. Is this some pet theory you've got? I think I've read everything there is to read on economics, and there's not much except for Smith and Ricardo…

GUSTAVE: Smith and Ricardo, an amazing double-act will jump through a hoop of fire wearing leg-irons, hair shirts and Spanish sombreros. Hugo, Ferdy has read the titles, the titles. He is trying to impress you.

FERDINAND: Will you shut up, Gustave? Stop making such a virtue out of your ignorance.

GUSTAVE: Smith and Ricardo. Pah!

FERDINAND: Go and do something elsewhere. Go on, I'm tired of you.

GUSTAVE: I don't do what you tell me to do.

FERDINAND: You're a stupid drunken baby, Gustave. Go on, leave us in peace for a while.

HUGO: There is no need…

FERDINAND: There are times when one must insist with Gustave. He is spoilt. We listen most of the time, we endure him for Edouard's sake. Go on Gustave, do some fishing.

GUSTAVE: I don't want to.

FERDINAND: Do some fishing or I'll sort you out!

GUSTAVE: Alright.

(*GUSTAVE goes to the boat, takes out a rod and reel and starts to thread the line, attach the hook and float. Pause.*)

FERDINAND: That's better. Yes, Hugo, money. Obviously it's interesting.

HUGO: I don't limit myself to money. My theme is bigger.

FERDINAND: But the main problems have been solved I think, you'll admit that. There is a steady improvement all round.

HUGO: Yes. The present system is creating wealth at a phenomenal rate, unprecedented in human economic history. There has never been such prosperity. Productivity is rising, communications improving, trade booming.

FERDINAND: So what are you saying that's so dangerous? That it will suddenly stop? Collapse?

HUGO: Oh no, it will go on like this. There may be temporary depressions, bad harvests, but in general the economy of Europe will carry on growing. I think we have thirty, forty years of it to look forward to. Yes, it will be a period of unprecedented development.

FERDINAND: Well, that's a relief.

GUSTAVE: Victorine, come and help me catch a fish.

VICTORINE: (*Getting up.*) Poor Gustave. Are you miserable? (*Strokes his head.*) It sounds as though the Suez Canal might work after all.

GUSTAVE: I wish I could sing an aria from Smith and Ricardo.

VICTORINE: Ferdy will get tough with you again.

FERDINAND: So, if you were an investor, Hugo, you'd recommend a working knowledge of economics?

HUGO: It is the science of the future.

GUSTAVE: Tran-ta-ra-ra! The briefest of overtures introduces Smith and Ricardo's latest musical masterpiece, a new opera entitled, 'Doom In The Diggings' or 'Holes In Very Fine Sand Are Impossible'. A hush, the hush of paper money sleeping on gold. The curtain rises on the forecourt of the Temple of Plenty. Pause. Enter Industry in a cast-iron helmet, bare-breasted and bathed in the light of Dawn, sharp eyes searching a silent horizon for smoke. Good morning! she trills to the welcoming hordes of Suez Canal labourers up to their ears in night-shift sand. Good morning! they roar in the key of B Minor. How goes it? She asks in a commanding contralto only rivalled by the assembled fog-horns of the British navy as a thousand ships sail into view, hurrying to be first through the new international waterway. Where are you all headed for, you mercantile matelots? thunders the bass-baritone from Boulogne who is playing Capital tonight. A golden future, sing the men of the merchant marine augmented by ten tenors from Trieste, two from Tannenberg and one from Toronto in favour of transatlantic trade. We are all going to make a f-o-r-t-u-n-e! How? boom a billion basses from Birmingham, Bali and New Brunswick. Ferrying flax, fodder, fol-de-rols and farinaceous foods to Hong Kong, Korea and Christmas Island, sings a solo soprano salivating sideways over her superlative salary. Exploiter! exhales an arsehole from Amsterdam! Materialist! moos an adroit but atrocious alto from Avignon 'aving acute agony with 'is 'igh A's and aitches. 'Oo cares? calls a counter-tenor to his crumbling coloratura who has tits trapped in the oddly included accordion in the almighty orchestra. No one! crescendoes a chorus of churls in chains on their way to China 'oping to re-open the opium trade. Ya got the money? Ya got the ending? Ya got the score? A final aria by a boy treble bleeding from the nose, entitled Man is monkey (Do ah win, do ah lose?) then take out the K and make it money, monkey without the K, without the kudos, without the Christ, without the credence, and the curtain comes tumbling down! Rapturous applause! Smith and Ricardo are called to the stage! Author! Author! We have a hit on our hands tonight! The Suez Canal is filled with champagne and the crocodiles weep with alcoholic remorse, of course!

FERDINAND: Edouard, I can't stand this fool any more. I'm going home.

BERTHE: Ferdy, don't be such a wet blanket.

FERDINAND: He is deliberately wasting our time.

GUSTAVE: Ferdy, I'll be quiet. I promise. (*Takes a jar out of the boat.*) You carry on with your apology for economics, Hugo. (*Pause.*) Well, go on. Ignore me. (*Opens the jar.*)

HUGO: Many of the basic principles of economics…

GUSTAVE: (*Taking out a live worm.*) Dug them in the garden this morning. The manure-pile is teeming with them, millions of red worms.

HUGO: (*Laughing.*) I surrender.

GUSTAVE: This is a Manet worm. See, Ferdy? He's wriggling. (*Holds it up.*) Edouard, part of the family portrait! Keep still you brute! Now, the hook…

VICTORINE: Well, don't show us! We don't want to see.

GUSTAVE: The worm is about to start his working life. Hugo is delighted aren't you? This Manet worm was useless until this moment, now it is about to become economically viable. It can't feel anything. It's quite stupid...but useful. Right? I'm going to put it on the hook...

(*VICTORINE slaps his hand and the worm drops to the ground. GUSTAVE goes to stamp on it but HUGO covers the worm with his foot, then picks it up.*)

HUGO: No. Give me the jar.

(*GUSTAVE gives the jar to HUGO. He puts the worm back, holds out his hand for the top. GUSTAVE hands it over. HUGO carefully puts it on, holds the jar up to look at the worms, then replaces the jar in the boat.*)

GUSTAVE: Then I'll have to use bread.

FERDINAND: (*Shrugging.*) I give up, Edouard, I give up.

(*GUSTAVE takes a piece of bread, goes to the boat, sits on the gunwhale, baits his hook with bread-flake, then casts into the river, settles the line, then sits very still. Pause. He turns, smiles at HUGO, winks, turns back. Pause. BERTHE pats FERDINAND's hand, gets up, smiles at HUGO, then walks down-stage.*)

BERTHE: Edouard, could you ask for a better life? (*Pause.*) Of us all you have got closest to doing what you want to do with your time. These are little arguments, pinpricks. Gustave does love you. When his brother is accepted and praised, you watch him then. What he wants more than anything is to see people buying your work. Then it will be alright. You will be completely vindicated. It is this in-between time, while you are building up your reputation, that is difficult for him. When you make the break-through, Gustave will be on top of the world. And, you know what else will happen? Ferdy will get less interested, because this is the kind of moment he enjoys – watching something grow. Remember I said that. We'll see if I'm right...

GUSTAVE: Ah!

HUGO: A bite?

GUSTAVE: A knock, a nibble. Here we go again.

HUGO: Strike then.

GUSTAVE: Which is exactly what you said to the Egyptians, you radical swine!

(*HUGO laughs.*)

BERTHE: The good thing about it is the way you keep us all together. We fight, who doesn't, but each day there is someone suggesting that we go here for dinner, go there for a walk. For me, I enjoy it when you join in and talk and tell us why you see people like you do, and why you choose one light in preference to another...the technicalities, the ideas, I know that you can't always explain down to the bottom level, but that's where this bond comes in. There is a bond. We all feel it, we've all got it. There have been times when I wished more than anything that I could be released from its responsibilities, cleaned and cured. I know Victorine gets the same way. But we always come back for more. You know why?

HUGO: The Suez Canal, my friend, is being dug by slaves.

GUSTAVE: Slaves, by definition, cannot stop work. If they do, they die.

HUGO: The Egyptian labourer is in the same position. Yet he chooses to starve. Why? (*Pause.*) When Rameses the Second started the original canal two thousand years ago, it was dug by slaves, the same slaves that built the Pyramids. This canal, two thousand years later, is being dug by slaves as well, and if they finish it in their present conditions of employment they will have raised an equal monument to the pharaohs of contemporary capitalism.

GUSTAVE: You mean there's been another canal?

HUGO: It was a failure also.

GUSTAVE: We're repeating a failure? I've invested my dead father's money in an ancient flop? Things are worse than I thought. The dead are investing in the dying.

BERTHE: We're moths round a flame. (*Turns to HUGO.*) Give Edouard ten francs and he'll paint your boils out for you. He could even improve the size of your brain. (*Pause. HUGO looks into the audience and laughs.*)

HUGO: That is the kind of help I need.

GUSTAVE: (*Twitching the rod.*) There's something moving down there. (*Pause.*) At last we know what the Sphinx is smiling at. Me, the small-time French investor, the small-time French revolutionary, the small-time French lover, the small-time French father, French letter, pox and leave.

VICTORINE: Will you tell us about your wife, please, Hugo.

HUGO: My wife?

VICTORINE: Tell us about her. Is she good-looking?

HUGO: My wife is a beautiful woman.

BERTHE: Are you sure?

HUGO: Of course I'm sure. She was the most beautiful girl in the town I lived in…by far. There was no one to match her.

BERTHE: Was?

HUGO: She could have had any husband she liked.

VICTORINE: How long have you been together?

HUGO: Twenty years.

VICTORINE: Hell.

BERTHE: No wonder he's in love with science. Twenty years? Twenty minutes is long enough for me. Where is she from?

HUGO: My home town. It's on the French border…

BERTHE: Don't be smart, Hugo. I mean what class is she from? The town doesn't matter.

(*Pause.*)

HUGO: She is from an aristocratic family.

BERTHE: I could tell.

HUGO: How?

BERTHE: The way you said beautiful.

HUGO: Her brother is the Prussian Minister of the Interior, her father was a Privy Councillor. How did I say that?

BERTHE: You might just as well have stuck your finger up my nose.

VICTORINE: Another one. (*Sighs.*) Paris is full of them. If they're not Prussians they're Russians, if they're not Russians they're Rumanians. Hugo, you're a deadhead with a beautiful aristo wife. We've known hundreds. You outnumber the poor.

HUGO: Exiles don't ask to be exiles.

BERTHE: And you've never been unfaithful to this aristo?

HUGO: I've not been unfaithful.

VICTORINE: I thought there was only one way to say that.

FERDINAND: Girls, this is very discourteous.

BERTHE: Get out. He can't get away with that. Come on, Hugo, you're telling lies.

FERDINAND: Don't answer. They're hopelessly nosey.

HUGO: I think perhaps I should.

BERTHE: See Ferdy? He makes up his own mind. Go on, tell us about how you've been faithful.

HUGO: When we left Prussia – let's say we were invited to leave for a while – we came here, to Paris. One of my wife's servants followed us here – a girl.

VICTORINE: Aha!

HUGO: She has been with us all the time. Then, after twenty years, she needs me. My servant comes to me and says she needs me. Up until that moment there was nothing. (*Pause.*)

BERTHE: You agreed?

HUGO: It was not a negotiation. She made it plain, I must have you with me. So I went. She even bought a new bed.

VICTORINE: You left your wife?

HUGO: No.

VICTORINE: You deceived your wife under her own roof?

HUGO: My wife knew. If anyone agreed, it was her.

BERTHE: That is magnificent! Hooray for such a wife. Bring her over here!

VICTORINE: And is your servant happy now?

HUGO: A child was born. I think that was what she really wanted.

BERTHE: Your child?

HUGO: A child.

BERTHE: Do you have children by the aristo?

HUGO: Yes, three daughters.

VICTORINE: How old are they?

HUGO: A little younger than you, but not too much.

VICTORINE: Are they good-looking?

HUGO: To me...yes. I think they are anyway.

VICTORINE: But you'd never let them be tarts, would you?

HUGO: With the world as it is, all of us are tarts, aren't we?

BERTHE: Well said, if you mean it. If you don't, shit on you.

VICTORINE: I think he means it. He's sentimental. Give me a few minutes and I could make him cry.

BERTHE: Hugo, if you stayed long enough I think we might need you. Be warned. You must have more than enough women in your life.

HUGO: They're all over the place. Every door I go through has a woman on the other side.

VICTORINE: Take us home with you. We'll polish your boots and buy the beds.

HUGO: There's no room. (*Gets up with the towel round his shoulders and a glass of wine in his hand.*) Monsieur Manet, you have good friends. (*Walks down-stage.*) That is a kind of genius in itself. (*Lowers his voice.*) May I ask, in confidence, if I am completely unknown to you? I was under the impression that Paris was one of my lucky towns…somewhere that actually remembered. Oh, it was a long time ago, years. You were a child no doubt, interested in other things. But if you are seeing things differently, and you feel that certainty – is there a more wonderful sensation? – of being close to the true reality –
I might have been instrumental in bringing that gift to you. We may be looking through the same pair of glasses, you through one lens, me the other. I am not asking you to admit anything at this stage. It is only a chance. Your pictures may be laughable. But if they sing aloud with change, if they ring out like bells over this city – well, you might try and bring my name to mind from all your schoolbooks and bibles. Not an arresting title, no. Think of your own process. You take the light, you make it manifest within the eye, you give it sense and proportion – perhaps. That is my style, too. We should talk…

GUSTAVE: (*Throwing the rod down.*) Close the Seine! All the French fish are migrating to Mexico! And you, river-god, you are the underwater, under-cover agitator who provoked the Egyptian fellaheen and made them throw down their shovels! I see now, you are a dangerous myth indeed! Stand up and fight!

HUGO: I deny all charges. I am innocent, your worship.

FERDINAND: (*Coming up behind him.*) Did you recognise your child?

HUGO: I beg your pardon.

FERDINAND: The servant's child. Do you accept the servant's child?

HUGO: Well, the position…

FERDINAND: (*Furiously.*) DO YOU ACCEPT THE SERVANT'S CHILD?

HUGO: What do you mean? He lives in our house.

FERDINAND: Your house, Prussian? You own it? Now, the child: does it have your name?

HUGO: What is my name?

FERDINAND: So, you don't own it. You have not given it your name. It is not called Moor.

HUGO: It is not called Moor.

FERDINAND: And you are not ashamed?

HUGO: The boy is the equal of the others…

FERDINAND: But you have not given him your name. You will not publicly admit that his blood is yours.

HUGO: His blood is his own. I do not contribute to that view of society. I reject inheritance.
(*Pause.*)

FERDINAND: Convenient.

HUGO: (*Angrily.*) I have already lost four children! Did I own those?

FERDINAND: Losing presupposes owning.

HUGO: When he grows up he can take any name he likes.
(*Pause.*) It is philosophy that needs my name, not children.

FERDINAND: If you say so. I don't know your thoughts.

HUGO: I can even forgive Christianity much because it taught us to worship the child, but I must remain absolutely conscious that my scientific discovery marks a development in the history of the human race, not one individual, no matter how precious. (*Pause.*) I can have a thousand children and still leave nothing of myself behind.

FERDINAND: I understand.

HUGO: Do you?

FERDINAND: Please accept my apologies. I did not mean to raise my voice to you.

HUGO: That was the agreement. She has the child. It was all she wanted from me…

FERDINAND: Yes.

HUGO: Do you think that there are not enough names that people can call me without my providing more? They attack my ideas, why should I give them the chance to attack me? She knows that, the mother knows that, she would never want to expose me to public censure…

FERDINAND: Of course.

(*From off-stage right a shout, 'Hello!'*)

VICTORINE: Quiet! What was that?

(*Off, 'Hello!'*)

BERTHE: It's the filth!

VICTORINE: Hugo, they sound very close…

(*Off, 'Hello!'*)

GUSTAVE: They're on the island!

FERDINAND: That's it, we've had it. They're going to find him here.

VICTORINE: Hugo, put my dress on, and the bonnet.

FERDINAND: Edouard, I appeal to you…sort this out.

(*HUGO drags the dress over his head. VICTORINE and BERTHE help him, putting the bonnet on his head. VICTORINE then drops her cloak and sits down, naked.*)

VICTORINE: Go and squat in the trees.

HUGO: Squat?

VICTORINE: Look like you're having a piss.

(*HUGO goes into the trees and stands there.*)

Not like a man, you twat! Like a woman. Squat!

(*HUGO squats. BERTHE drops the top of her shift and exposes a breast. GUSTAVE and FERDINAND freeze as ERIQUE enters. He is a thin, sharp man wearing white trousers and a vest.*)

ERIQUE: Excuse me. I'm looking for a friend.

VICTORINE: Will I do?

ERIQUE: I'm sorry to disturb you but it is quite important.

(*BERTHE snatches up a knife from the picnic and holds it against ERIQUE's back ribs.*)

BERTHE: What do you want? Don't turn round or I'll spear your kidneys. Papers.

ERIQUE: Back pocket.

GUSTAVE: Who is this friend you're looking for?

(*BERTHE carefully removes some folded papers from ERIQUE's back pocket and hands them to FERDINAND.*)

ERIQUE: That is my business.

VICTORINE: If you are the filth you had better start composing a farewell speech.

FERDINAND: What am I supposed to do with these?

BERTHE: Look at them. Who is he?

(*FERDINAND opens the papers and scrutinises them.*)

ERIQUE: (*Nodding at HUGO who is still squatting, his back to him.*) Who is that?

VICTORINE: My mother.

ERIQUE: What is she doing?

VICTORINE: She's having a piss.

(*Pause.*)

ERIQUE: She must have a bladder like a horse.

FERDINAND: His name is Erique Claraud…he's a pattern-maker.

HUGO: Erique, it is you…(*Turns.*)

ERIQUE: Karl, thank God we've found you…

HUGO: Sssh! (*Comes across to ERIQUE.*) I told you not to follow me.

ERIQUE: We were worried that you'd drowned. There's a boat at the top end of the island…

VICTORINE: (*Putting the cloak back on.*) You know each other…alright. That is fine.

BERTHE: (*Dropping the knife.*) He looks good doesn't he? Disguise is obviously your strong point, Karl. (*Puts her breast back.*)

HUGO: I came in illegally. You don't expect me to use my own name, do you?

BERTHE: To us, yes. So who are you?

ERIQUE: He is the guest of my organisation.

VICTORINE: And what is that?

ERIQUE: We have a friendly society.

VICTORINE: You think you're the only one?

ERIQUE: It's a working-men's organisation.

VICTORINE: So is ours, only the hours are longer.

FERDINAND: He works in the cannon-foundry at Billancourt Arsenal.

(*Pause. FERDINAND gives the papers back to ERIQUE. Pause. They look at HUGO. He starts to take VICTORINE's dress off. It is a struggle. No one helps him. They stare at him in silence.*)

VICTORINE: Careful! You're stretching it...

ERIQUE: Then give him a hand.

VICTORINE: No. (*Pause.*) It doesn't matter. I'll have to burn it now anyway.

(*HUGO holds out the dress to VICTORINE. She indicates that he should throw it on the ground where it was originally. He obliges, tossing the bonnet after it.*)

HUGO: Don't waste a good dress. Erique, have you got a few francs?

(*ERIQUE gives HUGO some money out of his pocket.*)

HUGO: Here, get it cleaned, and the towel. (*Offers the money.*)

VICTORINE: No.

(*HUGO keeps his hand out, then shrugs, gives the money back to ERIQUE.*)

FERDINAND: Will you go now?

HUGO: Have you any idea of the conditions these men work under?

FERDINAND: I am not asking for explanations.

HUGO: Half the artillery for the French army and navy is made at Billancourt...

FERDINAND: We're not involved and we don't want to be.

VICTORINE: What are you, an arms-dealer?

ERIQUE: No, he's not. You can cut that out...

VICTORINE: How do we know? What do you want from a cannon-foundry? Justice?

(*Pause.*)

HUGO: Where are the police now?

ERIQUE: They're a long way off now. There's nothing to worry about. We've got your clothes in the boat.

GUSTAVE: Burn them. Let him sail back to England like that.

ERIQUE: Now stop this. He is my friend, so watch out...

GUSTAVE: Get off our land! My land!

HUGO: Why have you turned against me? What is all the excitement about?

FERDINAND: A scientist with a gun? An economist with a cannon?

HUGO: You cannot just argue on paper...

FERDINAND: Not such a joke now, eh Gustave? You get rid of him…

ERIQUE: He'll go when he's ready.

VICTORINE: Two-faced bastard!

ERIQUE: Shut up! You don't know what you're talking about. (*Pause.*)

VICTORINE: If there's no blood in the streets then no one is having a good time. We were kids at the last lot. Berthe had to search for her old man under a ton of straw at the morgue!

BERTHE: I'll deal with that. (*Pause.*) But I can rely on you to hate Louis Napoleon, can't I?

ERIQUE: Hate him? Destroyed him! He has written a whole book against the Emperor! He's torn him to pieces!

BERTHE: Then I'd like the name of the sod who put him back together again.

FERDINAND: Listen, both of you, the revolution, if you can bless that brawl with such a name, was the Emperor's birthday. Without it France would still be a republic…after that fiasco you couldn't even talk about democracy. The revolution made the Emperor inevitable.
(*Pause.*)

BERTHE: I'd like to ask you a question for myself.

ERIQUE: Karl, let's leave these bourgeois pigs to get on with it. No questions! We're going.

HUGO: What is the question?

BERTHE: Why does a servant woman want you as the father of her child and your homeland close its borders to you? (*Pause.*)

HUGO: I'll send you a copy of my book.

BERTHE: I don't read much, even under pressure.

HUGO: In the revolution of eighteen forty-eight in Paris, I had cause to go into a brothel. There was a sign painted on the ceiling of every room – Respect Your Comrade Sister! I like to think that my servant, and my home, give me equal credit in their own way.

VICTORINE: You, in a brothel? With a beautiful aristo wife? Well.

HUGO: I went there to deliver some newspapers.

BERTHE: You went there to sell newspapers?

HUGO: They only cost a few sous.

BERTHE: You took them newspapers, you'll send us books. What have you got against tarts?

VICTORINE: You're a stinking priest!

ERIQUE: Bitch, you'll get the back of my hand!

HUGO: No need, calm down…yes, Victorine, if I must be called a priest because I have beliefs…

FERDINAND: A scientific priest with a gun. Your creed must be complicated.

HUGO: Not at all. I am a materialist. I detest poverty.

GUSTAVE: You assured me that you had no shares in the Suez Canal.

(*Pause.*)

FERDINAND: Materialism is already triumphant! That is Capitalism!

HUGO: It must be adapted to the needs of the majority. As a faith it must fit the poor. There are two virulent diseases – Christianity and Capitalism.

GUSTAVE: A logical diagnosis by an impoverished Jew. (*Pause.*) In those pants even a man as deceitful as you cannot keep a secret.

ERIQUE: Shit! I'm not having that!

(*ERIQUE hits GUSTAVE, knocking him down. FERDINAND grabs ERIQUE's arms.*)

HUGO: That was a stupid thing to do. Go and stand over there and keep quiet!

(*FERDINAND releases ERIQUE who walks to the left and stands by himself, his back to GUSTAVE. HUGO offers GUSTAVE his hand. He takes it. HUGO pulls him to his feet.*)

Are you hurt?

(*GUSTAVE shakes his head, pulls his hand away.*)

Come to England, Gustave. Come and see me. I could use you. I could train you. Yes, I could. You have a lot to offer me. I could use you like you will never use yourself. Being with you here has upset me. I cannot stand waste. When I send you back to France, you should have a chance to outstrip Edouard. (*Pause.*) No? Take some time to think about it. If you do change your mind, come and visit me. My name is Doctor Marx and I live near Hampstead Heath in London. You will find me walking on Parliament Hill any day after lunch. (*Walks down-stage.*) Well, now I'll get out of your way so you can carry on with your work. I hope your view of reality is not as unpopular as mine is with the authorities. Perhaps you can get away with more in painting. We will leave from another part of the island, I don't think there is much danger of us being seen. Do you care if I am? (*Pause.*) Your manners are impeccable. If they arrest me, you and I might get closer together. There are Hanging Committees and Hanging Committees. (*Pause.*) And tell your brother that my offer is sincere. I can give him the chance to make something of his life.

ERIQUE: Karl, I think we should be getting back if you don't mind…

HUGO: Goodbye, Monsieur Manet, and good luck. (*Turns, walks back.*) Goodbye to all of you, and thanks for sharing your wine with me, (*Pause.*) Gustave…

(*GUSTAVE does not respond, his back turned to HUGO. HUGO whispers over his shoulder.*)

Tombs in Rome, graves in Egypt. That's not a wise investment. Sell them out and join us.

(*HUGO exits left with ERIQUE.*)

FERDINAND: (*Clapping his hands.*) Back to your places. There's not much light left.

(*BERTHE, VICTORINE, FERDINAND and GUSTAVE swiftly rearrange the scene until it is set exactly the same as the opening of the play, then slide into their original poses and positions.*

Lights fade to Blackout.

The picture is Edouard Manet's 'Dejeuner sur l'Herbe' which now hangs in the Musée d'Orsay, Paris.)

The End.

LIVINGSTONE AND SECHELE

For Nkas

NOTE

David Livingstone was born in Blantyre, Scotland, in 1831 and first set foot in Africa at Capetown in 1841 as a doctor/missionary headed for the free territory of Bechuanaland on behalf of the London Missionary Society. He married Mary, daughter of Robert Moffat, another Scottish missionary, in January 1845 and three months later made his first contact with the Kwena tribe and their chief, Sechele. By the end of the year Livingstone had sufficient influence with the chief to persuade him to move his people to a new settlement at Chonuane in order to be close to a permanent water-supply as the area was suffering from a severe drought. Six months later the move had to be repeated, this time to Kolobeng, 40 miles to the north, as the river dried up.

David Livingstone died of malaria and exhaustion in the Bengweulu Swamps of present-day Zambia in 1873, his wife Mary pre-deceasing him by eleven years at the mouth of the Zambesi, also of malaria. Sechele died of old age in 1892. The date of Mokokon's death is not recorded.

Characters

DAVID LIVINGSTONE
aged 35

MARY
his wife, aged 25

SECHELE
chief of the Crocodile People, aged 38

MOKOKON
his favourite wife, aged 25

Livingstone and Sechele was first performed at The Traverse Theatre, Edinburgh on 15 August 1979, with the following cast:

LIVINGSTONE, John Shedden

MARY, Ann Scott-Jones

SECHELE, Joe Marcell

MOKOKON, Muriel Odunton

Director, Peter Lichtenfels

Set in Kolobeng in the Kalahari Desert

ACT I: August 1848

ACT II: March 1849

R, a large circle chalked on the floor; L, a square of equal dimension. The upstage sectors of each form are built up into walls. Where they touch is an empty door frame with two English wooden chairs facing each other. An unhung door leans on L. Beneath the wall R is a bed of skins: beneath the wall L is a mattress made up into a perfect oblong of pure linen with two goosedown pillows. At the centre of the circle R (SECHELE'S rondavel) is a large stone quern; at the centre of the square (LIVINGSTONE's cabin) is a wooden table with a bulky object beneath it covered with canvas. Carved wooden stools, Victorian candlesticks, enamel plates, wooden cups are intermingled through both rondavel and cabin, a mixture of British and African styles at the level of simple living.
The walls are whitewashed, the floors the colour of red earth.
PRE-SET
Two balls of dough: one on the quern; one on the table.

ACT ONE

Blackout. Out of the darkness the voices of two women with Scottish accents singing very softly, to the tune of 'Auld Lang Syne'.

ABCD
Eh-EFG
HIJKLM
NOPQ
RSTU
VWXYZ

Lights fade up on MOKOKON pounding dough at the quern and MARY punching dough at the table. They synchronise their pounding with the alphabet learning song, building it up until it is strong, joyful and loud. MARY is dressed in plain blouse and skirt, MOKOKON in brilliant tribal finery.

Enter LIVINGSTONE from L with a Bible. He sits in the chair at L of the touching-point of rondavel and cabin, the empty door-frame, and starts reading. The women sing on, hammering out the lesson and their work, glancing at each other through the door-frame, laughing.

Enter SECHELE from R in his suit of skins, a wide-awake hat, military boots, flicking himself with a fly-whisk. As he passes MOKOKON he caresses her backside and the rhythm falters, picks up and continues. SECHELE sits in the chair R of the empty door-frame, takes off his hat, puts aside his fly-whisk, then leans across, takes LIVINGSTONE's hand and kisses it. LIVINGSTONE tugs it away, stands up.

LIVINGSTONE: Ladies, may we have the soft pedal for a while? Or even silence? Will you come to prayer?

MOKOKON: I have a lot to do.

SECHELE: Come and practice.

MOKOKON: I've already got the hang of it. You get down on your knees.

SECHELE: If you don't pray with me you'll get beaten.

MOKOKON: Now I know that Jesus is merciful.

(MOKOKON kneels with SECHELE, LIVINGSTONE and MARY. As MOKOKON presses her hands together they are seen to be white with the flour she has been making.)

LIVINGSTONE: Dear God, guide us through our studies so that Thy holy word be made plain to this man. Give me the gift of explanation, and him the wonder of understanding. Through Jesus Christ, the great physician to our sickness, the missionary to our ruined world. Amen.

SECHELE: Amen.

MARY: Amen.

MOKOKON: Huh.

(*SECHELE smacks the side of MOKOKON's head. She glares at him.*)

MOKOKON: Alright, alright. Amen.

LIVINGSTONE: (*Getting up.*) I think the ladies might get about their household chores while we do this detailed work on the Scriptures, Sechele. It is not for the superficial mind, you understand? And Mokokon is not sympathetic.

SECHELE: How can a woman see into the mind of Saint Paul?

MARY: His mother might have.

MOKOKON: Nothing is true because it is written down. (*Pause.*) Ask the people who cannot read.

MARY: Moko, don't reject the gospel because it needs thinking about.

SECHELE: It is beyond her. She is stupid, bless her. But I want a Saint Paul to happen to me, I must be struck down by God so that I can accept Christianity. I pray for it every day. I look forward to a thunderbolt of iron and fire. Wham!

MARY: God loves you now, Sechele. You don't have to wait for him to knock you about.

(*MOKOKON and MARY return to their work, making bread in their different ways.*)

SECHELE: David my love, shall we get started?

LIVINGSTONE Let's go back to where we left off yesterday. The Acts of the Apostles, chapter nine, verse seventeen.

SECHELE: Great stuff. A strong man Saint Paul.

LIVINGSTONE: And Ananias went his way, and entered into the house; and putting his hands on him said, Brother Saul, the Lord, even Jesus, that appeared unto thee in the way as thou camest, hath sent me, that thou mightest receive thy sight, and be filled with the Holy Ghost.

SECHELE: Yes, yes, yes, this is the best part. Ah, it is a sweet moment of history. Let me say it, David, my heart's blood. Watch the holy words fit in my mouth, appearing...And immediately there fell from his eyes as it had been scales; and he received his sight forthwith, and arose and was baptised.

LIVINGSTONE: You've learnt that well.

SECHELE: To see God you must first go blind. A good, solid smack in the head, over I go. What shall I do? Put thorns in? Stare at the sun? Jump off a cliff?

LIVINGSTONE: Sechele, you don't have to follow Saint Paul to the letter.

SECHELE: It is the one I find easiest to understand. It is the power of God.

LIVINGSTONE: It may not happen that way. Don't anticipate, just be ready.

SECHELE: But I am as great a heathen as he was. He persecuted the Christians. I did. He murdered Christians. We, the Crocodile People, murdered Christians. So, what he got, I must get. Where is Damascus?

LIVINGSTONE: Don't think about Damascus. Here, at Kolobeng, in this desert, you will find Christ, and quietly, with me.

SECHELE: And rain, David?

LIVINGSTONE: That is another question altogether.

SECHELE: Four years, David. I have loved you for four years and there has been no rain.

LIVINGSTONE: You can hardly blame me for that.

SECHELE: Other chiefs hate the Word and they have rain. I listen, admire, relish it from your lips, and I have nothing. For you I have moved my people from one dried-up river to another, hoping for better luck. God sent Saint Paul a light. Could he not send me some rain, just a couple of drops?

LIVINGSTONE: That is not what you must expect. The drought is a test which your tribe must pass...well, maybe it's now an examination.

SECHELE: Will you lie down with me and let us talk about it?

LIVINGSTONE: No further discussion is needed.

MOKOKON: The People want you to make rain, Sechele.

SECHELE: How can I displease the man I love by making rain?

MOKOKON: They're getting angry.

SECHELE: David won't agree, if I make rain in the old way, he will leave me and go to another chief.

MOKOKON: Who is more important? The People or David?

SECHELE: David.

MARY: Dear God, send water into this desert so that the tree may straighten up and grass appear beneath the feet of children. The drought has gone on long enough.

LIVINGSTONE: Woman, curb your prayers!

MARY: They have a right to criticise...

LIVINGSTONE: They live in the desert. Where do you find no rain?

MARY: The tribe didn't choose to live in the Kalahari...they were driven.

LIVINGSTONE: But they choose to stay heathen, they choose not to listen.

SECHELE: Mary, we will never have faith because God has been good to us. It all depends on me, on the explosion. One day I will go off like a gun and fly into the brain of Jesus Christ. All I regret is that it has taken two thousand years for this system to trek down here from Jerusalem, which is only two thousand miles. A mile a year? That is slower than dung wears off the sole of your foot. Why did no one come before and tell us? Now, that is what I criticise. You were a long time coming, my love.

LIVINGSTONE: Thousands live and die without God and without hope though the command went forth of old –

Go ye into the world and preach the gospel. Blame
the churches.

SECHELE: I do. When will the Pope become a Christian?

LIVINGSTONE: I am here now. There is no cause for
complaint. The good news has arrived. Why don't
you listen?

SECHELE: The best thing for me to do is go to London.

MARY: You wouldn't like it.

SECHELE: It is the City of God.

MARY: More like the Devil.

MOKOKON: Have you been there?

LIVINGSTONE: I lived there. There's nothing for you in
London. Your duty is here, amongst your own
countrymen, not being stared at like a wild beast as the
children in a strange town do to me. I have always been
opposed to exhibiting real or supposed converts prize-
cattle fashion.

SECHELE: I don't mind being admired.

MARY: But you'd object to being laughed at. You're better
off here at home.

MOKOKON: Home? Home was Mabotsa where you
moved us from: home was Chonuane where you moved
us from. This isn't home. It's a place no one else wants.
(*Pause.*)

LIVINGSTONE: We'll find a plateau, with a navigable
river to the coast. No fever, no tsetse-fly. A good, healthy
climate, fertile soil. Then you'll meet some friends. We'll
bring out the poor working people from England and
Scotland to live with you, side by side, give them some
sunshine and you some sense.

MOKOKON: Are they all like you?

LIVINGSTONE: No, we have a great variety of folk like
yourselves.

MOKOKON: But you're poor, aren't you?

LIVINGSTONE: In material things.

MOKOKON: Why bring us more poor men? We have
enough already.
(*Pause.*)

MARY: David's idea is to put the best features of both
nations together.

81

SECHELE: Myself and David. That combination would be astounding. We could rule the world. Two great friends would make one great, lovely king of life.

LIVINGSTONE: Sechele, don't think in those terms. What you've got to do is embrace the Lord and put your house in order, give up your reliance on Europe, keep yourself pure and uncontaminated by all kinds of heathenism, and be independent. Accept no interference from British, Dutch, Matabele, anyone!

SECHELE: How can I? I'm your slave.

LIVINGSTONE: You're not! I'll not have you saying that! Don't ever repeat it in my presence. The Boers have slaves, not me. I own nobody.

(*Pause. LIVINGSTONE is very agitated.*)

So don't make things worse. See me? I'm a poor escapee from the anvil and loom, a slave myself once, for pennies. When I met the Boers you know what they asked me to do? Preach to you a text that you were below them! Then, they said, I can stay. They'd hang all us missionaries on the same gibbet, as would the governor of Cape Colony if he could. We're a nuisance because we don't teach subjection.

(*Pause.*)

MARY: Freedom is best. If you must be obedient, obey God.

MOKOKON: If we have your God, and that is the God of the poor people in England, and they come out here to live with us...that will be very convenient.

MARY: David has said it many times. Brothers in Christ become brothers in Caesar. A new state could be made, blending all the qualities. It's not such a dream when you think about it.

SECHELE: (*Loudly.*) I have not given permission for any more Scotsmen or Englishmen or Irishmen or any men of any kind to come here! This is not just sand, it is my garden, what there is of it. (*Pause.*) There is only one David.

LIVINGSTONE: My face is like ten thousand others. Ten years ago it was paler, and I was thinner, and when I woke in the morning my eyes were rosy with last night's candlelight reading. I'm nothing special, Sechele.

SECHELE: You will not invite any more people to come here! Only my David!

LIVINGSTONE: You can't squash my ambition simply by bellowing at it. There's room. My millions at home don't have to live like mice in a meal-kist. Out here they can stretch themselves and find a happy existence. You'll never bully me out of that.

MARY: That will be only when you find the Promised Land...won't it?

LIVINGSTONE: But it's there, somewhere in the north.

SECHELE: David, when it rains here, we will have everything we want. There is no need to look any further. You found this magnificent spot for us. I don't think it can be improved upon.

LIVINGSTONE: I think there's a lot of looking left to be done.

MOKOKON: It will mean a journey for someone.

SECHELE: We are finished with travelling. He will take our chances here by the Kolobeng. David's not going anywhere.

(*Pause.*)

LIVINGSTONE: Would you like to see some pictures?

MOKOKON: Oh yes! Pictures! Pictures!

SECHELE: I will help.

LIVINGSTONE: Move your stuff, Mary.

(*LIVINGSTONE takes the cover from the object under the table. It is a magic lantern. MARY clears the table, LIVINGSTONE sets up the magic lantern so that it points at the back wall of the cabin.*)

MOKOKON: Which ones will we see? I like the wedding, the feast, the driving out of the church, the star, the shepherds, in the garden, the mountain...

SECHELE: They are not the most important. First, there is the face of Christ. Always look for that in every picture of David's. Someone saw Him.

MOKOKON: And London, the Queen, show us those...

MARY: Afterwards, afterwards.

SECHELE: We should bring the rest of the family in. They will be hurt if they hear that we have had the pictures and they have not been invited to see them...

LIVINGSTONE: I think we'll have one wife at a time Sechele, if you don't mind. They do tend to chatter during my instruction. It is unfortunate but...

MARY: Oh let them come in, David.

LIVINGSTONE: (*Furiously.*) This is not an entertainment!

SECHELE: Ssssh!

(*LIVINGSTONE lights the oil lamp. Lights dim. The picture is thrown in a wavering image onto the back wall. MOKOKON claps her hands with delight. It is the crucifixion.*)

LIVINGSTONE: Jesus Christ who died for us all. Any questions?

SECHELE: Any questions, Moko?

MOKOKON: I've asked them all before.

MARY: Well, ask them again. David might come up with more convincing replies.

MOKOKON: That man is supposed to be God?

LIVINGSTONE: He is God.

MOKOKON: The Romans nailed him like that and he could not stop them.

LIVINGSTONE: Would not stop them.

MOKOKON: Why?

LIVINGSTONE: Because he was dying for us all.

MOKOKON: Then why are we still dying?

LIVINGSTONE: That is only a temporary affair. By sacrificing Himself in this way, Jesus showed us the road to eternal life, through divine love.

MOKOKON: Oh. Is that what you say, Mary?

LIVINGSTONE: Yes, it is.

(*Pause.*)

MOKOKON: That is the son?

MARY: That's right.

MOKOKON: Where is the father?

SECHELE: Inside the son. The Holy Ghost is there also.

MOKOKON: Why do you think that?

LIVINGSTONE: That is the basis of the Holy Trinity.

MOKOKON: Did He say, my father is inside me…up on the cross?

SECHELE: And the Holy Ghost.

LIVINGSTONE: Not in so many words.

MARY: He said, 'Father, into Thy hands I commit my spirit,' then he said to his mother, Mary, 'Woman, behold thy son,' then to a disciple, 'Behold thy mother,' meaning she should take him under her wing, then He said, 'My God, my God, why hast thou forsaken me,' and, to the thief on one side, 'Verily, unto thee I say, today shalt thou be with me in Paradise,' then, 'It is finished.'

MOKOKON: He said something else. It must have slipped your mind, Ma-Mary.

LIVINGSTONE: And what might that be?

MOKOKON: I thirst.

(*Pause.*)

LIVINGSTONE: Excellent, Moko. You've a retentive memory, a blessing. The Romans gave Him vinegar, the same Romans came to Scotland and built a wall to keep us out. Why? Because they didn't want to share the Word. But we climbed over and listened to the good tidings, hidden in the bushes by their campfires, barbarians like yourselves. Now, you chose the book for study last week, Sechele. I presume you've done your homework?

SECHELE: Every day. Moko helped me.

LIVINGSTONE: That's very good, Moko. I'm glad you take such an interest.

SECHELE: Have you got a picture of Isaiah?

LIVINGSTONE: Lined up and waiting.

(*LIVINGSTONE changes the picture in the magic lantern. It is an Old Testament scene.*)

SECHELE: Which one is Isaiah?

LIVINGSTONE: The one on the left.

SECHELE: No, that is…

LIVINGSTONE: That is Isaiah.

SECHELE: The last time we saw that picture, David, my ambrosia, you said that man was Moses…

LIVINGSTONE: What have you got for us, Sechele? Did Isaiah say anything to you?

SECHELE: As you know, he is my favourite with Saint
Paul; a man who speaks from strength. It is a very
powerful piece of thinking.

LIVINGSTONE: Fifty-five, twelve! For ye shall go out with
joy and be led forth with peace: the mountains and the
hills shall break forth before you into singing, and all the
trees of the field shall clap their hands!

MARY: Thirty-three, six! And wisdom and knowledge shall
be the stability of thy times, and strength of thy
salvation; the fear of the Lord is his treasure!

LIVINGSTONE: Sechele?

SECHELE: (*Taking a piece of paper out of his pocket.*) Yes,
here's one...er, I can't see what I've written...a
moment...(*Holds it in the light of the magic lantern.*)

MOKOKON: I will make waste mountains and hills, and
dry up all their herbs; and I will make rivers islands and
I will dry up the pools! Behold, at my rebuke I dry up
the sea; I make the rivers a wilderness: their fish stinketh
because there is not water, and dieth of thirst!

LIVINGSTONE: (*Angrily.*) Forty-one, seventeen! When the
poor and needy seek water, and there is none, and their
tongue faileth for thirst, I, the Lord, will hear them!

SECHELE: Yes, here it is. Er...chapter twenty-two, verse
thirteen. And behold, joy and gladness, slaying oxen and
killing sheep, eating flesh and drinking wine; let us eat
and drink for tomorrow we die.
(*Pause. LIVINGSTONE blows out the oil lamp in the magic
lantern. Slow lights up as he dismantles the equipment.*)

SECHELE: Is that all we're having? That was a bit short,
wasn't it?

LIVINGSTONE: We're getting nowhere.

SECHELE: But David, it's very helpful. Moko has made
great strides forward.

LIVINGSTONE: You're a polygamist man, a sinner in
depth. The poor woman is one of the wives who must go.
A Christian can't have five wives.

MOKOKON: Why not, if he can afford it?

LIVINGSTONE: How can I teach her, or you, anything
while we're still fighting this problem? One wife,
Sechele, one! If not, no baptism, ready or not.

MOKOKON: Which one?

MARY: It has to be the first one he married.

MOKOKON: That isn't the one he wants. He wants me.

SECHELE: Did I say that? Who said you could speak for me, eh?

MOKOKON: Me! Who warms your bed? Me! The others spend all their time with their mothers. I am the first wife.

LIVINGSTONE: That can't be.

MOKOKON: My father kept him in his chieftainship, fought for him when they tried to bring him down. He owes me this marriage, and he likes it. He won't say it, but it is the truth. Look at him. Without my father he was half a chief.

(*Pause.*)

SECHELE: I must have more time to think about it.

LIVINGSTONE: No. If you think I'm going to spend the rest of my life waiting for you to sort out your seraglio, you're mistaken. It's nigh on four years, Sechele, and you're still messing about, procrastinating. I've got work to do for God, and if you won't open your ears I'll find other chiefs who will. There's the whole of the north waiting, millions of souls up there. If you won't accept Christ in the next seven days, you and your Crocodile People will have to come down with the dust and I'll move on.

SECHELE: Don't be hasty. Give me time. It's a big decision.

LIVINGSTONE: I can't hang about any longer. Living on hope for four years, putting up with whims and fancies, repeating myself...Sechele, Christ is God! He can save you and your people. That is all there is to it. Accept Christ and civilisation will follow, protection from the Boers, trade, the tribe will get stronger, your luck will change...

MOKOKON: Yah!

MARY: It will, I've seen it happen before. Look at my father's work with the Fish People and the benefits they have reaped...

MOKOKON: We are not the Fish People!

SECHELE: Go to bed, Moko.

(*Pause. MOKOKON goes to the pile of skins and lies down.*)

SECHELE: Take no notice of her. She does not speak my mind, David. It is pure self-interest in her case. Who are the Crocodile People now? No one. We are refugees. What do we live off in this wasteland? Locusts and wild honey. We have no pretensions. You are right to chide me.

MARY: You want to be a Christian, don't you?

SECHELE: Oh yes, very much. It is only the people who prevent me. They hate Christianity.

MARY: The Jews hated Jesus.

SECHELE: True. But he had a lot of help, all of which I must look to my beloved David to provide. He is my father.

LIVINGSTONE: I'm not your father. Your father was a tyrannical old heathen who got his just desserts from what I understand; a disgusting old rogue.

SECHELE: That he was, darling. A wicked man. He deserved to be murdered. The Crocodile People deserved to be ruined by the Matabele, as we were. When Mzilikasi took all my cattle and burned down my village, he was well within his rights as an unknowing instrument of God Almighty. What surprises me, David, my angel, is that natural justice has left me alive at all. It would be better for the desert stones if I did not abuse them with my shadow.

LIVINGSTONE: The severe trials through which your tribe has been passed during the past twenty or thirty years were designed by God to produce humility and make your mind more susceptible to the influences of the gospel and my coming amongst you. But will you use this preparation? No. All that time and trouble for nothing. I'll bid you good night.

SECHELE: Mary, soften his heart for me.

MARY: David has given you a fair trial in many ways.

SECHELE: But it has taken your father twenty years to get anywhere.

MARY: Sometimes he gave up with people. You don't take your own soul seriously, Sechele. I know you. I see the twinkle in your eye. We are only an amusement to you.

SECHELE: No, you're not. I look upon the gospels in a sober and cool manner and I believe them for myself, but I must believe them for my people. I am their god, as you know, and my obscene father is supposed to be mine, and so on. When I am baptised, it is for all the tribe, acting as their leader. That is what holds me back. For as much as I love you, they hate you. They are blind, like Saint Paul, fallen down, like Saint Paul, but the scales are still there on their eyes like a snake. (*Weeps.*)

LIVINGSTONE: Not impressed. To bed, Mary.

SECHELE: These are real tears, my lamb!

LIVINGSTONE: Aye, we've seen them before. Sleep well.
(*LIVINGSTONE and MARY get ready for bed. SECHELE wanders over to MOKOKON.*)

SECHELE: You've made me angry.

MOKOKON: Then I will suffer for it.

SECHELE: David is going to leave me.

MOKOKON: He's been saying that for the last two years.

SECHELE: This time he means it.

MOKOKON: He is selfish. It only means he is tired of the Kalahari.

SECHELE: No, never. Christ would not come down here from Jerusalem, but David has come all the way from Glasgow. That is real love, a love that travels. When you are shifted, Moko, you whine, you grieve, you make a noise. All you are fit for is lying in one place. Most of my cattle can do better than you when it comes to moving. (*Pause.*) What are you doing down there?

MOKOKON: Nothing.

SECHELE: What makes you think I prefer you to the others?

MOKOKON: You eat more of my bread.
(*SECHELE gets into bed with MOKOKON and makes love to her. Lights dim R, fade up on LIVINGSTONE and MARY kneeling down by the bed to pray L in nightgowns.*)

LIVINGSTONE/MARY: Lord God most merciful...

(Uproar from SECHELE and MOKOKON, laughter, screams.)

LIVINGSTONE: Give it a rest will you, man!

SECHELE: Ssssh!

MOKOKON: What are you doing? Come back!

SECHELE: Start again, David. I am with you. I must pray to God before I go to sleep.

LIVINGSTONE: Try then, try hard. *(Pause.)* We confess that we have sinned, through our own fault...

MOKOKON: You speak for yourself!

LIVINGSTONE: Heathen whore! And in common with others, in thought word and deed, and through what we have left undone...

MOKOKON: I tell you, David, by what I have here in my hand, I am a decent, properly married woman!
(LIVINGSTONE leaps up and storms through to the rondavel.)

LIVINGSTONE: Will you shut that concubine up while I address myself to my maker?

MOKOKON: Why do you say WE? We confess? I don't confess, I haven't done anything.

MARY: *(From the cabin.)* David, she's being difficult for the sake of it. Come back. Don't rise to the bait.

LIVINGSTONE: And you say nothing, Sechele.

SECHELE: I daren't. She's got a grip like a vice.

LIVINGSTONE: Then I'll pray with my wife. I don't think God would open his ears to a man in your predicament. I'm disgusted and tomorrow I'm definitely leaving. *(Goes back to the cabin.)* Filthy bloody heathen ways! Dirty atrocious devil!

MOKOKON: Yah-yah-yah-yah!

SECHELE: Moko, when you let go there is going to be a massacre here.

MARY: Ignore it, David. There are moments of African life that you have to turn your eyes from. There's no real harm done. Come on...pray with me and leave them to their own devices.
(MARY makes LIVINGSTONE kneel down. He is shaking with rage and disgust.)

LIVINGSTONE: There's no more Christian affection between those two than there is between my riding-ox and his grandmother.

MARY: Don't be so hasty, hush now. It doesn't matter, none of it matters. Only the work. Let us finish our prayer.

LIVINGSTONE: I'd rather be in the Union workhouse or back in the mill. I can't stand it, Mary...

MARY: We ask to be forgiven. By the power of your Spirit turn us from evil to good, help us to forgive others, and keep us in your ways of righteousness and love; through Jesus Christ our Lord. Amen.

(LIVINGSTONE sighs. MARY holds him. SECHELE and MOKOKON are lying very still, listening.)

LIVINGSTONE: That was the right thing to do, keep going. I'm obliged to you, Mary. I'm alright now.

SECHELE: You are the apostle to the Crocodile People, David!

LIVINGSTONE: So I am. And you'll know it when I'm gone.

(LIVINGSTONE and MARY get into bed. Pause. Suddenly SECHELE pounces on MOKOKON and beats her up in bed, but ends up making love to her.)

SECHELE: You disobeyed me! Where is my wonderful Scotsman now? I have lost him. He hates me.

MOKOKON: Good! Good! Good!

SECHELE: I will kill you if he leaves. If I find a witch; the witch must be wiped out. What do you think you are?
(Pause.)

LIVINGSTONE: Mary.

MARY: Yes?

LIVINGSTONE: I am tossed like a ball into a large country.

MARY: Isaiah, twenty-eight, eighteen.

LIVINGSTONE: Do you think I'm cut out for this work?

MARY: So shall they fear the name of the Lord from the west...

LIVINGSTONE: Fifty-nine, nineteen. But can I preach?

MARY: Oh yes. You make them tremble.

LIVINGSTONE: You wouldn't say I was tedious when I was preaching? Just banging on, no inspiration. (*Pause.*) I get a pain nowadays in the upper right lung after about forty-five minutes of a sermon at full tilt. What it is, I don't know but it's acute. A cold sponge on the chest didn't help at all. It produced a convulsion, palpitations. (*Pause.*) Mary.

MARY: Yes?

LIVINGSTONE: I think my days are few. I won't live long, I know it.

MARY: For the grave cannot praise thee, death cannot celebrate thee. Thirty...

LIVINGSTONE: What concerns me is that I won't get the work done. I'll die here with this...villain. Oh Mary, this isn't how I saw it. All the mountain of my labour has brought forth a ridiculous mouse. Is this my forte? Lying within earshot of that animal, interpreting his noises and moods?

MARY: He is the key to the Kwena. If Sechele accepts the Lord, in twenty years we will win the whole tribe for Christ, for ever.

LIVINGSTONE: Is that enough for me?

MARY: It is for my father.

LIVINGSTONE: Flies, wolves, grasshoppers on my turnips, the Boers accusing me of gun-running, no money...and a man who has more than his share of the unfelt wants of the soul. My mind is troubled with the afflictions of others. They are truly slow of heart. When will they learn wisdom?

MARY: When thy learn patience.

LIVINGSTONE: You're on the side of all my obstacles.

MARY: No. But I believe in grinding on. They have to be worn down slowly.

LIVINGSTONE: All this bother and bluster and blarney will receive a quietus before many years. (*Puts his arm round her.*) What a hush takes place as the shades of death close around us. When we have finished our work, please God let us be rocked to rest on Abraham's bosom. (*Pause. MOKOKON and SECHELE groan, breathe, laugh.*)

Benighted, barbarous savage. I can't understand why he's so partial to the prophet Isaiah. He doesn't offer much hope to a sinner like Sechele.

MARY: Oh, I don't know. There's or...Behold I will do a new thing, now...

LIVINGSTONE: ...it shall spring forth; shall ye not know it? Good old forty-three, twenty.

(*LIVINGSTONE makes love to MARY, slow blackout. Slow lights up with a red tinge. Dawn. SECHELE gets out of bed, dresses and pads over to LIVINGSTONE and MARY who are still asleep.*)

SECHELE: David!

MARY: (*Waking.*) What do you want?

SECHELE: I must tell him the good news.

MARY: Let him sleep for a while longer. It's the Sabbath.

SECHELE: Mary, it has happened.

MARY: Sechele, go back to your own place and we'll talk later.

SECHELE: God struck me.

MARY: (*Pause.*) I'm very pleased.

SECHELE: It has happened. I am converted.

MARY: Well, wait for a while and I'll get dressed...

SECHELE: Mary, I want David to be the first Christian to hold me in his arms after my conversion.

MARY: He is sound asleep. He gets very crusty if you face him with problems first thing.

SECHELE: I won't waken him, just steal a kiss. (*Pause.*) I'm not a problem.

MARY: If you're not, Sechele, the word has lost its meaning overnight.

SECHELE: Do you think it will be alright for a kiss? A little one?

MARY: If you must, but gently. On the cheek.

(*SECHELE leans over LIVINGSTONE and kisses him on the mouth. LIVINGSTONE wakes up with a shout of fear.*)

LIVINGSTONE: Get off! What's this?

MARY: Nothing to worry about. Calm down. Sechele has something to tell you.

SECHELE: I want to be baptised. Embrace me, brother.

(*Hugs LIVINGSTONE.*)

LIVINGSTONE: (*Struggling free.*) Give over, will you? Now what's this...

MARY: He seems to be genuine...

LIVINGSTONE: Yes, yes, like the other times.

(*SECHELE lies full-length next to LIVINGSTONE in one quick movement.*)

SECHELE: You have persuaded me.

LIVINGSTONE: Get up man! Get off my bed!

SECHELE: I am your child now.

LIVINGSTONE: (*Jumping out of bed.*) Out of here!

SECHELE: I will put away all my surplus wives.

(*Pause.*)

MARY: Truly?

SECHELE: Truly.

LIVINGSTONE: If you renege on this one, Sechele, I'll leave the same day.

SECHELE: I have made up my mind. It came to me in a dream.

LIVINGSTONE: You'll divorce your surplus wives? Four will have to go, you know.

SECHELE: All of them if you like. What do I need with wives when I have Christ and you?

MARY: Sechele, I'm delighted. Thank the Lord and praise His name.

(*MARY takes SECHELE's hand.*)

SECHELE: Thank you, Ma-Mary.

LIVINGSTONE: Keep one wife, you'll need one. It's better that way.

MARY: David, show the chief you're pleased. It's a great moment for you. He's your first convert.

LIVINGSTONE: Yes, it's marvellous. Well done, well done. Now the Devil's children will be hustled and we'll show the world a thing or two.

(*He holds out his hand. SECHELE takes it, then pulls LIVINGSTONE into his arms and hugs him. He struggles free.*)

SECHELE: I want to be baptised today.

LIVINGSTONE: No, caution. I think you should wait a
couple of months, just to be sure. I must be certain that
you'll not backslide on me.

SECHELE: Two months? Months!

LIVINGSTONE: This is the most important decision
you've ever taken. For a little while you can worship at
the shrine of the goddess, prudence. Then we'll give you
to Christ in surety. Congratulations. Now, if you'll
excuse me, I must relieve myself of a burden.

*(He exits. SECHELE looks at MARY. She shrugs, then
follows LIVINGSTONE off. SECHELE returns to
MOKOKON who is still asleep, stands by her for a while,
bends down, strokes her head.)*

SECHELE: Moko.

MOKOKON: What?

SECHELE: You have done it for me.

MOKOKON: Well...

SECHELE: Where I asked myself, does that terrific feeling
come from? From me? From you? Impossible. It comes
from God. He has been striking me for years and I didn't
know it, every night. My dear, you were the instrument
of God last night, and I thank you very humbly.

MOKOKON: I don't know what you're talking about.

SECHELE: David says I must desire God, inside.

MOKOKON: *(Pause.)* Don't use me like that. You're making
it up.

SECHELE: Saint Paul had to fall down in the road, but I
had it softer. *(Pause.)* You have helped to make me into
a Christian.

MOKOKON: *(Getting up.)* You are sick with love for that man.

SECHELE: Didn't I do the same for you? You must have
felt it, in there.

MOKOKON: No.

SECHELE: Are you saying you felt nothing?

MOKOKON: Sechele, leave me out of it. Do what you like.

SECHELE: You are confused. That was God in us last
night. He has been there all the time, the father inside
like David says. We have every reason to believe now.
You will be baptised as well.

MOKOKON: I will not!

SECHELE: I command it!

MOKOKON: You stupid man. David, David, David. When your people are hungry, you feed David; when they are sick, you care for David; they say if they die, will you bury David?

SECHELE: Moko, I will be allowed one wife. Now, I have an argument. If I am to be a Christian – which I am – then my wife should be a Christian as well. If you do it, now, it can be you, before the others start queuing up for baptism.

(*Pause.*)

MOKOKON: This crocodile is not a chameleon.

SECHELE: Then you'll have to go back to your family.

MOKOKON: He's got you twisting and turning. Everything you say is an excuse you've thought up for keeping him. What's so beautiful about the man?

SECHELE: He is good for the tribe. Count how many guns we have since he came. If the Matabele or the Boers attacked tomorrow I would kill them with eighty quick shots. Bang! Bang! Bang! Bang!

MOKOKON: Hunters, traders, anyone will sell you guns.

SECHELE: David gives me guns, all sorts of guns, guns of men and guns of God.

MOKOKON: We will see what the people say. I'm going to tell them.

SECHELE: Do that. And mention that I take Christ for them, not just for myself. I'm doing them a favour.

MOKOKON: Listen for the sound of laughter.

(*MOKOKON exits. SECHELE kneels down at the quern.*)

SECHELE: Jesus, I have taken this step beyond the edge of my understanding and I need to hold your hand, but I do not bother to reach out. There is no hand waiting. You were in the desert and you must remember the likelihood of mirages, seeing water that was not there. That is how I feel. David is my oasis and you, I pray, will be the spring beneath.

(*Enter LIVINGSTONE. He sees SECHELE praying and stands quietly behind him, then kneels down so they are side by side.*)

SECHELE: So, I will start walking towards an image in the air. If you exist, don't move away. I have to be baptised, so give me some firm ground to stand on.

LIVINGSTONE: God, make his faith stick.

SECHELE: (*Shuffling towards LIVINGSTONE on his knees until their shoulders and knees are touching.*) David, I have released the news.

LIVINGSTONE: God knows already. (*Edges away.*)

SECHELE: I am sending Moko away.

LIVINGSTONE: (*Pause.*) Who will look after her?

SECHELE: Her mother. Is it right to ask God to watch over a heathen?

LIVINGSTONE: He does, whether you ask or not. He was responsible for her creation.

SECHELE: He was the father inside the father on the night…

LIVINGSTONE: Dear God, grant this man clarity of mind. Clean out all his confusions, settle all his disturbances and storms. For myself, I am unspeakably pleased to have struggled and won his soul for Thee.

SECHELE: Let him stay for ever. I know he wants to be with me, but wishes to be a great man. Tell us an approach. Wiping out the Boers, destroying the Matabele, bringing rain…(*Puts his arms round LIVINGSTONE's shoulder.*) Give him fame, God! Give him fame! (*Blackout. LIVINGSTONE and SECHELE exit. Lights up on MOKOKON facing MARY.*)

MOKOKON: I am going away now.

MARY: What do your parents think?

MOKOKON: That Sechele has lost his mind, which he has.

MARY: Are they angry?

MOKOKON: Everyone is angry.

MARY: Perhaps you stirred them up?

MOKOKON: I wish I could.

MARY: If you succeeded in getting rid of us, things would not get better. There is no future for you out here without God. You would starve in the soul and in the stomach.

MOKOKON: I have no soul.

MARY: (*Covers her ears.*) No!

MOKOKON: When you're dead, you're dead!

(*Pause. MARY takes her hands away.*)

There are small yellow men in this desert who have been here all the time. When they die someone scrapes a shallow hole for them and they are tumbled in and covered up. It is the only time words are said over them and they are these: You have all that belongs to you. Go your way and leave us to get what we can from the ground.

MARY: Moko, if you only know how wrong you are, the great love God has for you...

MOKOKON: It is not as great as the love I have for my husband.

(*MOKOKON exits. MARY is very upset, takes up the Bible and holds it to her breast, closes her eyes, then suddenly opens her eyes, opens the Bible and stabs a finger downwards. Pause. She reads it. As she does this, LIVINGSTONE enters unseen by her.*)

MARY: Saint Luke...Beware of the scribes, which desire to walk in long robes, and love greetings in the markets, and the highest seats in the synagogues and the chief's room at feasts...

LIVINGSTONE: <u>Chief</u> room at feasts. (*Takes the Bible from her.*) Don't let me catch you playing at that again. Sometimes your kind of innocence is difficult to live with, Mary.

MARY: He doesn't know what he's doing.

LIVINGSTONE: They regard the body, with its appetites and desires, as the whole of Man. They have no curiosity about God and eternity. Their little dried-up devil of a divinity lives in a hole in a dry river-bed and has one leg and a stiff brain from lack of thought. Religious ideas are like broken planks to them, floating down the streams of ages from a primitive faith.

MARY: What are you trusting to?

LIVINGSTONE: A push, a nudge. It will come. He can wait two months.

(*Enter SECHELE.*)

SECHELE: Well, my Moko has gone. She made a lot of noise, but she's gone. (*Sits down.*) I have a special favour to ask.

LIVINGSTONE: Whatever is in my power.

SECHELE: I want Moko to see me baptised. I think it might impress her.

LIVINGSTONE: She can't have any relationship with you, you know that?

SECHELE: Of course. I have my...oldest wife, and that is that. But it will do Moko good to see the actual process whereby I am saved...

LIVINGSTONE: Stand in the hope of being saved, to be more accurate.

SECHELE: Yes. Make a start.

MARY: You must write to Moko, as a friend.

SECHELE: You will help me write every Sabbath.

MARY: Once she has got over this, I think we must try and get her to accept Christ.

SECHELE: What better husband?
(*Pause.*)

LIVINGSTONE: Sechele, I am going to give my wife Communion now.

SECHELE: I will watch.

MARY: David...

LIVINGSTONE: Not until you are baptised.

SECHELE: David, surely a man in my state of mind should be encouraged to observe the mystery, even if I am not allowed to take part in it?

MARY: (*Pause.*) I don't mind then.

LIVINGSTONE: It's the most solemn moment.

SECHELE: That is my mood. Being divorced four times in one day made me go into a serious frame of mind.

MARY: Stay with us then and watch. I hope it gives you comfort.

SECHELE: Thank you.
(*LIVINGSTONE prepares the table with bread and wine and the Bible.*)

SECHELE: David, will you build into this Communion a prayer to God that he separates, in the minds of my Crocodile People, Christ and hunger?

LIVINGSTONE: I'm afraid the order of service is as laid down by the Congregational Church of Scotland.

SECHELE: Then I will make one up myself.

LIVINGSTONE: (*Pause.*) Aye, well, free expression is allowed – as long as you say it quietly.

SECHELE: Perhaps I should do it separately?

LIVINGSTONE: If that's what you'd prefer.

SECHELE: You have taught me to open my mind to God, to speak to him directly so that is the way I intend to do it.

LIVINGSTONE: Face to face, nothing in between, no interference or embellishment; the individual with his creator.

SECHELE: Absolute honesty. So, there is one thing which I did in the past for which I must ask God's forgiveness; then I'll move on to another subject.

LIVINGSTONE: As you wish. We have all the time you need.

SECHELE: (*Kneeling, hands together.*) Some years ago, my Redeemer, I sent a present to my relative Bubi, who was, at that time, running half of my Crocodile People for me, having stolen some of my authority. Bubi, being a cautious man, treated my gift with suspicion and said the right spell over it in case I had sent him something dangerous to his health. This spell consists of passing a red-hot iron over the article and singing some scraps of an old song. Lord, forgive me for sending my relative Bubo a cask of gunpowder. It is unlikely but I pray he has an easy time in Paradise. (*Pause.*) If I am forgiven for this, Lord, then I am prepared to forgive you for the last twenty years…

LIVINGSTONE: Sechele, no…

SECHELE: I must clear it up! Silence! I cannot leave it aside. Jesus, you, so David says, sent the Zulus of Tshaka against the emaNgaweni so that they drove them from their land…

LIVINGSTONE: I was not that specific!

SECHELE: So the emaNgaweni attacked the Hlubi and drove them from their land, and the Hlubi attacked the

Wild Cat People and drove them from their land, and the Wild Cat People attacked the Mist People and drove them from their land and, God, they became man-eaters! Was that not enough shame for everyone? No. You, and Isaiah, and Saint Paul, spurred the Wild Cat People to kill the Fish People then the Matabele to murder us, the Crocodile People and steal the land from under us. Since then the Matabele have killed the Baboon People, the Lion People, the Buffalo People, the Python People, the Rhinoceros People and the Rain People, all cousins of our nation. All this I understand. Sixty, fifteen: for behold, the Lord will come with fire, and with his chariots like a whirlwind to render his anger with fury, and his rebuke with flames of fire. And twenty-four, three: for the land shall be utterly emptied and utterly spoiled for the Lord has spoken this word. BUT, all this happened before we were brought the good news. We did not know what was needed. If you had offered salvation under threats of this happening to us, we would have jumped at it. (*Pause.*) No matter now. You are forgiven for the last twenty years. I am forgiven for Bubi. We have balanced things out. Amen.

LIVINGSTONE: Sechele, I can't tell you how wrong all that is...

SECHELE: Nothing to do with you. Our God and I have settled it. I will not bring it up again. I think we are both satisfied.

LIVINGSTONE: I can't just let it pass. It's entirely erroneous and most upsetting...

(*Enter MOLOKON with a bundle on her head.*)

MOKOKON: I have forgotten something of mine.

SECHELE: Ah, Moko, stay for a while.

MOKOKON: No, I have to catch up with the others. I left my...mirror.

SECHELE: If you stay for a minute you can watch Mary having Communion.

LIVINGSTONE: That would not be in order I'm afraid.

(*MOKOKON goes to the bed of skins and finds a small mirror.*)

SECHELE: If she watched through the mirror, would that be alright?

LIVINGSTONE: Sechele, no.

MOKOKON: I'm going.

SECHELE: If I write to you, will you write to me?

MOKOKON: I cannot see Communion, Sechele.

(*MOKOKON exits. Pause.*)

LIVINGSTONE: Sechele, I'll warn you now. This is the most sacred moment in a Christian's life and if you attempt to debase it I'll have no hesitation in throwing you out. My wife's soul and my own deserve some respect and we demand reverence such as we practice ourselves. (*Pause.*) So don't follow any peculiar instinct of your own. Keep absolutely silent and watch. Let us worship God. (*MARY remains standing. SECHELE sits in his chair.*)

LIVINGSTONE: This is the day which the Lord has made.

MARY: Let us rejoice and be glad in it.

LIVINGSTONE: It is good to give thanks to the Lord.

MARY: For His love endures for ever.

(*MOKOKON reappears, still with her bundle, the mirror on a string round her neck. She peers into the rondavel and is not observed as the others are intent on the service.*)

LIVINGSTONE: We pray for the nations of the world, our own country, all who work for unity and witness, those in trade and industry, members of the professions, all who serve the community, the sick and suffering, victims of injustice, the lonely and bereaved, or families, friends and neighbours, all who need our prayers.

(*During this prayer MOKOKON creeps through the rondavel until she is closer to SECHELE who is sitting in his chair, fascinated. LIVINGSTONE is performing the service from memory, eyes closed. MARY has her head bowed.*)

LIVINGSTONE: Here the words of Jesus Christ. I am the bread of life, he who comes to me shall not hunger, he who believes in me shall never thirst.

(*MOKOKON takes a knife out of her skirt and holds it close to the back of SECHELE's head, then produces a small bag of dust which she dips the knife into.*)

LIVINGSTONE: He who comes to me I will not cast out. Hear the story of the Lord's Supper as it was told to us by Saint Paul. I received from the Lord what I also delivered…
(*MOKOKON holds the blade over SECHELE's head and taps it so dust gently falls down onto him.*)
…to you, that the Lord Jesus on the night when he was betrayed took bread, and when he had given thanks, he broke it, and said, 'This is my body which is for you. Do this in remembrance of me.'
(*MOKOKON takes the mirror and holds it close to SECHELE's head, then passes her hand over the image, puts her hands to her mouth and swallows.*)

LIVINGSTONE: In the same way also the cup, after supper, saying, 'This cup is the new covenant in my blood. Do this, as often as you drink it, in remembrance of me.'
(*MOKOKON squeezes her breast onto her palm, then licks it.*)

LIVINGSTONE: For as often as you eat this bread and drink the cup, you proclaim the Lord's death until he comes.
(*MOKOKON slides away and exits. LIVINGSTONE breaks the bread and gives a piece to MARY. SECHELE is riveted, leaning forward in his seat.*)

LIVINGSTONE: Take, eat; this is the body of Christ which is broken for you.
(*MARY and LIVINGSTONE slowly chew and eat the bread. SECHELE gets halfway out of his seat with excitement but LIVINGSTONE suddenly darts a glance at him and he subsides.*)

LIVINGSTONE: (*Handing MARY the cup.*) This cup is the new covenant in the blood of Christ, shed for you and for many, for the remission of sins: drink of it.
(*MARY drinks deep. LIVINGSTONE takes the cup from her and drinks himself. SECHELE holds out a hand, sinks to his knees, begs for a drink.*)

SECHELE: Make it rain. Make it rain.

LIVINGSTONE: Wisht ya, this wine was not for water.
(*Blackout.*)

End of Act One.

ACT TWO

Lights up on SECHELE dressed in a long mackintosh, wellington boots, and a red knitted cap. He is pouring water out of a Duke of Wellington painted jug into a cup and then back again, chanting 'Waterloo, Waterloo,' sometimes wetting his lips with the water. Enter MARY, nine months pregnant, carrying washing which has been drying.

MARY: Don't let David catch you doing that.

SECHELE: Waterloo, Waterloo! I was shouted at outside my own hut. Before I was baptised I would have shot them down. Sechele, Sechele, you are lost. So, I turned both cheeks and shuffled off. You are a beautiful elephant mother now. (*Pats her.*) To think, another King David.

MARY: Or Bathsheba. There are no guarantees, you know.

SECHELE: It must be due now. You have been carrying that child for years.

MARY: Any day now.

(*Enter LIVINGSTONE, now dressed in a sailor's peaked cap, a pea-jacket and white duck trousers. MARY starts folding the clothes.*)

LIVINGSTONE: Expecting a change in the weather, Sechele?

SECHELE: Maybe a storm on the ocean. Where are you going?

LIVINGSTONE: Nowhere. Aren't you hot?

SECHELE: The Duke of Wellington cools me down.

MARY: Is anyone else coming to the prayer meeting?

SECHELE: Only Moko.

LIVINGSTONE: Is she getting any nearer to asking for baptism?

SECHELE: I think so. She has hung around here for six months. It can't be for any other reason. She hates me, personally. Her father has threatened to kill me. I have had unpleasant visits from three of her brothers – all of whom I would have shot dead if I wasn't a Christian now – the only attraction must be the truth.

LIVINGSTONE: I feel such a fool giving a sermon to two people.

MARY: We're always interested in what you've got to say, David.

LIVINGSTONE: But I must have practice and, you know, that pain in the upper lung is almost conquered. I'll make it short.

SECHELE: Moko can't be far away. She never is. I'll go and round her up.

LIVINGSTONE: Only if she wants to. I'll have no strong-arm tactics.

SECHELE: I have no strong arms except yours, my redeemer. (*Exits.*)

LIVINGSTONE: What does he look like?

MARY: What do you look like? Have you joined the navy?

LIVINGSTONE: Practical garb. They arrived in the last charity supplies. No one else wants them, even Sechele. (*Pause.*) The Kalahari is a kind of sea.

MARY: They heckled him again just now. I feel so sorry for him.

LIVINGSTONE: He must sit it out. They'll come round.

MARY: They said he was a white man's creature.

LIVINGSTONE: So he is if Christ is white.

(*SECHELE enters towing MOKOKON.*)

SECHELE: Here she is. She was skulking at the back, hoping to hear a few scraps of grace.

MARY: Hello, Moko, come in and sit down.

(*MOKOKON sits down on a stool, her hands in her lap.*)

LIVINGSTONE: Come on, Moko, this isn't the girl we knew. Where's your smile? Don't look so doleful. (*Pause. MOKOKON smiles timidly. LIVINGSTONE pats her on the shoulder.*)

SECHELE: I got her in with the promise that I would be allowed to read some of Johane Bunyana aloud as my piece. That seemed to impress her.

MARY: I think we'd enjoy that ourselves, Sechele.

LIVINGSTONE: No one else out there interested?

SECHELE: No, except to throw stones.

(*Pause.*)

LIVINGSTONE: Remember the martyrs.

SECHELE: I do, dear God, I do. (*Pause.*) In former times, when a chief was fond of hunting, all his people got dogs. If he was fond of dancing, or beer, they did a lot of that to join him in his pleasures. But in my case it is different. My only joys are in David and the Word of God, and not one of my brethren will join me. In this tribe things are going downhill.

MARY: In twenty years, Sechele, this will be a totally Christian nation. I know it.

SECHELE: How long will I live? Ah, I forgot. For ever.

LIVINGSTONE: Can you stop doing your chores now, Mary? I think we've got our full complement. Would you like to kick off with the first prayer, Sechele? Remember, quite spontaneous, straight out, nothing between you and God.

SECHELE: (*To MOKOKON.*) Watch this. (*He places the Duke of Wellington jug on the table.*) We give you thanks that you loved the world so much that you gave David and your only Son so that everyone who has faith in them will not die but have eternal life and water like the Duke of Wellington, a great soldier whose spirit I must consult as to my strategy of defence against the Boers who threaten me from the east, the Matabele from the north, the British from the south.

LIVINGSTONE: Sechele, I think you'd better read from Johane Bunyana instead.

SECHELE: How dare you interrupt my prayers? Fie! This is a private moment. I am opening my heart. (*Pause. LIVINGSTONE shakes his head, sighs. MARY touches his hand.*)

SECHELE: Are you saying that the Duke of Wellington is not in Heaven?

LIVINGSTONE: My own preference has always been for passive resistance. I'm not sure that it's right to fight for anything in a military way.

SECHELE: God, give me my prayer back. I will have to think again. You do one, David.

LIVINGSTONE: Mary first. She is on the edge of something great and vast.

MARY: (*Coolly.*) Guide the nations in the ways of justice, liberty and peace; and help them to seek the unity and welfare of mankind. Give to our Queen and to all in authority...

LIVINGSTONE: (*Riding over MARY in a sudden spontaneous outburst.*) Dear Jesus, in the midst of this dreary drought it is wonderful to see the ants running about with their accustomed vivacity! I put the bulb of a thermometer three inches under the soil in the sun at midday, and found the mercury to stand at fifteen twenty to fifteen forty; and if certain kinds of beetles were placed on the surface, they ran about and, in a few seconds, expired. But this broiling heat only augmented the activity of the long-legged black ants! They never tire! Their organs of motion seem endowed with the same power as the human heart which never becomes fatigued but beats on, driving us forward to that sphere to which we fondly hope to rise. (*Pause.*) Lord, where do these ants get their moisture? Can it be that they have the power of combining the oxygen and hydrogen of their vegetable food by a vital force so as to form water, H_2O?
(*Pause. LIVINGSTONE slumps, sits down in a chair. SECHELE looks at MOKOKON.*)

SECHELE: There. Now can you doubt he is God's friend? Consider the ant.

LIVINGSTONE: Go to the ant, thou sluggard, consider her ways, and be wise. Proverbs six, six. (*Pause.*) Feel quite knocked up. This heat is stifling.
(*SECHELE takes a woven fan and cools LIVINGSTONE then offers him a drink of water out of the Duke of Wellington jug.*)

SECHELE: David, this is Jonathan speaking. Refresh yourself.

LIVINGSTONE: Why aren't there more people here? Mary, what have we done wrong? We're being punished, that's obvious. But why? (*Breaks down.*) Jesus does not come to judge.

(MARY comforts him, looks up at SECHELE and indicates that he should go. SECHELE beckons MOKOKON to follow him. She stands up, now full of herself, stretches, saunters past MARY, takes SECHELE's arm and is led out by him. Pause. MARY holds LIVINGSTONE's head to her breast. Looking thoughtful.)

MARY: There, there now. You've just boiled over for a moment. It's only to be expected.

LIVINGSTONE: No, it's not. Not in a trained man. *(Gets up, walks about desperately nervous.)* See these hands? Shaking. Why am I shaking? Mary, this is my life's work and I can't take it.

MARY: David, my father went through the same despair in the early days. That's my first memory, you know. And he had the most terrible tribal wars to contend with, armed invasions, stand-up fights...I've seen him sitting in a chair without moving for a day and a night.

LIVINGSTONE: His approach was wrong.

(Pause.)

MARY: My father?

LIVINGSTONE: Allowing himself to become a man of blood.

MARY: David, the Wild Cat People were going to wipe out the station and every convert he'd made. Someone had to organise their defence.

LIVINGSTONE: Right. So now who is going to have the impossible job of saving the Wild Cat People? Would you like to be the missionary who attempted that? The whole Christian endeavour has been mismanaged here from the start. No wonder they're so stiff-necked. And what was the chief of the Fish People doing?

MARY: You know full well the man was incompetent.

LIVINGSTONE: *(Pause.)* The apostles moved around. They didn't stay in one place. They made flying visits. Corinthians, Galatians, Ephesians, Philippians, Colossians, Thessalonians, gave them the Word and pushed on. It was a touch, a kindling. They didn't squat with the tribes and simmer!

MARY: That was when the Word was brand-new.

LIVINGSTONE: It should strike like lightning, then flash on, and on. An onward movement should be made whether men will hear or will forbear.

MARY: These people have short memories. If something comes and goes it is just another light in the sky, a dagga-dream, some kind of vision. They must be given substance and example, like you give them.

LIVINGSTONE: No. Mary, I'm a very unattractive personality, I know that. My charm is in my absence. Listening to my own voice is as painful to me as it is to my audience.

MARY: That is a silly thing to say.

LIVINGSTONE: It's true nonetheless. God gave me few natural talents for some reason. I can think, I can walk and that's about it. Sometimes, in sin it is, I know that, I'm of the opinion that God was mean when he made Livingstone...

(*LIVINGSTONE goes to MARY and she takes him in her arms while he cries.*)

Now what did I do that for? (*Standing up, leaving MARY's arms.*) That is unaccountable in the extreme. I'm ill, pressure on the brain probably.

MARY: You've been working too hard.

LIVINGSTONE: For a congregation of two and a half? Ha!

MARY: Let's go to Kuruman for a while and stay with my parents. They'll understand...

LIVINGSTONE: No, there are a thousand jobs to be done here. Gardening. Digging. Engineering even. Mending guns, always mending guns. Mending broken legs, drawing teeth...everything but winning over souls for Jesus. I'm not a missionary, Mary, I'm a handyman. I am the working folk of the Kwena all by myself.

They hardly lift a finger. Do this for me, do that. It's a trap, Ma-Mary.

MARY: That's not true. You're teaching them useful skills. It helps.

LIVINGSTONE: I'm doing things they should be doing themselves. If I handed the whole lot back to the witch-doctor, how many more would perish? A few. And why?

Not gallstones or pneumonia, dearie, spirits sitting up
trees or crawling round the kraal at night whistling.
What am I working for?

MARY: Don't think like that. I swear to you, David, Africa
will be a Christian continent through men like you.

LIVINGSTONE: Do you think Sechele is sincere?

(*Pause.*)

Well?

MARY: As much as he can be.

LIVINGSTONE: I'd like a plain answer, not skidding off
round a corner.

MARY: He was always drawn to you.

(*Pause.*)

LIVINGSTONE: The man frightens me sometimes.
I honestly doubt his sanity.

MARY: Is it madness to love a man like you?

LIVINGSTONE: Madness is not seeing the frontiers.
He crosses any line he feels like. If they were walls he'd
float over them. Love has to have a consistent walk
and conversation with God or it is a poisonous
companionship. (*Touches his right chest.*) Hush, there it
goes. I'd like that old king of terrors to stop giving me
such a squeezing when he feels like it.

MARY: Lie down for a while. I'll make you some tea.

LIVINGSTONE: No tea. (*Lies down.*) Perhaps they pray in
secret in the bushes. You think so? Maybe they're
ashamed. They take it as a sign of unmanly weakness to
change their minds. Steal cattle? Oh yes. Rob the Devil?
– Not likely.

MARY: Sechele sets great store by your friendship. Isn't that
to be valued? We have to live together, even with our
different customs...

LIVINGSTONE: Socialism has but sorry fruits amongst
these unsophisticated specimens of humanity. They
misinterpret their emotions. (*Falls asleep.*)
(*Pause. MARY waits until LIVINGSTONE is breathing
deeply, then scoots out through the rondavel and comes back
immediately holding MOKOKON by the ear. She thrusts her
into the rondavel, then claps a hand over her mouth.*)

MARY: Keep still, you wicked girl. Don't make a sound or you'll really be in trouble. (*Takes her hand off MOKOKON's mouth.*) Wait. (*She feels MOKOKON's breast, then puts a hand over her stomach. Pause. She hisses and groans in despair.*)

MARY: How long?

MOKOKON: Two months.

MARY: Who?

(*Pause.*)

I said, who?

(*Pause.*)

You're proud of yourself, aren't you? You've undermined all our work and made us look fools. But I'll tell you something funny, it's him who'll regret it. Have you told him yet?

MOKOKON: No.

MARY: I expect he's too stupid to notice. (*Pause.*) Are you going to tell him?

MOKOKON: I'm his wife, I can have his child any time I like.

MARY: You're not his wife any more and that baby is illegitimate.

MOKOKON: It is the child of the chief of the Kwena!
(*Pause. MARY sits down.*)

MARY: Has any other man been near you?

MOKOKON: As many as you.

MARY: I suppose it's pointless to ask if you feel any guilt?

MOKOKON: I am proud of it.

MARY: (*Pause.*) If God will forgive me, I will let you have every piece of cloth, jewel, knife, every possession of mine, providing you agree to go away and dispose of that infant elsewhere.

MOKOKON: Dispose?

MARY: Its birth will set the cause of the Christian gospel back an untold distance if it is known that Sechele fathered it on you after his baptism.

MOKOKON: So who is more powerful?

MARY: Oh, you are Moko, you are. Who can doubt it?

MOKOKON: I won.

MARY: Will you do as I asked?

MOKOKON: Oh, no.

MARY: What do you hope to gain?

MOKOKON: He will throw you out.

MARY: Because he proved to himself that he was a weak man who could not resist temptation? (*Pause.*) I don't think you understand men, Moko.

MOKOKON: He is a joke to his own people, to the chiefs of other tribes. He will not bear it much longer. When this child is born, he will want to worship that, not David. Then we will put you two upon a donkey and send you on the north track to Egypt so you can feel good. (*Pause.*) My son will be the saviour of the Crocodile while you two Romans march off and get out of the way.

MARY: You've been seeing too many pictures, Moko.

MOKOKON: It was simple. A pot of beer, me, a little girl with no friends, and then there was no Bible for Sechele. You left his mind.

MARY: You don't surprise me, Moko. We knew he wasn't completely firm.

MOKOKON: He was for me.

MARY: That will be enough of that, thank you.

MOKOKON: Why don't you go now before the people kill you?

MARY: They have no intention of killing us.

MOKOKON: Someone has started saying that if you died there would be rain.

MARY: I wonder who that could be?

MOKOKON: It happened before. Two seasons before Sechele was born a Christian doctor and a Christian captain came to the homelands we had before Mzilikasi drove us out. There had been no rain. So they were given to the crocodiles. Then rain came and the crops were good. Sechele's father had done the right thing.

MARY: You think some old customs are worth reviving?

MOKOKON: David has put a spell on Sechele. Until it is broken there will be no rain. That is what everyone is saying. He has stolen his soul.

(*MARY gets up with some difficulty, walks over to MOKOKON and slaps her across the face. MOKOKON is knocked backwards onto the bed of skins, hissing and snarling. MARY pauses, starts to speak, but thinks better of it and goes through the door-frame into the cabin.*)

MOKOKON: And who is the father of that thing in your belly? Your husband or holy God? Must I have mine in the kraal with the cows?

(*Enter SECHELE to the rondavel wearing a knitted red cap, an old red threadbare jacket, moleskin trousers, stockings the colour of soil, and his Wellington boots. The jacket and trousers are too short for him.*)

SECHELE: Get off there! What are you trying to do to me?

(*MOKOKON gets to her feet slowly, holding her stomach. SECHELE points to the door and beckons her to get out. MOKOKON exits. SECHELE walks through the rondavel and stands peering through into the cabin.*)

SECHELE: Boo-hoo, thou mighty man of valour. What's this? Lying down on the job?

(*MARY lifts her face and looks at him with pure hate in her eyes. SECHELE frowns, is taken aback, half smiles, then realises that MARY's expression is connected with MOKOKON. He retreats, then kneels at the quern with his head in his hands. MARY gets up and follows him through.*)

SECHELE: That is you, Ma-Mary. I know you are there.

MARY: You hopeless great baby. Why?

SECHELE: She is my friend. I could not have her sitting outside, waiting.

MARY: Did you think you were deceiving God?

SECHELE: That is impossible. (*Stands up.*) Nor his mother.

MARY: All Mokokon is interested in getting what she wants.

SECHELE: She seduced me.

MARY: Not the most difficult thing in the world, I should think.

SECHELE: But it is over now. Twice it happened, in January. Ma-Mary, I lasted four months since I sent her out. Next time it will be...for ever...now, it is for ever. I will not lie with that woman again, not if all women died tomorrow, present company excepted.

113

MARY: She hasn't told you, has she?

SECHELE: Moko? There is nothing to tell.

MARY: She is with child.

> (*SECHELE closes his eyes, sinks down on his knees again and bangs his head on the ground, groaning loudly. LIVINGSTONE wakes up and comes through.*)

LIVINGSTONE: What's up with him?

MARY: I'll tell you later. Leave him.

> (*MARY walks away from SECHELE, pushing LIVINGSTONE back into the cabin.*)

LIVINGSTONE: Is he ill?

MARY: No. Forget him for a minute.

> (*SECHELE groans louder and gets to a kneeling position, holding his head, swaying backwards and forwards, then he tears off his coat and shirt, seizes his fly-switch and starts to flagellate himself.*)

LIVINGSTONE: I'm not putting up with this. Hey, Sechele, cut that out now.

SECHELE: Oh, I have sinned, I have sinned!

LIVINGSTONE: (*Snatching the fly-whisk out of his hand*) We'll have none of that popish nonsense here! Pull yourself together man, stand up. You're behaving like a big soft booby. Now, what's the matter?

> (*LIVINGSTONE lifts SECHELE to his feet.*)

SECHELE: Beat me, please.

LIVINGSTONE: No more claptrap!

SECHELE: David, my heart's love, I am the most miserable of men.

LIVINGSTONE: Tell me what it is. I'm not a mind-reader.

> (*Pause.*)

MARY: (*Flatly.*) Moko is having a baby.

LIVINGSTONE: Moko? I didn't notice anything…

MARY: She is only two months gone.

> (*Pause. SECHELE crumples to the ground again. LIVINGSTONE does not move.*)

LIVINGSTONE: And it's his?

> (*MARY nods.*)

> Christ. (*Pause.*) Aye, whip yourself, whip yourself, you useless, sinning, cannibal beast! (*Takes up the fly switch*

and flogs SECHELE.) Where is she? Bring her to me! Bring me that raging harlot!

(*MOKOKON enters, she has been listening from outside. LIVINGSTONE throws down the fly-whisk and goes through to the cabin, sits in his chair, then shoots out a foot and kicks SECHELE over. MOKOKON picks SECHELE up, straightens him out.*)

LIVINGSTONE: Come over here. (*Laughs, holds his chest.*) Christ in Heaven.

(*SECHELE limps across with MOKOKON. They stand in front of LIVINGSTONE.*)

Your confession has loosened all my bones. I feel I should sink through the earth and run away. You cannot imagine the lancinating pangs that this betrayal has caused me. They fall on my soul like drops of aqua fortis upon an ulcerated surface.

(*MOKOKON raises her eyes in mocking despair and tuts insolently. SECHELE hurls her to the ground.*)

SECHELE: Prostrate yourself!

MOKOKON: (*Getting up.*) To you, yes! To him, no!

(*SECHELE throws himself down on top of her and grabs her hair, banging her head on the floor.*)

SECHELE: Isaiah! I did not listen to Isaiah!

MOKOKON: David keeps you in the desert! It fits his Bible!

SECHELE: Beg his forgiveness!

MOKOKON: Yah!

LIVINGSTONE: But draw near hither, ye sons of the sorceress, the seed of the adulterer and the whore! Against whom do ye sport yourselves? Against whom make ye a wide mouth and draw out the tongue? Are ye not children of transgression, a seed of falsehood?

MOKOKON: Leave us alone! Get out! Go away! Go back to Glasgow! Yah!

SECHELE: You see what I have to deal with, David, my sweetheart?

(*Kicks MOKOKON.*) There is no peace, saith the Lord, unto the wicked. Apologise!

MOKOKON: Yah!

115

SECHELE: You are wrong!

MOKOKON: Isaiah! Chapter four, verse one. And in that day seven women shall take hold of one man, saying, we will eat our own bread and wear our own apparel, only let us be called by thy name... SEVEN, never mind five!

LIVINGSTONE: Fifty, verse one: This saith the Lord, where is the bill of your mother's divorcement, whom I have put away?

MOKOKON: What's that got to do with it? I'm no one's mother!

LIVINGSTONE: Yet.

MARY: You're an arrogant girl, Moko. You take what you like from the good book, you deliberately misinterpret its meaning...

SECHELE: Not Sechele. Isaiah is clear to me, clear as Saint Paul in his light. (*Continues beating MOKOKON up.*) I will kill her, David.

LIVINGSTONE; You'll do no such thing. God will punish her, and you. This does not impress me, Sechele. The whole exercise is a failure.

SECHELE: (*As he plucks the finery and ornaments off MOKOKON.*) Because the daughters of Zion are haughty and walk with stretched-forth necks and want eyes, walking and mincing as they go, and making a tinkling with their feet, therefore the Lord will smite with a scab the crown of the head of the daughters of Zion and the Lord will discover their secret parts! In that day the Lord will take away the bravery of their tinkling ornaments about their feet and their chains, and their bracelets, the ornaments of their legs and their headbands and their ear-rings and their nose-jewels...three, sixteen!

LIVINGSTONE: This is all to no avail, Sechele. I have raised a rampant vacuum.

SECHELE: David, she would not leave me alone. She hung about. In the morning I'd find her under the eaves by the door, waiting.

LIVINGSTONE: My heart is broken. I can no longer be a teacher here.

SECHELE: (*Clasping LIVINGSTONE's knees.*) No, you must never leave me. I repent! I am saved!

LIVINGSTONE: You are an apostate. Trusting you is a waste of time. Your world is an easy place. That curious inability to put things square within yourself has proved the end of our connection. I've got no more to say.
(*Pause. SECHELE gets to his feet.*)

SECHELE: Speak to him for me, Ma-Mary.

MARY: You are banned from fellowship with us until further notice. You are not permitted to worship with us, or take Communion.

SECHELE: No, no...you are casting me out.

LIVINGSTONE: (*Angrily.*) What do you do with devils?

SECHELE: David, how can you be so hard? Now I am nowhere.
(*LIVINGSTONE starts to exit. SECHELE bars his way.*)
The people don't want me, you don't want me, the Boers don't want me...what am I to do?

LIVINGSTONE: That's up to you.

SECHELE: But I can be forgiven. It says so!

LIVINGSTONE: You will do it again!

SECHELE: I will not. She goes!
(*Pause.*)

MOKOKON: Sechele, I am the only one left who truly wants you.

SECHELE: (*Spits.*) Yah!
(*Pause. LIVINGSTONE sighs. MOKOKON remains defiant, staring at MARY.*)

MOKOKON: Now you have not only taken away my husband but orphaned my child. I will sit outside with the cattle until this one is born and by then this great man of yours will have changed. King David was unfaithful to his wife, and he will find a way of leaving you.
(*MOKOKON exits. SECHELE sits in LIVINGSTONE's chair. MARY closes her eyes, her hands crossed over her womb.*)

LIVINGSTONE: And the first thing you can do, you great ninny, is to stop her talking to my wife like that. I won't have it, ye hear? Who does she reckon she is? Cleopatra?

I tell you, she wouldn't get away with that kind of thing where I come from...come on, get out of there, up, up... (*SECHELE gets out of the chair. LIVINGSTONE picks up the door.*)

You're going to help me hang this.

SECHELE: David...

LIVINGSTONE: I want it up before tonight. I want it firmly fastened and sound-proof if you're going to run a bordello in there.

SECHELE: Not now...

LIVINGSTONE: (*Slamming the door on the floor.*) Yes, right now. Get over there and guide the hinges over.

(*Unwillingly SECHELE takes one side of the door and helps LIVINGSTONE carry it over. MARY goes to help as well.*)

LIVINGSTONE: Don't you touch it, not the way you are. We'll do it.

(*MARY exits, the two men steady the door to get it over the hinge holes. They lower it and miss.*)

LIVINGSTONE: Ya stupid clot, ya shifted it!

SECHELE: I am sorry, David.

LIVINGSTONE: Keep your hand steady, for God's sake!

SECHELE: Yes, David.

(*They try again, and miss. LIVINGSTONE crashes the door down in a fury.*)

LIVINGSTONE: Ya useless eejit! Can't ya do a simple thing like that? Can't I trust you with anything at all?

SECHELE: Forgive me, David.

LIVINGSTONE: Stop farting about in God's name! Get yourself sorted out! D'ya think I've got time to waste on this kind of thing?

SECHELE: I am truly sorry, David.

LIVINGSTONE: (*As they try again.*) Aye, that's all very well coming out with I'm sorry and that, but ya don't try, do ya? It's all too bloody easy for you because it doesnae mean anything (*They miss again.*) Christ aam up to here wi ya shit 'n Hell! (*Hurls the door down.*) See you, if ya mess me around one more time I'll knock ya senseless, ya numbskull! Aa've nair met such a gormless lout in ma life!

SECHELE: Perhaps it would be easier if one of us did it?

LIVINGSTONE: NO! Ye do a door together. One fae the top, the other fae the bottom. (*Pause.*) You stay at the bottom.

(*Pause. They pick up the door, steady it, then slide it over the hinge rods. LIVINGSTONE opens it, closes it, opens it, closes it, then beckons SECHELE to go through. SECHELE obeys. Pause, with SECHELE looking at him through the open doorway, LIVINGSTONE slams the door shut in his face, turns on his heel and storms out. Pause. SECHELE picks up his fallen chair, sets it so it is back in its old position facing the doorway, sits down, fixes his eyes on the closed door in an unblinking stare and takes up his fly-whisk, cradling it in the crook of his forearm like a sceptre. Lights start to dim.*)

SECHELE: (*Sings, brokenly, then becoming firm.*)

GIVE ME JOY IN MY HEART, KEEP ME PRAISING,[*]

GIVE ME JOY IN MY HEART, I PRAY!

GIVE ME JOY IN MY HEART, KEEP ME PRAISING,

KEEP ME PRAISING TILL THE BREAK OF DAY.

(*Blackout.*)

SING HOSANNA! SING HOSANNA!

SING HOSANNA TO THE KING OF KINGS!

SING HOSANNA! SING HOSANNA!

SING HOSANNA TO THE KING!

(*LIVINGSTONE and MARY enter in blackout and light a candle, then get ready for bed. SECHELE remains in his chair, looking at the door.*)

MARY: You feel better now you've walked some of that steam off.

LIVINGSTONE: I'll never feel better about him. I don't think anyone's ever let me down with such a bump.

MARY: David, he's only a man...

LIVINGSTONE: He's full of wind...

MARY: Well, I think there's a lot of good in him. I blame her for it most. She did it quite deliberately to offend us.

LIVINGSTONE: Who's the chief of the Kwena? Sechele or her? The man's got a responsibility; he has to give moral leadership.

[*] Hymn number 26: New Church Praise – melody edition © public domain

MARY: Of all the chiefs I've met...

LIVINGSTONE: Mary, that lot your father deals with are all rabbits. All they're after is a gunsmith. They kid him along. (*Pause.*) Sechele has something else, another quality which he's betrayed. You don't go against your own talent, especially if it's of the spirit. That's what he's done.

(*LIVINGSTONE and MARY kneel down to pray at the bedside.*)

LIVINGSTONE/MARY: Our father in heaven, hallowed be your name...

(*SECHELE joins in from the other side of the door. LIVINGSTONE and MARY stop. SECHELE stops. They start again. He starts. He persists right through the Lord's prayer.*)

LIVINGSTONE/MARY: Your kingdom come, Your will be done on earth...(*Pause.*)

SECHELE: ...as it is in heaven. Give us this day our daily bread. Forgive us our sins...(*Pause.*) as we forgive those who sin against us. Do not bring us to the time of trial but deliver us from evil. (*Pause. Then speed up.*) For the kingdom, the power, and the glory are Yours now and for ever, amen.

(*LIVINGSTONE angrily snuffs the candle. He and MARY get into bed.*)

SECHELE: Good night, David. Good night, Mary. God bless you.

(*Silence. SECHELE quietly hums and sings his hymn to himself, occasionally sighing, flicking his whisk in the dark.*)

LIVINGSTONE: (*Suddenly quite loudly, pitched so SECHELE can hear.*) I've had reports from travellers that there is talk of a lake to the north called Ngami. To reach it you must trek through the worst part of the desert where the only water for man and beast is a peculiar sort of melon called a kengwe or keme or a cucumis caffer. The elephant revels in this fruit as does the rhinoceros, although naturally diverse in their choice of pasture. Various kinds of antelope feed on them with equal avidity and lions, hyenas, jackals and mice, all seem to

know and appreciate the common blessing. (*Pause.*)
But some are sweet, and some are bitter. This duality of
flavour is combined in some, as it is in a red eatable
cucumber about six inches long and about an inch and a
half in diameter. It is a bright scarlet colour when ripe.
Bees convey the pollen from one to the other. (*Pause.*)
Around this lake are millions of men who are waiting for
the Word. I am thinking of going there. (*SECHELE hums
and sings on, flicking his fly-whisk.*)

MARY: Go to sleep now.

(*Enter MOKOKON. She goes over to SECHELE, takes his
hand and puts it on her stomach.*)

MOKOKON: There. Feel that.

SECHELE: (*Still singing, incorporating the words.*) Go away.

MOKOKON: Come to bed.

SECHELE: Go away. Go away. Go away.

MOKOKON: Don't you want me?

SECHELE: No, no, no.

MOKOKON: Why?

SECHELE: God doesn't want you.

MOKOKON: Who wants him?

SECHELE: Poor Moko.

MOKOKON: Come to bed.

SECHELE: You can lie there if you like. I am waiting for
this door to open.

MOKOKON: Will you remember how comfortable it was?
(*Lies down on the bed.*)

SECHELE: David will allow me to lie in his bed if I am
sick. He will give me his medicines and cut my growths
out with his knife, pull out my rotten teeth, feed me
morphine to make me sleep. (*Pause.*) I love God because
he is David's.

MOKOKON: Sechele, come away from that door. He is
destroying you.

SECHELE: All the Crocodile People will become
Christians, every one of them. (*Loudly.*) I promise you!
They have had the opportunity and they have not learnt.
The guilt is on their heads!
(*MOKOKON lights a candle.*)

MOKOKON: Read to me.

SECHELE: David, if I am dying, bring me to your bed.

MOKOKON: Read me Johane Bunyana. Come away from the door.

(*Shows him the book.*)

(*SECHELE grunts, gets up, gently takes the book, then falls face down onto it on the bed, weeping. Abruptly he stops, lifts the book to the candle flame.*)

SECHELE: You have to read a part.

MOKOKON: No, you just read to me.

SECHELE: I will read the part of Hopeful and you will do Christian.

MOKOKON: Sechele...

SECHELE: Do it! (*Pause.*) From here. I will make a start. I never thought that by awakenings for sin, God at first begins the conversion of a sinner...

MOKOKON: (*Stroking his head.*) Sechele, are you reading or thinking?

SECHELE: Sin was yet very sweet to my flesh, and I was loth to leave it. I could not tell how to part with mine old companions, their presence and actions were desirable to me. Ah, Moko, Moko. The hours in which convictions were upon me, were such troublesome and such heart-affrighting hours that I could not bear no, not so much as the remembrance of them upon my heart. (*Pause. MOKOKON has her hand inside his shirt.*) Your turn now.

MOKOKON: You are my one love.

SECHELE: Christian says: Then, as it seems, sometimes you got rid of your trouble? Then Hopeful says: Yes, verily, but it would come into my mind again; and then I should be as bad, nay worse than I was before. Then Christian says...

(*MOKOKON takes the book out of his hand, puts it down, blows out the candle. Pulls him down into the bed. Pause in darkness. Lights up slightly, enough to reveal MOKOKON leaving SECHELE and slipping out of the rondavel's circle and squatting outside it. SECHELE sleeps on. MARY suddenly sits up.*)

MARY: Ah. (*Pause.*) David! David, wake up. (*Nudges him.*) Come on.

(*LIVINGSTONE turns over, putting his back to her.*)

MARY: It's starting.

LIVINGSTONE: Ach, you go on for hours. There's plenty of time.

MARY: I'm getting up.

LIVINGSTONE: Carry on. Take a walk, that'll do you good.

MARY: You'll have to collect some water together from somewhere.

LIVINGSTONE: Why didn't you save some from the washing?

MARY: David…

(*MARY grabs his shoulder. A labour pain hits her and she sucks in her breath, exhales, bends her head.*)

LIVINGSTONE: Alright?

MARY: They're very strong for so early.

LIVINGSTONE: They probably started while you were asleep. Come on, I'll walk you around.

MARY: What about the water?

LIVINGSTONE: We'll find some.

(*MARY gets up. LIVINGSTONE dresses and helps MARY.*)

LIVINGSTONE: Hold on. I'll just have a word with Sechele.

(*LIVINGSTONE knocks on the door. SECHELE wakes up.*)

LIVINGSTONE: Sechele! May I come in?

SECHELE: The door locks on your side.

(*LIVINGSTONE opens the door and enters the rondavel.*)

LIVINGSTONE: Ma-Mary has started her labour. I am going to need some water.

SECHELE: Water? There is no water.

LIVINGSTONE: Will you send out some men to cut melons for me? I must have fluid of some kind. Ask about.

SECHELE: I will do that.

LIVINGSTONE: Thank you.

(*LIVINGSTONE closes the door and takes MARY off R. SECHELE goes over to MOKOKON.*)

SECHELE: Get some water.

MOKOKON: For her I'll make some water. It will be born dead.

SECHELE: Sssssh! Unsay that.

MOKOKON: I have cursed her womb like I've cursed the rest of her. It will be born dead. She will die. He will die. Their oxen will die. Their waggon will lose its wheels.

SECHELE: Gather all the water in the village, every drop. If you fail I will kill you as a witch. (*Gives her the Wellington jug.*)

MOKOKON: You would never harm me.

SECHELE: Moko, if any harm comes to David's child, I will beat your brains out with my own club. Water!

MOKOKON: You are trying to make them hate you even more. The people are dry.

SECHELE: They have some, everyone has some put aside. Collect it and bring it here. No one must refuse or I will deal with them in a very tough way.

(*MOKOKON exits. Enter LIVINGSTONE. He goes straight through the cabin, opens the door, without knocking.*)

LIVINGSTONE: Sechele, what have you heard about Ngami?

SECHELE: Ngami? Nothing.

LIVINGSTONE: That's not true.

SECHELE: David, would I lie to you?

LIVINGSTONE: Yes. (*Pause.*) How far is the first river north?

SECHELE: How should I know...

LIVINGSTONE: Does the Koloberg connect with the Nuatuane River? How far is it across the thickest desert? Two hundred? Three hundred? Four hundred?

SECHELE: A thousand at least.

LIVINGSTONE: I have it from another source that it is less than half that. And there are fountains on the route at a place called Boatlanamet, Lopepe, Zentle, Mathulane, Nohokotsa and Bakwrutse. They're at regular intervals until you come to another river which runs into the lake.

SECHELE: David, you have beer there already, my beloved.

LIVINGSTONE: I'll need men, guides...

SECHELE: How is Mary?

LIVINGSTONE: I've drawn up a guesswork map. Would
you like to see it?

SECHELE: I am getting some water for you.

LIVINGSTONE: Come through, come through. I've made
a map of my proposed trip. (*Walks through to the cabin.
SECHELE follows him.*) It's my opinion that it lies
somewhere around twenty degrees latitude. (*Uncovers the
magic lantern and starts to set it up on the table.*) I shall
have the privilege of first preaching Jesus and the
resurrection on the shores of Lake Ngami.

SECHELE: We will build a church. When the rain comes
we will have moisture for making bricks...

LIVINGSTONE: I cannot help earnestly coveting the
privilege of introducing the gospel into a new land, new
people, and maybe into a new language. Yes, I'm
thinking of taking up translation...
(*MARY enters, unsteady.*)

MARY: Whew, strong now. Oh...
(*She reels. SECHELE takes her arm, leads her to the bed
and helps her sit down.
LIVINGSTONE lights the oil lamp. The picture of the
crucifixion appears on the wall as the lights lower.
LIVINGSTONE swiftly changes it to a hand-drawn map
showing his route from Kolobeng to Lake Ngami.*)

LIVINGSTONE: Ngami means Great Water. See here,
that's us. This high ground to the immediate north is
there for a fact, we know that...

MARY: Ah!

SECHELE: Hold my hand, Ma-Mary.

MARY: It's so hot. There's no air in here. Can we have the
door open?

LIVINGSTONE: I have had it reported that the river going
into the lake has a periodic flow and the reeds on its
fringes comprise the homelands of populous tribes which
have as their main diet fish, shoals of which descend with
the new influx of water...

SECHELE: David, Ma-Mary would like the door open...

LIVINGSTONE: My informant could give no scientific reason for the rise of the water except that he has heard that a chief who lives in the north part of the country kills a man annually and throws his body into the stream after which the water begins to flow...

MARY: Ah!! Here we go again...

SECHELE: Oof, what a grip you have, Ma-Mary. Wait. (*Stands up. Leans over and blows the oil-lamp out. Lights quickly up.*)

LIVINGSTONE: You won't see my image in this light.

SECHELE: Anything you want. Men, riding-oxen, guns... I will help you.

LIVINGSTONE: It'll take two months to get the expedition together.

SECHELE: (*Delighted.*) Two months! Two months! And you'll come back, you'll have to come back...

MARY: David, did you manage to get any water?

LIVINGSTONE: Mary will stay here I think. She won't be fit to travel not with a yowling infant...

SECHELE: Ma-Mary will be safe with me. I will take care of her.

MARY: Oh no, I'm coming with you, David. You're not leaving me behind.

LIVINGSTONE: Out of the question I'm afraid...

MARY: I've lived all my life in Africa. I didn't marry a missionary to get left behind.

LIVINGSTONE: Mary...

MARY: No! I'm perfectly capable...I'm stronger than you!

LIVINGSTONE: Fever, Mary. The northern areas are teeming with fever...

MARY: Then why do you think your precious plateau and the healthy highlands are up there, eh?

LIVINGSTONE: That will be through the fever belt. We'll have to walk just about all the way. There's virulent tsetse that will bring down the draught oxen.

MARY: Then I'll walk...

LIVINGSTONE: With an infant?

MARY: Yes, lashed to my back like a native girl. David you cannot leave me behind. If I don't come with you now, I'll never be in your company.

LIVINGSTONE: Mary…

MARY: This is not what I was wed for! You're getting shut of me.

LIVINGSTONE: Mary! (*Pause.*) Let your affection be towards God, much more than towards me. I hope I shall never give you cause to regret that you married me, but whatever friendship we feel towards each other, let us always look to Jesus as our common friend and guide, and may he shield you with his everlasting arm from evil.
(*Pause.*)

MARY: I will return to it. Mary Moffat is no stay-at-home!

LIVINGSTONE: On future journeys I may take you…perhaps; but not this one. We don't know who or what we shall find up there.

SECHELE: I will divorce Moko again!

LIVINGSTONE: Once is enough under rational law. This last time was an adulterous relationship and the work of the prince of the power of the air. This is no time to talk about it.

SECHELE: Eloi, eloi, lama sabachthani.

LIVINGSTONE: You'll make me beholden to you if you'll use those holy words for the fit occasion, of Christ crying on the cross and not a part of this sordid interlude of your life. Apt pupil you may be, Sechele, but you've no sense of appropriate context.

SECHELE: They fit my heart. My God, my God, why hast thou forsaken me?

LIVINGSTONE: Maybe she should go to her mother and father at Kuruman?

SECHELE: (*Desperately.*) No, she is better here. I will guard her with my life. When you get back she will be safe, the child will be happy and well, there will be no problem at all.

MARY: Sechele, it might be easier for me to go to Kuruman after all.

SECHELE: No. How can you travel? It is impossible.
   (*Pause.*)
MARY: I was thinking of the Boers. You know what they
   think about David. If they found me here, alone, it could
   be bad.
SECHELE: We would fight them and beat them with
   passive resistance.
   (*Pause. MOKOKON enters with the Wellington jug brimming
   with water.*)
LIVINGSTONE: (*Calling.*) Who is that?
MOKOKON: It is all the water of the Crocodile People.
SECHELE: Bring it through.
   (*MOKOKON comes through the door and stands by the table
   with the jug. LIVINGSTONE moves the magic lantern to
   make room for it. Pause. MARY stiffens.*)
MARY: Ah-ah, ooh…
SECHELE: What a child it will be, such strength!
MARY: This is terrible…
LIVINGSTONE: You're doing well. Nothing to worry
   about. Breathe deeply.
   (*MARY convulses and lets out a horrified scream of pain.
   Pause. MOKOKON runs to her and slips her hands under
   her arm-pits and into a full nelson.*)
MOKOKON: Down, down, no crying, no sorrow, come out,
   all back, here I am Lord, down, down, down. It is all
   unknotted and unsaid. My tongue is clean.
SECHELE: David, my heart's love, while we have water
   here, baptise me again.
LIVINGSTONE: When I get back, if you've behaved
   yourself properly.
MOKOKON: Isaiah, one, seven and eight: your land,
   strangers devour it in your presence and it is desolate, as
   overthrown by strangers. And the daughter of Zion is left
   as a cottage in a vineyard, as a lodge in a garden of
   cucumbers. Five, thirteen: people are gone into captivity,
   because they have no knowledge and their honourable
   men are famished, and their multitudes dried up with
   thirst. I take Christ now.

SECHELE: I will never let you down again.

LIVINGSTONE: Clear the decks. Give the doctor room to work.

(LIVINGSTONE pushes MARY back, raises her knees, covers her with a sheet.)

LIVINGSTONE: Will you be so good as to wait next door? *(SECHELE and MOKOKON stand up, pause, then go through to the rondavel. Pause. LIVINGSTONE looks round. SECHELE closes the door. A great yell from MARY, half in terror, half in triumph. Blackout.*

Lights up on LIVINGSTONE holding a baby bundled in a bloody sheet, MARY flat out behind him sighing, SECHELE and MOKOKON kneeling.)

MARY: Glory to God in the highest and peace to his people on earth!

LIVINGSTONE: *(Dipping his fingers into the water.)* In the name of Jesus Christ, our Lord, I baptise you Thomas. May you cling to Him all the days of your life. *(Makes the sign of the cross on the baby's head.)* Amen.

MARY: Amen.

SECHELE: Amen.

MOKOKON: Amen. All praise to Christ who conquered the crocodile. *(LIVINGSTONE holds out his wet fingers. SECHELE licks them dry.)*

LIVINGSTONE: Learn again. Start at the beginning. Persevere and He will come to you, from darkness into light.

MOKOKON: *(Singing, to 'Auld Lang Syne.')*

ABCD
EH-EFG
HIJKLM
NOPQ
RSTU
VWXYZ.

ALL:

ABCD
EH-EFG
HIJKLM

NOPQ
RSTU
VWXYZ.
(*Blackout.*)

The End.

RICHARD III PART TWO

For Clio

Characters

GEORGE ORWELL

RICHARD III

CICELY

PRINCE EDWARD

LOUISE

PRINCE RICHARD

McMASTERS

LOVELL

ELIZABETH WOODVILLE

CHRYSOSTOM

A NOTE ON THE CHARACTERS

GEORGE ORWELL: born Eric Blair in India, 1903. Went to Eton, joined the Burma Police, then became a writer. Fought for the Republican cause in the Spanish Civil War. His most popular books are *Animal Farm* (published 1945), and his last novel *1984*, written in 1948. Died of tuberculosis in 1950.

RICHARD III: born 1452, Fotheringhay, last son of Richard, Duke of York, and Cicely Neville. After his brother's death (King Edward IV) in 1482, he was designated Protector. Crushing a conspiracy by Elizabeth Woodville (King Edward's widow) to seize power, he accepted the suggestion that the sons of his brother were bastards by reason of Edward's alleged first marriage to Eleanor Butler, and ascended the throne himself. His nephews (the Princes in the Tower) were placed in custody.

LOVELL, FRANK: born 1950, educated at Ampleforth and the London School of Economics. Did postgraduate work in retail dynamics and ergo-selling at the Massachusetts Institute of Technology before joining the United Nations as an adviser to the Commission on Entertainment Shortfalls in the Third World. Moved to the Ministry of Sport (Indoor Games Division) in 1983 as Sales Promotion Director. Awarded Queen's Commerce Medal. Hobbies: dialect poetry and country dancing.

LOVELL, FRANCIS: born circa 1450, educated with Richard at Middleham in Yorkshire by the Earl of Warwick. Became Richard's High Chamberlain and fought with him at Bosworth, but escaped, re-appearing at a later rebellion against Henry Tudor by Lambert Simnel posing as Prince Edward. Escaped again and disappeared. In 1708 a skeleton was discovered seated at a table with bread and wine, in a secret vault under Minster Lovell, his house.

McMASTERS, GEORGE: born 1951, educated at the local grammar school and St. Andrews where he graduated in Business and Commerce Studies with International Relations as a subsidiary. Worked for Ford Motor Company, Dagenham and Detroit, then the International Leisure Council as Chairman of Card-Games Regulations Standardisation Committee. Joined the Ministry of Sport (Indoor Games Division) in 1982 as Marketing Surveys Controller. Hobbies: gliding and the scouting movement.

McMASTERS, GEORGE: born 1451, Peniquick, near Edinburgh, of poor parents. Apprenticed to a merchant banker in Edinburgh and rose to become a partner. Made an alderman in the year before Richard III invaded Scotland and demanded the surrender of the city. As one of the principal negotiators he was considered responsible for the arrangement whereby the English King was allowed to enter Edinburgh unopposed. Unable to remain in the city after the withdrawal of the English army, he accompanied King Richard to London and became the chamberlain of Cicely, Duchess of York. Died in 1499 of jaundice.

ELIZABETH WOODVILLE: daughter of Earl Rivers and widow of Lord Ferrers, a Lancastrian supporter killed at Saint Albans, by whom she had two children. Married Edward IV secretly on May Day 1464 and bore him three children – Edward and Richard (the Princes in the Tower), and Elizabeth who later married Henry Tudor. After the marriage, Henry Tudor locked her away in a nunnery in Bermondsey. Died 1492.

EDWARD V (born 1470) and RICHARD, DUKE OF YORK (born 1474): the 'Princes in the Tower', sons of Edward IV and Elizabeth Woodville. Dates of death unknown.

CICELY, DUCHESS OF YORK: born 1414, Raby in County Durham, daughter of Ralph, Earl of Westmorland. Aunt of Warwick the Kingmaker. Had twelve children, only seven of whom survived infancy – Edmund (killed in battle), Edward IV, George, Duke of Clarence (executed for treason by Edward IV, his brother) and Richard III (killed at Bosworth) were her sons. After Richard's death she retired to her castle at Berkhamsted and lived as a religious recluse until her death in 1495.

CHRYSOSTOM, CHRISTOPHOLOUS: born circa 1446 in Constantinople, son of a Byzantine church craftsman. When the city was besieged by the Turks in 1450 the child was taken north to Dubrovnik where he was later apprenticed to the painter Mappani. After arguing with his master, he switched to glass-making and travelled throughout Central Europe and then the Mediterranean, working in Milan for the Sforza, in Rimini for the Malatesta, and Florence for the Medici. Went to France and Burgundy in 1482-3 and arrived in England at the height of his international reputation. On his return to his home in Genoa he established a glass factory and built up a major industry which was transferred to Venice twenty years later by his natural son Georgio. Date of death unknown.

LOUISE PENHALYGON: born 1960, Penzance. Graduated from Exeter Technical College in Audio-Visual Aids in 1979 and joined the Imperial War Museum as a demonstrator of early gas equipment. Became Projects Co-ordinator Grade III at Ministry of Sport (Indoor Games Division) in 1983. Hobbies include ornithology and playing records.

NOTES

The rôles shown as doubled in the original production are recommended as being played that way in any casting; but the roles of PRINCE EDWARD/CICELY and LOUISE/RICHARD may he performed as separate parts. RICHARD III and GEORGE ORWELL must be doubled.

Two acting levels help with the flow of time-shifts in the play between 1948, 1984 and 1484. Scene changes are not recommended, except by using direction of dialogue, music and strategic moves. The play should flow between its locations.

Whenever possible McMASTERS and LOVELL should change from 1984 to 1484 costume and vice versa in order to identify the time they are working in, but this should not impede the action and may occasionally be dispensed with, once the convention has been established. As a general rule, LOUISE is not intended to make stage exits, but moves to and from the control areas.

A textile backdrop showing the Betrayal game board, (the design of which is left to the imagination of the director and designer), can be used as a cover for the stained-glass window, then drawn aside as curtains on the final scene.

The Death and Nativity cards should be large, simple and able to be produced from the main rostrum beneath the Betrayal board, either as flip-overs, or hinged panels. The plastic punch-cards out of the Betrayal box itself must be exact copies.

The chess-table, chairs, stools and other stage furniture used should have a heavy medieval feel and tone in order to contrast with the chrome dazzle of the electric piano. Two ultra modern chairs in chrome and plastic can be used for McMASTERS and LOVELL in a position, or on a level where 1984 action is predominant.

The music can be played by the acting company or an orchestra. Notes on the music are provided with the score at the end of the text.

Instruments used in the original production were: lute-guitar, rebec, Nordic lyre, psaltery, dulcimer, guitar, electric piano, glockenspiel, sopranino and tenor recorders, penny whistle, percussion. Wherever possible, the instruments should be used as helpers and illustrators of the action, almost as secondary characters. They can be handled, tuned, knitted into the story to give the impression of RICHARD III being a man who loved music and surrounded himself with instruments as well as men.

Richard III Part Two was first performed by Paines Plough at the Traverse Theatre Club, Edinburgh on 24 August 1977, with the following cast:

GEORGE ORWELL, Stephen Boxer

RICHARD III, Stephen Boxer

CICELY, Harriet Walter

PRINCE EDWARD, Harriet Walter

LOUISE, Diana Kyle

PRINCE RICHARD, Diana Kyle

McMASTERS, Robert McIntosh

LOVELL, Eric Richard

ELIZABETH WOODVILLE, Fiona Victory

CHRYSOSTOM, Joe Marcell

Director, Edward Adams

ACT ONE

The Betrayal board background is revealed as the lights go swiftly up. GEORGE ORWELL, dressed in pyjamas and dressing-gown, stands in front of the board, a typescript in his hand. He places it on the chess table. The chess-board is still set for a game which has been abandoned. Some of the pieces have been knocked over. Stage left is a control area where LOUISE is sitting. She wears a tee-shirt with 'Indoor Games' across the chest. All the instruments are stacked or placed here, also a tape-deck and amplification system. LOUISE remains in shadow, an electric piano keyboard in front of her.

ORWELL: My name is George Orwell and I have written a book, here. As a socialist all my life – too late to find another word for what I believe in – the book perturbs me. I don't feel at all easy about it. My agent thinks it will be misunderstood and fail. I'm afraid I got a little upset as that was a conclusion I had come to myself. I have set it in 1984 – this being 1948. It is an arbitrary date but it is the future. So that means I am being prophetic, which is alarming in itself. This I do not attempt to excuse. We must have prophets, ask the government, and a dying one has always been conceded a certain status, indulged. (*Coughs.*) I have TB, a contagious disease of the lungs passed on spittle. My book may drown in a flood of it. More than anything, I don't want this book of mine sensationalised in its more trivial aspects. After a decade of war against fascism – on which I have some opinions – my main theme needs to be politically clear. For example, I say that in 1984 the middle-class will adopt the uniform of the working-class and prance around in overalls; and that the new television-sets appearing everywhere will mean the end of private life by this time. Perhaps I am going too far. Could be. My argument that English socialism will be turned into a machine of oppression by successive gangs of university lecturers, technocrats, scientists and publicity men, all of rigorous middle-class background like myself, ah, that is what will be taken up. I will suffer for that. I will be accused of betraying the cause; and that will be painful. I will be accused of betraying my own past; and that will be agonising. (*Coughs. Takes a handkerchief out of his pocket, covers his mouth, looks at it, grimaces, puts it back in his pocket.*) What I am deeply concerned about in 1984 is the wilful destruction of historical truth by over-powerful, self-righteous governments. Real history is a law, like gravity. There is no greater power in the human present than the human past. The present is the past. Winston Smith, the hero of my book – called after Churchill who wasn't averse to rewriting history himself, in imitation of Stalin we could say – Winston Smith works in the Ministry of Truth as an expert operator of Doublethink. That's his job. Let me illustrate. (*Setting up the fallen chess-pieces one by one.*) Stage One – you make up a story for propaganda purposes. Stage Two – you deliberately believe that story yourself. Stage Three – you force yourself to forget that you created it. Stage Four – you accept it as history. So history is plastic. Its patterns are in a state of constant disturbance. (*Pause.*) How did we get into this position? Why did we allow ourselves to become so arrogant as to think that we have the right to re-shape the past? These were lives people led, they happened, happened in their terms, not ours. History belongs to the people who lived it first! They have a right to be heard, always. (*Pause.*) But ought I to post this book to my publishers? My enemies will do everything in their power to discredit me for having written it. They will give me no peace. (*ORWELL exits, taking the typescript. General lighting up. LOUISE takes up a microphone, flicks a switch on the console.*)

LOUISE: (*Over loudspeakers.*) This is the final call for delegates to the Ministry of Sport Indoor Games Division Conference for sales executives and operatives to go to the Danube Room. Will all delegates please go to the Danube Room where the conference is about to begin.

(*LOUISE switches off the amplification system. LOVELL and McMASTERS enter in smart, clean pressed overalls which look tailor-made, carrying two game boxes. The top one reads 'Big Brother'.*)

McMASTERS: Introductions are hardly necessary, but this is Louise Penhalygon, Projects Co-ordinator...

LOUISE: Hello.

McMASTERS: Frank Lovell, Sales Promotion Director, Indoor...

LOVELL: Hello.

McMASTERS: And I'm George McMasters, Marketing Surveys Controller, Indoor. Now, if any one of you is worried about this conference, forget it. 1984 has been a record year for the Indoor Games Division, thanks to you, the best sales team I ever worked with. You're terrific, every single one of you.

(*McMASTERS puts the game boxes down, the lid of one still hidden.*)

LOVELL: 1984 has been a marvellous year, marvellous. Our George Orwell promotion has been a fantastic success. The Big Brother unit became the top-selling board-game in the Common Market – 909,771, plus an export figure to trade areas outside the EEC of 801,567. Phenomenal. I've never imagined Orwell's ideas had such pull.

McMASTERS: But this coming year, 1985, has got to be even better. New targets have been set and we have to hit them. It really is export or die. Now Orwell's comic novel is well-known, all those jokes, Big Brother, Newspeak, Doublethink, they've been enjoyed for thirty years. But he is nothing beside the figure at the centre of our new project.

(*LOUISE plays a chord on the electric piano.*)

LOVELL: He's notorious!

(*Another chord, building.*)

McMASTERS: Our greatest villain!

(*Another chord, building.*)

LOVELL: A political monster!

(*Another chord.*)

McMASTERS: The archetype of all cold-hearted killers! (*Final swelling chord.*)

McMASTERS/LOVELL: Richard the Third!

McMASTERS: The game? Betrayal! (*Shows the lid of the box.*)

LOVELL: It will be a world-beater.

McMASTERS: Monopoly, look out. Diplomacy, forget it. (*LOUISE changes to softer, more reflective music, LOVELL speaks over.*)

LOVELL: So at the heart of the game, there's a man, and a mystery? Was he guilty? Did he murder so many?

McMASTERS: Henry the Sixth's son, Henry the Sixth, his own brother Clarence...and the Princes in the Tower? There's a tale that touches everyone. The boys. The boys. Did he kill the boys? And if he did...why? Tantalising stuff. (*Opens the game.*)

LOVELL: All we know is that they disappeared, and no one ever admitted that they were dead. So, our game takes place in the right environment – speculation! You play Betrayal on Monday – he did. You play Betrayal on Tuesday – he didn't. That's the kind of zesty, quicksilver fun we can offer. I tell you, we're on to a winner! (*Music fades out. Enter ELIZABETH WOODVILLE.*)

McMASTERS: Pieces. Let's have a look at the pieces. Once again our backroom boys have done us proud. Look at this. Have you ever seen such detail? Such finish? And the style is exact. Real quality.

LOVELL: Elizabeth Woodville, widow of King Edward, mother of the Princes. (*Enter PRINCE EDWARD and PRINCE RICHARD.*)

McMASTERS: And here are the boys. The tall one is Edward, the uncrowned King, shoved aside by his uncle on his way to the throne. The short one is Richard, Duke of York. Look at that. Beautiful craftmanship. See the way they glide across the board.

ELIZABETH: Come and play chess until your Uncle Richard arrives. That will pass the time.

PRINCE EDWARD: Mother, no more games, please. That's all we've done since father died, play games.

PRINCE RICHARD: Why don't you do something to get us out of here?

ELIZABETH: I will, I will. Don't forget I've been virtually under house-arrest myself for the last year. I'm working on getting you free, you must trust me. Now, chess. A game will keep you occupied. But when you hear Uncle Richard coming I want you straight back upstairs so we can all come down together and face him as a family...

PRINCE EDWARD: I don't want to see him. I hate his guts.

PRINCE RICHARD: So do I.

ELIZABETH: You will do as you're told. I want you both to be on your best behaviour. Give your uncle no cause to criticise you. If you do, you could spoil everything. Sit down at the table. Edward, you take the black, Richard, the white.

PRINCE RICHARD: I had white last time. I want the black.

PRINCE EDWARD: Don't be so stupid, as if it mattered. Come on then.

ELIZABETH: You know how to play?

PRINCE EDWARD: Vaguely. Mother, we're really sick of amusing ourselves. We want you to do something! Uncle Richard will never let us go...

ELIZABETH: This is the king. This is the queen. This is the bishop, knight, castle. These are the pawns. Checkmate means the king is dead.

PRINCE EDWARD: I'd kill him if I had the chance.

PRINCE RICHARD: Mother, if there's kings and queens and bishops and knights on the board, why aren't there princes?

ELIZABETH: You should know why. They're all locked up in the castles.

(*ELIZABETH exits.*)

LOVELL: See what I mean? We're offering so much. We can really break through into the big time with Betrayal. 1985 is the five hundredth anniversary of the Battle of Bosworth at which Richard the Third was killed. Remember Bosworth. Important. Significant. The end.

McMASTERS: The final square. The pay-off.

LOVELL: Betrayal-teeming with these marvellous medieval characters – kicks off on Christmas Eve 1484 at Berkhamsted Castle, gallops excitingly through winter, spring and summer and ends in August, the day of reckoning.

(*PRINCE EDWARD and PRINCE RICHARD start to play chess.*)

McMASTERS: Hear him coming? Over the hill, down the lane. A cold, cold day but you can see quite clearly. The King is coming.

LOVELL: Into the courtyard, off his horse, up the steps, through the door, into the corridor...this is the game, and this is the man!

RICHARD: (*Off.*) Hello! Anyone at home? I'm here!

(*PRINCE EDWARD and PRINCE RICHARD sweep the chess pieces away into a bag and run off, terrified. Enter RICHARD III in a long cloak, bent over, hunchbacked.*)

Where is everyone? Rouse yourselves! The King is here! God, it's cold. Where are you all? (*Whisks off his cloak to reveal a mandolin on his back. He takes it off.*) Come on down! Let me see you!

(*McMASTERS and LOVELL put on medieval surcoats which cover the tops of their overalls.*)

LOVELL: Sire.

McMASTERS: Sire.

RICHARD: There you are. No, no, up, up. No formalities. Where have you been hiding? Come here. (*Embraces them.*) How are my old friends? Steady as ever. Let me look at you both. Never was a king so fortunate in his friends. I've missed you both.

McMASTERS: Welcome to Berkhamsted, sire. We've been waiting for you.

LOVELL: Hello, Richard. You've made good time.

RICHARD: Where's my mother?

McMASTERS: She's in the middle of a lecture given by a wandering friar on the practical uses of self-denial. She'll cut the household budget and then tell us to blame it on God.

RICHARD: Is she well, in herself?

McMASTERS: Stronger than ever. I don't know how she does it.

RICHARD: Go and tell her I'm here and that I'd like to see her.

(*McMASTERS exits.*)

Has Elizabeth arrived yet?

LOVELL: She has.

RICHARD: I expect you were pleased to see her.

LOVELL: As a drowning man delights in water.

RICHARD: I'm sure she has her good points.

LOVELL: Maybe, but I'm not risking my life looking for them.

RICHARD: Bear with her for my sake. I need her here. I'll explain later.

(*Enter McMASTERS with a robe for RICHARD.*)

McMASTERS: Your mother has a few prayers to finish, then she'll be with you. God is in a chatty mood today.

(*Enter ELIZABETH with PRINCE EDWARD and PRINCE RICHARD. PRINCE EDWARD is coughing.*)

ELIZABETH: There you are Richard, at last. The boys and I have been listening for your horse.

RICHARD: He's a quiet walker. Hello Elizabeth. (*Kisses her.*) And what's this, Edward?

PRINCE EDWARD: I have to stay in bed.

PRINCE RICHARD: He's very ill. He coughs so much he keeps me awake at nights.

RICHARD: That is worrying. Is their bedchamber warm and dry, Frank?

LOVELL: The best in the house.

RICHARD: And you Richard, how is your voice? As pure as ever? I hope you will sing for me later. I boast about the voices of my nephews.

ELIZABETH: He will be glad to. I think Edward should go back to bed now, with your permission.

RICHARD: Edward, we will cure this cough. Use your mind, your will-power. Think to yourself – this cough does not exist. Believe it, and the cough will go away. Go on, say it. This cough does not exist.

PRINCE EDWARD: This cough does not exist. (*Coughs.*)
    I knew it wouldn't work.

PRINCE RICHARD: He doesn't know what he is
    talking about.

ELIZABETH: Richard, don't be insolent.

PRINCE EDWARD: I'm not a bastard!

PRINCE RICHARD: Neither am I!

PRINCE EDWARD: My father was king. I should be king…

ELIZABETH: Edward, stop it!

PRINCE RICHARD: And if he's not king, I should be.
    I'm next.

ELIZABETH: Get upstairs this minute…

RICHARD: No, no, let them go on. Anything else you want
    to say to me? You might as well get it all off your
    chest. No?

LOVELL: They want a good thrashing, the pair of them!

RICHARD: Quiet, Frank.

ELIZABETH: I'm sorry, Richard. They have behaved
    disgracefully…

PRINCE EDWARD: We're sorry too, aren't we?

PRINCE RICHARD: Yes, to the bottom of our hearts.

PRINCE EDWARD: We learnt something for you, Uncle.

PRINCE RICHARD: It's not much, but we worked hard at
    it. I'm ready.

PRINCE EDWARD/PRINCE RICHARD:
    The Cat, the Rat, and Lovell our dog,
    Rule all England under an hog.

LOXTELL: I'll break your bloody necks!
    (*PRINCE EDWARD and PRINCE RICHARD run off.
    RICHARD stops LOVELL following them.*)

RICHARD: Leave them, Frank. They are only children.
    Thank you for the entertainment, Elizabeth.

ELIZABETH: It had nothing to do with me. If my sons pick
    things up out of the gutter it is not my fault. It is you who
    has charge of their education. But I will, with your
    permission, go and see to it that we have no more
    embarrassing outbursts. May I?

RICHARD: Of course.
    (*ELIZABETH exits.*)

LOVELL: Some chance you've got of having a peaceful
Christmas with her around. She'd cause a riot in
a graveyard.

McMASTERS: She put the boys up to it. They'd never dare
talk to you like that without her support. That was all
carefully rehearsed.

RICHARD: Quite likely. But she is my brother's widow,
and my present policy is to contain her mischief, and her
sons, and let her live. (*Pause.*) Now, this is to go no
further at this time, but news has come from agents in
France that Henry Tudor plans to invade England next
summer and seize the throne.

LOVELL: God's teeth! As soon as that? We're not ready
for them.

McMASTERS: With what army? What money?

RICHARD: French army, French money. And some help
from friends at home. (*Pause.*) You see why I wanted
her here?

McMASTERS: Dame Elizabeth?

LOVELL: Who else?

(*Enter CICELY, Duchess of York, unseen.*)

RICHARD: Tudor is negotiating to marry her daughter. If
he is successful his plan is to unite York, the lady, with
Lancaster, himself, and bring the realm together. Only
the boys stand in his way. They are Elizabeth's
bargaining factor.

LOVELL: Jesus Christ. That woman would haggle over
how many pennies to put on a dead man's eyes.

CICELY: Kill her. Hello, my son. Did you have a good
journey? Yes, kill her. God understands acts of political
necessity, he must do, otherwise the world would have
fallen to pieces years ago.

RICHARD: Mother...

CICELY: The woman is not to he trusted. You've got
thinner and you look tired. Why are you so kind to her?
'To deliver thee from the strange woman, even from the
stranger who flattereth with her words.' Proverbs, chapter
two, verse sixteen...

McMASTERS: (*In unison.*) Proverbs, chapter two, verse sixteen…

CICELY: I would have no hesitation in disposing of the bitch. I am sorry if my castle is cold but it has been empty for months. Kiss me. We have been very busy preparing for you. This, I said, must be his best Christmas.

(*Enter ELIZABETH holding up a handkerchief spotted with blood.*)

ELIZABETH: Look, Edward has coughed blood. (*Pause.*) I'm not saying that it's anyone's fault but blood is blood. That is very worrying. (*Pause.*) Oh let us not enter into any debate on the subject. Brr, there's a draught from somewhere…

(*Enter CHRYSOTOM, a magnificently-dressed negro wearing an enormous Renaissance hat and carrying a jewelled bag and a long white-washed board. They recoil.*)

CHRYSOTOM: (*Chuckling.*) Hello. It's very cold out there. (*He takes off his hat and executes a phenomenally contrived bow.*) That's how they do it in Burgundy these days. Silly, isn't it?

LOVELL: Hold it right there!

CHRYSOSTOM: Harmless, harmless. A wanderer. I am expected.

McMASTERS: Identify yourself! This is a royal household!

CHRYSOSTOM: From Byzantium. My father was in mosaics, I am in glass. A chip off the old rock.

LOVELL: How did you get here?

CHRYSOSTOM: I am the result of a clandestine cultural exchange between Africa and Asia Minor.

McMASTERS: Right, you stay where you are. Don't move. Drop everything. Keep absolutely still. Put your hands where I can see them.

(*Pause. CHRYSOSTOM is searched, his bags examined during the next sequence. RICHARD watches him, wary.*)

LOVELL: (*Picking up the board.*) What's this?

CHRYSOSTOM: I could be a fakir.

McMASTERS: Say that again, slowly.

CHRYSOSTOM: A fakir. An Indian comedian. They induce mirth in their audiences by lying on a bed of nails. As you can see, I have come strongly under the influence of western civilisation. I have had all the nails pulled out. No, not at all. I never even bothered to put them in. (*Pause.*) This is my sketching board, for my designs. Have you finished fondling me?

LOVELL: Sire, I don't like the look of this character...

CHRYSOSTOM: Tomorrow I'll try harder. I've only changed my codpiece twice today and I have a huge selection of ridiculous hats.

RICHARD: What are you doing here?

CHRYSOSTOM: I have an invitation to spend Christmas here from the King's mother. (*To ELIZABETH.*) Here I am and thank you for asking me. I have kept a careful list of my expenses so far...we can take my home base as Genoa for the moment, but I think we'll have to keep the fee open for negotiation as the exchange rate for rose nobles has been dropping against all the major European currencies as a result of your persistent political unrest...

ELIZABETH: I am not the King's mother.

CICELY: That is me. You must be the craftsman I ordered.

CHRYSOSTOM: Rather the executive you asked for.

CICELY: Have you the mystery of making coloured windows?

CHRYSOSTOM: I possess it.

CICELY: This man is here at my invitation. His name is Chrysostom.

CHRYSOSTOM: Call me Chris. (*Looking at RICHARD.*) Is this the subject?

RICHARD: This is the King.

CHRYSOSTOM: I see a lot of kings but few men. (*Looks at the window.*)

CICELY: I did not think you would be black.

CHRYSOSTOM: Neither did my father.

RICHARD: Mother, I want this to be a family Christmas...no business.

CICELY: Richard, you are the last of my sons, the last of my men. You came to me late in life and you were the smallest, and the weakest, needing most from me. So, I love you best of all my children, and now you are King

of the English. When you die I want there to be
something beautiful, something timeless to keep you in
the public mind. I will pay for it.

CHRYSOSTOM: You want a timeless window? Timeless
comes expensive.

CICELY: Isn't that the quality of great art?

CHRYSOSTOM: One shared with great lies. But you're the
customer and you are gifted with unfailing, relentless
rectitude.

CICELY: Will you agree, Richard? He has a fine reputation.

RICHARD: What for? His tailor?

CHRYSOSTOM: (*Bowing again.*) Sire, it is a pleasure for the
world's best stained glass window maker to meet the
world's most bloodstained widow maker.
(*Pause.*)

RICHARD: You believe all you hear?

CHRYSOSTOM: If one circulates, one lives with rumour.

RICHARD: Mother, I will have to be persuaded.
This creature has no natural part in a Christian festival.

CHRYSOSTOM: King, what am I selling? What can I do
for you? Why should your mother pay me for something
so fragile, so insubstantial as a stained glass window? I'll
tell you. You need a new image.

LOVELL: That's what we've been telling him.

CHRYSOSTOM: You've got to change the way that people
think of you.

McMASTERS: When you say 'Richard the Third' to anyone,
pow! I want to see their eyes light up and their hands head
straight for their wallets!

CHRYSOSTOM: The Good Prince must have a good image.
He's got to concentrate on that, keep in the public eye,
shape what is known, disguise that which might confuse,
cover up that which is unsightly.

LOVELL: Be practical...

McMASTERS: Cultivate the right approach...

CHRYSOSTOM: Well, the way I look at it is this – image-
making is a whole new business when you see it in
relation to politics. It suddenly has power, importance.
Up until now the industry has been crude, rudimentary –

look at the work of your English portrait painters, it's laughable, useless – it hasn't been adapted to your needs.

ELIZABETH: You're preparing to idealise him. Is that what you want, Mother-in-law?

CICELY: You balance extremes with extremes. Let him do it, Richard.

RICHARD: One window? What will one window achieve? Will all the people of England come to Berkhamsted to see it?

CHRYSOSTOM: Copies, facsimiles, hand-outs, brochures, leaflets...

LOVELL: Posters, medals, coins, clothes, badges...

McMASTERS: Shields, flags, buttons...I can see it!

LOVELL: So can I!

McMASTERS: You'll make a fortune!

CHRYSOSTOM : So will I.

RICHARD: In the face of such universal enthusiasm I can only say – go ahead.

LOVELL: Go ahead. May I speak to Mr Caxton?

McMASTERS: Caxton speaking. What can I do for you?

LOVELL: Big order coming your way. By appointment to the King.

CHRYSOSTOM: Tell him not to forget my commission.

McMASTERS: What do you want? Two-tone litho? Silk-screen? How many thousand? How many million? How many copies from the original?

ALL: (*Sing.*)

REPRODUCTIONS, REPRODUCTIONS, LET THE IMAGE BE WIDESPREAD,

REPRODUCTIONS, REPRODUCTIONS, THE SPECIES NEVER DEAD,

INTRODUCING WILLIAM CAXTON WITH HIS HUG AND SQUEEZE AND PRESS,

INTRODUCING WILLIAM CAXTON WHO CAN MULTIPLY A YES OR A NO OR A QUICK QUICK SLOW,

OR A SIGH OR A THOUGHT OR A BATTLE FOUGHT,

OR A PRAYER OR A NOTE FROM THE DEEPEST THROAT,

OR A LOVE OR A LIE OR A DON'T SAY DIE.

REPRODUCTIONS, REPRODUCTIONS, CIRCULATION, OUTLETS, SALES,

REPRODUCTIONS, REPRODUCTIONS, THIS SYSTEM NEVER FAILS,
INTRODUCING WILLIAM CAXTON WITH HIS COMMA, O AND
STOP,
INTRODUCING WILLIAM CAXTON WHO IS GETTING TO THE TOP
OF THE BOTTOM, SEE THE 'I'S, YOU DOT 'EM,
GIVE THE Q LITTLE TAIL, ALPHABETICAL SNAIL
GIVE THE J BLOODY HOOK FOR A JUDGE'S BOOK
HAVE THE B WITH A BREAST YOU'LL FIND THAT SELLS BEST

REPRODUCTIONS, REPRODUCTIONS, GET THE SCREW DOWN ON
THE PLATE,
REPRODUCTIONS, REPRODUCTIONS, THE LADY'S PERIOD IS LATE,
INTRODUCING WILLIAM CAXTON WITH HIS BLACK, PROPHETIC
HANDS.
INTRODUCING WILLIAM CAXTON WHO GAVE REPRODUCTION
GLANDS
AND AN ORGAN, CONCLUSION FOREGONE,
SUCCESS, HIT THE HEIGHTS WITH YOUR NAME IN LIGHTS,
TELL THE WORLD, HERE'S THE TRUTH, GRAB A NATION'S
YOUTH,
DO A RUN, THOUSANDS COME AND THE CAMPAIGN'S WON.

LOVELL: It's the answer, sire. This way you can change the
situation instead of allowing the situation to change you.

RICHARD: Leave us alone. I would like a private word
with this peacock.

(*McMASTERS, LOVELL. CICELY, ELIZABETH exit.*)

I let it pass at the time, but are the insults necessary for
your art? Does it pay to be so provocative?

CHRYSOSTOM: Europe is full of gossip about you. Is it
true that you have had the sons of King Edward
murdered in the Tower of London?

RICHARD: (*Pause.*) You will see them here, with your own
eyes. That apart, watch your tongue.

CHRYSOSTOM: My apologies.

RICHARD: So, they talk about me?

CHRYSOSTOM: You are a man who...attracts much
speculation.

RICHARD: Henry Tudor knows how to broadcast lies. In
that he is more skilled than I. As for battle, that is
another matter.

CHRYSOSTOM: They say he has a good chance against you.

RICHARD: He has never fought in his life, except from well to the rear. Tudor is a coward.

CHRYSOSTOM: Sire, all Europe's monarchs exhibit their military prowess from a safe distance nowadays. It is the new style. I have seen them, at ease, surrounded by maps, messages…having refreshments, drunk, with women…

RICHARD: That is a fashion we will not adopt here.

CHRYSOSTOM : It seems to make kings live longer.

RICHARD: As what? (*Pause.*) A king leads. If he creates a risk, then he must share it. These are not kings you are talking about. They are desk-clerks.

CHRYSOSTOM: The window. May I have a free hand?

RICHARD: It is your mind my mother is paying for, not mine.

CHRYSOSTOM: One idea has just occurred to me during our discussion. We might think about introducing this motif. (*Shows RICHARD a skull design.*) I have used it a lot recently. There has been plague in Paris and Milan. It has been a good seller, very popular. We might find a place for it in our design.
(*Dances and sings.*)
SIR, EMPEROR, LORD OF ALL THE GROUND,
HIGH PRINCE, SON OF A NOBLE HOUSE,
YOU MUST GIVE UP YOUR GOLDEN APPLE,
YOUR BLADE-SCEPTRE, TREASURE-TROVE,
AND WITH ALL DANCE MY WAY,
HOLDING HANDS WITH ADAM'S CHILDREN AS THEY GO,
SOME GOING QUICK, SOME GOING SLOW,

PEOPLE LOOK ON THIS SHELL,
THE GESTURES IN AN ANTIQUE DANCE,
SEE WHAT YOU ARE AND WHERE YOUR NATURE LEADS,
FOOD FOR WORMS, UNINSTATED TRASH WITH ONLY WORDS,
AND DEAD SONS FOR REMEMBRANCE.
HERE HE SITS WHO IS A KING,
ALIVE BUT DEAD, A DOOMED, INANIMATED THING.

I HAVE NEVER LEARNT TO DANCE WITH HOPE,

BUT ONLY AT THE MASS WITH SAVAGE STEPS,

WHO IS THE HARDEST IS THE MOST WISE,

THE KING WOULD BE BETTER WITH THE DANCER'S EYES.

(*CICELY, LOVELL and McMASTERS re-enter. During the dance, which should be in the spirit of the danse macabre, LOVELL reveals a large card showing a skull based on CHRYSOSTOM's design which has been seen by RICHARD. CICELY kneels down at the end of the dance. LOVELL and McMASTERS take off their medieval surcoats and revert to their 1954 costumes. McMASTERS takes a plastic punch-card out of the Betrayal box. It is the skull design again, perforated. RICHARD and CHRYSOSTOM withdraw.*)

CICELY: I confess to Almighty God...

McMASTERS: This is the new design for the joker in the Chance pack...

CICELY: ...that I have sinned exceedingly in thought, word and deed...

LOVELL: When a player gets this joker he keeps it and when he finds himself disabled or out of the game through forfeits, landing on a penalty square, falling into a trap, then he plays this card and it gets him going again...

CICELY: ...through my fault, through my fault, through my most grievous fault...

McMASTERS: If the player finds himself in a one-to-one situation then he can use the card and take a gamble by inserting it into the game computer. Each card is punched up to provide a different solution...see here...the eyes...the teeth. The player might win, the player might lose...it's a last ditch ploy. You only use it if you think the odds are stacked against you. What the computer prints out, that's fate...

CICELY: I confess to adultery. I confess to pride. I confess to keeping my mouth shut.

(*McMASTERS turns over another card which has a picture of an infant, smiling.*)

McMASTERS: In contrast, the Nativity Card. (*Shows punch card of same design.*)

LOVELL: Each of the fifty noble family Dynasty Sets – all players must accumulate at least five by the inter-marriage share-out by the banker – must wait for a Nativity Card before they can start to plot for the throne and actually get on the board...

CICELY: I allowed the offspring of a common soldier to sit upon the throne of England, knowing the law that the illegitimate cannot inherit. Edward, as should have been seen from his tastes, was not his father's son. He was a bastard, Lord, as you know. (*Pause.*) But I let him be king. What brings low the House of York will be my sin. I have sent to the Pope for a full pardon with goods and money. Upon my death I need the document tied around my neck with ribbon and buried with me.

LOVELL: By placing the Baby in the game computer the player opens out a whole new permutation which can lead, with luck and some skilful manipulation of resources, to the ultimate objective. First-born to throne.

McMASTERS: I can't stress enough the importance of these two cards – our friend old Hollow-Eyes, and Smiler here. They activate the game. Without them a player is hamstrung, useless. Be sure to point that out to all retailers, all demonstrators...Watch out for the child and the bones...

(*LOVELL offers CICELY a crucifix which hangs round his neck. She kisses it, gets up. LOVELL and McMASTERS put their surcoats back on. RICHARD and CHRYSOSTOM come forward.*)

CICELY: Now, we'll leave you to come up with some good ideas. Is there anything else you need?

CHRYSOSTOM: No, thank you. If I may just...be around, part of the group, take a few notes, sketch...that will be fine.

CICELY: Good. Now, Richard, we would like some of your time. A quick word.

RICHARD: Mother, no state business...

CICELY: We sympathise with you about the death of your son, all of us. It was a bitter blow. But it is not the end of the world, not the world you live in. You must shake it off, come to terms with it.

LOVELL: It's the luck of the draw, some children never make it…

RICHARD: Shut up, Frank.

LOVELL: Yes, sire.

CICELY: You cannot afford to grieve so long. Strength is what matters. Show you're strong. Control it…

RICHARD: Have you finished?

CICELY: It's for your own good.

RICHARD: The matter is closed.

CICELY: I will not have the death of one boy responsible for the decline of this kingdom! You have the hammer and the anvil to make more children, make them…but you have one kingdom, one time, one life, one responsibility. To succeed. Be a great king, a memorable king, a king who will be part of the future…on his own terms.
You determine how people think, you regulate what people do, you interpret life for them, you…

RICHARD: Mother…

CICELY: Let me finish.

RICHARD: I need time to get over my boy's death. It is cruel not to give me time.

CICELY: There is no time. You are losing your grip. You are playing into your enemies' hands. While you grieve, they congregate; while you mourn, they multiply.
(*Pause.*)

RICHARD: You feel this way, Frank? George?

McMASTERS: Yes, it's gone too far.

LOVELL: Right.

RICHARD: And you kept it to yourselves?

LOVELL: Until now. As your oldest friend I respected your grief, but now we must put that aside and think of the future. We must plan, get ready…

RICHARD: There was no better child, so good, so content, so advanced for his age. He could read by the time he was three. He could write by the time he was four. He could sing from written notes in his fifth year. A child for a new age. A child for a new time.

LOVELL: Richard, the boy is dead!

RICHARD: What a king he would have been.

CICELY: Then the father must do what the child intended. Think of your son inside yourself. There he lives. That is his future. What better way to keep him alive?

RICHARD: Mother, don't you understand? I was never worthy of him. I could not live up to my own child.

(*Enter ELIZABETH and PRINCE RICHARD.*)

CICELY: That is an emotional nonsense. He was unformed, a jelly yet, far from manhood. What do you know about him? Dreams, hopes, perhaps some truth in them, but all of it guesswork. But look at you – experienced, strong, full-grown. As far as fitness for power is concerned there is no comparison. Child means incompetent, Richard. Child means unready.

ELIZABETH: Child means threat. Child means needle.

PRINCE RICHARD: (*Sings.*)

CHILD MEANS A MAN WITHOUT BEARD OR VOICE.

CHILD MEANS A MAN WITHOUT MORTAL FEARS.

ELIZABETH: (*Sings.*)

CHILD MEANS A WOMAN WHO WILL REJOICE,

CHILD MEANS A WOMAN IN LABOUR'S TEARS.

CICELY: (*Sings.*)

DON'T ADMIRE THE UNLIT FIRE, THE ABSENT FLAME,

THE PLAYER WHO IS NOT YET READY FOR THE GAME.

SAVE YOUR RESPECT, TRY TO PROTECT THE IDEAL OF ADULT,

AND WHEN YOU FIND THE PERFECT POWER, EXULT, EXULT!

RICHARD: (*Sings.*)

CHILD IS THE ME OF YESTERDAY,

CHILD IS THE PERSON WHO HAUNTS MY BONES.

ELIZABETH: (*Sings.*)

CHILD IS THE BIRD IN THE MONTH OF MAY,

CHILD IS THE NIGHTMARE'S MOANS AND GROANS.

CICELY: (*Sings.*)

YOU WILL FIND THE HUMAN MIND IMPROVES WITH AGE,

ABJURING EXCESS, RANDOM RAGE,

PETULANCE, THE BABY'S DANCE, THE TANTRUM IN THE DARK,

PREFERRING CALCULATION, MAKING MARK.

PRINCE RICHARD/ELIZABETH/CICELY/RICHARD:
(*Sing.*) CHILD MEANS AN ARGUMENT IN AGE,
CHILD MEANS A FEAT OF MEMORY,
CHILD MEANS A BIRD IN A HUMAN CAGE,
CHILD MEANS A KNOWLEDGE OF HISTORY,
CHILD MEANS A MAN WHO IS ALL REGRET,
CHILD MEANS A WOMAN WITH FADING LOOKS,
CHILD MEANS THAT LIFE IS NOT OVER YET,
CHILD MEANS A MARKER WITHIN THY BOOKS.
(*Lights change. TV chimes played by LOUISE.*)

ELIZABETH: This is a party political broadcast on behalf of the Tudors. Richard the Third was in his mother's womb for two years and when he was born he had hair down to his waist and a full set of teeth. His first conscious act was to bite clean through the nipple of his wet-nurse. This ugly, vicious infant was deformed – a withered hand, club foot, crooked back. Turning him over in his cradle was a physiological nightmare. Undersized, weak and sickly, he managed to stagger through his early years to boyhood. At the age of eight he was further pushed towards pathological abnormality when his father and brother Edmund were decapitated by the genial, fun-loving forces of Margaret of Anjou. From that moment on this abortive, paranoid personality became obsessed with murder and unnatural crime. At number eleven Downing Street the Chancellor, Sir Thomas More, described him as a symbol of evil rather than flesh and blood while William Shakespeare reports in the Globe today that he actually overheard the leader of the Plantagenet party say 'I am determined to prove a villain and hate the idle pleasure of these days.'
(*TV chimes out. Lights change back.*)

RICHARD: The lies that Tudor spreads about me!

LOVELL: Henry Tudor does what he must. He says, I'm out to win. I'll do what I can, do what needs to be done. Frenchmen, Germans, he doesn't care. He's a very practical man. Don't underestimate him, it will do you no credit.

RICHARD: He is preferred to me. I have improved the law, reduced taxation, protected our towns, been as fair as

I can. But this man is preferred to me. I say a king has to
earn his place. What has he done?

CICELY: He has put up his sign and opened his shop.
That is all.

RICHARD: You trust people, they let you down. You give
them gifts, they throw them in your face. You hold out a
hand of friendship, they break your fingers. Why? Why?

CHRYSOSTOM: (*Sings.*)

NO ONE KNOWS BUT DE LORD
WHY DIS SUFFERING IS SO,
BUT ONE THING DAT WE KNOW,
SUFFERING IS HERE TO STAY.

ALL: (*Sing.*)

YEH, YEH, YEH, YEH,
DAT MUCH IS RELIABLE IN LIFE

CICELY: (*Sings.*)

NO ONE KNOWS BUT DE LORD

ALL: (*Sing.*)

NO ONE KNOWS BUT DE LORD
NO ONE KNOWS BUT DE LORD
BUT WHAT DOES DE LORD KNOW?

HE KNOWS MAN BORN TO DIE,
HE KNOWS MAN BORN TO DIE,
HE KNOWS MAN HORN TO DIE,
DAT AINT MUCH TO LEAVE US WITH.

RICHARD: (*Sings.*)

LORD NOW TAKE THOU MY TROUBLES
AND SORT THEM OUT FOR ME.

ALL: (*Sing.*)

AND SORT THEM OUT FOR HIM!

RICHARD: (*Sings.*)

FOR I HAVE ONLY A SHORT TIME HERE
AND THOU HAST ETERNITY.

ALL: (*Sing.*)

THOU HAST ETERNITY!
NO ONE KNOWS BUT DE LORD,
NO ONE KNOWS BUT DE LORD,
NO ONE KNOWS BUT DE LORD,

BUT WHAT DOES DE LORD KNOW?

HE KNOWS MAN BORN TO DIE,

HE KNOWS MAN BORN TO DIE,

HE KNOWS MAN BORN TO DIE,

DAT AINT MUCH TO LEAVE US WITH.

RICHARD: (*Sings.*)

I JUST WANNA LIVE IN PEACE, LORD

JUST LIKE AN ORDINARY MAN.

ALL: (*Sing.*)

JUST LIKE AN ORDINARY MAN!

RICHARD: (*Sings.*)

I WANNA EAT AND SLEEP AND LAUGH, LORD.

PLEASE HELP ME IF YOU CAN.

ALL: (*Sing.*)

PLEASE HELP HIM IF YOU CAN.

(*Repeat chorus.*)

CHRYSOSTOM: Now the Lord, he says, tell me some of the troubles you've seen. Give me a list of the lies, give me a boxful of betrayals. I can take it, says the Lord.

ALL: (*Sing.*)

HE CAN TAKE IT, SAYS THE LORD,

HE CAN TAKE IT, SAYS THE LORD,

THAT AINT MUCH TO LEAVE US WITH.

CICELY: (*Sings.*)

OH HE SAW HIS DADDY CUT DOWN

AND CROWNED WITH A PAPER CROWN!

RICHARD: (*Sings.*)

THEY MURDERED A BROTHER OF MINE

AND DROWNED ANOTHER IN WINE.

ELIZABETH: (*Sings.*)

HE KILLED OFF MY BROTHER AND SON,

THAT'S HOW HIS KINGDOM WAS WON.

CHRYSOSTOM: The Lord has heard, and now he says, Richard, boy, turn the mind from governing the land and have a try at ruling of the people. Stop being so organic and symbolic and integrated with the nuts of nature. Forget the farmyard, yea! Forget the bull, forget the fox, forget the hog. Be-e-e rational, and national, be sane, be Greek baby, be re-born!

RICHARD: (*Sings.*)

PEACE IS MAN'S RICHEST POSSESSION
AND LEADS HIM HOME TO HEAVEN,
PEACE OF SOUL, PEACE OF MIND,
PEACE FROM PLAGUE, PEACE FROM WAR.

THERE'S WISDOM IN WHAT YOU SAY,
ADVICE NOT TO BE FORGOTTEN,
THE CHOICE IS MINE,
AN OLD AND TRUSTED, OR A NEW LINE.

(*Scream off. Enter PRINCE RICHARD running to ELIZABETH. She catches him in her arms. LOVELL and McMASTERS start taking off their surcoats.*)

PRINCE RICHARD: I think my brother Edward is dead!
(*Pause. LOVELL covers the Nativity Card with the Death Card.*)

ELIZABETH: Richard, I would like a word with you...

LOVELL: (*Sings.*)

NOW, THESE ARE THE RULES OF THE GAME,
ALL PLAYERS GET TREATED THE SAME,
NO PLAYER CAN USE HIS OWN DICE,
NO VIRTUE CAN CHOOSE ITS OWN VICE.

ALL: (*Sing.*)

NOW, THESE ARE THE RULES OF THE GAME,
ALL PLAYERS GET TREATED THE SAME,
NO PLAYER CAN USE HIS OWN DICE
NO VIRTUE CAN CHOOSE ITS OWN VICE.

ALL PLAYERS ARE GIVEN A CHANCE,
YOU CAN ACT, YOU CAN SING, YOU CAN DANCE,
YOU CAN BREED, YOU CAN DIE, YOU CAN STEAL,
YOU CAN FREEZE, YOU CAN FRY, YOU CAN DEAL.

(*Dance.*)

ON YOUR WAY, FOTHERINGHAY,
GOOD THROW, LUDLOW,
THREE AND CARRY, CANTERBURY,
A GO YOU LOSE, BACK TO BRUGES,
FIDDLE 'EM, MIDDLEHAM,
BALK AT YORK,

TAKE A CHANCE CARD AND THEN ADVANCE TO CARMARTHEN,
DARN IT, BARNET,
TRY AGAIN, AMIENS,
YOU SEEM TO BE HEADING FOR A SHOW-DOWN AT EDINBURGH,
TILT OF THE BOARD, STONY STRATFORD,
LUCKY MAN, NOTTINGHAM,
IN THE RED, BERKHAMSTED,
WHAT YOU WORTH, BOSWORTH.
NOW THESE ARE THE RULES OF THE GAME,
SHAKE THE DICE WHEN I CALL OUT YOUR NAME,
THROW A THREE OR A FOUR AND A FIVE,
AND WE'LL SEE WHO IS STAYING ALIVE.

(*General exit. Lights fade to blackout.*)

End of Act One.

ACT TWO

Enter characters to instruments. The 'Peace' theme is played as the lights brighten. Enter ORWELL in an overcoat and muffler, carrying a parcel. Music fades. LOVELL and McMASTERS are in 1484 surcoats.

ORWELL: I feel guilty about 1984, as if it were a trick. But it's not. Nor is it a stab in the back. (*Coughs, brings the bloody handkerchief out of his pocket.*) As perhaps my last book – you want to try writing and coughing as a routine rhythm – I would have liked to give it a more hopeful, idealistic note, less pessimistic, paranoid even. Can I do that with the way English socialism is going? When it happens, and this is the tragedy, people will not realise. It will have grown round them, become familiar. Continuous war, continuous conflict, state of emergency, backs to the wall, a relentless crisis day in day out...so you must do this, you must do that. Very easy. The screen, the man who asks all the questions for you, then answers them – who is he but your friend? Your brother? (*Coughs.*) I say that now, this year, history has to be made sacred. Our past must be preserved as it was!
The socialism we are growing into invites us all to be children, and me a dying man. Am I going to suck a dummy on my death-bed? Well, it's ready to go off. It will get bad reviews, oh yes. Orwell has followed the classical pattern: revolutionary, radical, revisionist, reactionary, cradle to grave, Labour to Conservative. My old friends will call me all the names under the sun. (*Coughs.*) What else can I do with my experience? Ignore it? Shall I go to the Post Office? I honestly don't want to. I care about how I will be remembered and I'd rather it was for my honesty and my support of the working-class than for my books. But it's written. I wrote it, fully aware of what I was doing. 1984 was inside me. (*Coughs.*)
A stamp, the red box, a slow walk back. That is the immediate future. I hate this book and all it stands for. (*Exits.*)

ELIZABETH: (*Coming forward.*) My big brother Anthony
was a writer. He was the author of the first book printed
on William Caxton's new printing-press. He had enjoyed
a wide experience of life and travelled beyond the Alps
in search of the Holy Grail, and as diplomat for my
husband, King Edward. While he was in Florence at the
court of the Medici in the late sixties, he was at the
house of a lawyer having dinner. Upstairs, the lawyer's
wife was being delivered of a baby. At the point when
the physician went to cut the umbilical cord, the child
shouted out, very loudly '*Affila quel coltello*', 'sharpen that
knife'. Later, my brother saw the child and heard it
christened with the Devil's name of Nicholas. Then he
left the house and never saw the Machiavelli family
again, but always remembered them with fear
and wonder.

McMASTERS: (*Sings.*)

THE EARTH WILL NOT BE THE CENTRE,
PHILOSOPHERS WILL TORMENT HER:
LIFE'S WHEEL WILL TURN ON AN AXIS
OF GOOD COMMERCIAL PRACTICE:
READ, WRITE OLD GREEK, NEW ITALIAN,
FILE GOD'S HEAD OFF YOUR MEDALLION,
SCRATCH MAN'S HEAD THERE,
BASED ON THE DEVIL'S, IF YOU DARE.

A STRAIGHT ROAD HAS NO RADIUS,
OUR FATHER, NOT DOMINE DEUS,
AMERICA'S HORIZON,
ROYAL SPANISH LINES IS DESIGNED ON:
FLY SHIP, SWING STAR, NAVIGATOR,
NEW FOUND LAND WILL COME LATER,
SCRIBE THAT WHITE PAGE,
HOLD UP OLD ATLAS, OUR NEW AGE.

ALL: (*Sing.*)

THE WORLD SPINS, ARGUE THE SUN IS STILL,
CLIMB INTO EDEN BY STAIRS OF WILL,
DISPUTE, DEFY YOUR OWN DESTINY,
ASK CHRIST TO LIST WHAT HE'S DONE FOR THEE:

WHICH BUILDER RAISED UP IN HELL?

WHOSE TONGUE IS HUNG IN THE LEPER'S BELL?

GO FIND THY GATE.

CHANCE IS THE LATCH, THE HINGES FATE.

(*Exit CHRYSOSTOM and CICELY. Enter RICHARD.*)

RICHARD: You wanted to see me?

ELIZABETH: We have things to talk about.

RICHARD: Elizabeth, I am genuinely sorry. I know how you must feel.

ELIZABETH: Save your sympathy. I can cope. What I want to know is where we go from here?

RICHARD: I will arrange a state funeral, Frank will see to it...

LOVELL: Christ, no! That's the last thing we need.

ELIZABETH: He's right, Richard. The rumour was always that you had killed Edward. Now he's dead, while in your care. Think about it.

McMASTERS: You'd be playing straight into Tudor's hands.

RICHARD: Obviously there will be repercussions, but I'll just have to weather the storm.

LOVELL: It is a storm which will drive you from the throne.

RICHARD: There is no alternative. I will simply tell the truth. He can be examined by physicians...

McMASTERS: Sire, it wouldn't work. At a time when the people must start believing in you, trusting you, admitting the boy's death would be madness. It's out of the question.

ELIZABETH: I have a suggestion to make. Richard, I want Henry Tudor to marry my daughter, in case he beats you this summer – which is a gamble, but he could, it's a calculated risk – don't shake your head, as a soldier you must know the chances of war. But to marry my daughter, Tudor must have her made legitimate. If she is legitimate, the boys are legitimate. If the boys are legitimate they have a right to the throne. So, Henry Tudor seeks the deaths of my sons, and the hand of my daughter. That is my predicament. So, as nature has killed Edward, I will use it. But Tudor must only know Edward is dead at the right time. That is crucial.

RICHARD: And when is that?

ELIZABETH: When the marriage contract is signed, sealed and delivered and I have agreed to the murder of Edward and young Richard as my daughter's dowry.

LOVELL: God's teeth...

ELIZABETH: (*Blazing.*) What else have I got to give? Your king has impoverished me, taken all I have in the world!

RICHARD: So young Richard must die as well?

(*Coughing off. Enter PRINCE RICHARD with a yo-yo. Crosses the stage, exits.*)

ELIZABETH: He will be dead by spring.

(*RICHARD exits.*)

LOVELL: During the break some keen lads came up with a few questions. One was – what is going to be the cost of Betrayal?

McMASTERS: What market are we aiming for? We're dealing with death, we're dealing with destiny.

LOVELL: This is a game for the family. It must be enjoyed together. Mothers and sons, husbands and wives, uncles and nephews.

McMASTERS: And games are a need. They are an interpretation of existence. There is no real choice. You must play. Betrayal is a need, a mental must. Be that strong with the dealers.

(*LOVELL, McMASTERS and ELIZABETH mime the burial. CHRYSOSTOM enters.*)

CHRYSOSTOM: They buried the dead Prince under the cellar floor of the castle. Lovell and McMasters did the dirty work. By the light of a candle an uncrowned King of England was tumbled into a muddy pit. His sceptre was a stone, his orb a pebble, his crown clay. Lovell tried to recall as much of the Mass for the Dead as he could, having heard it often of recent years, but one part slipped his mind. I could not prompt him, being a stranger here, but it runs thus – 'Brethren, we will not have you ignorant concerning those who sleep, that ye sorrow not'.

(*Enter RICHARD.*)

CHRYSOSTOM: Sire, will you sit for me?

RICHARD: Not now, Greek. I have lost my wish to be
remembered.

CHRYSOSTOM: A few moments of your time.

RICHARD: I said no. I have disfigured myself.

(*CICELY enters.*)

CICELY: I demand to know where my grandson is buried!

ELIZABETH: It is better that you do not know.

CICELY: I am not addressing myself to you. Richard, why
has that poor boy been shovelled away as if he were some
still-born brat in a stinking village?

RICHARD: Mother, it was necessary.

CICELY: As a royal prince his body must be exposed so
the people can see he is dead. It matters. It is important
to them.

ELIZABETH: He is not dead.

CICELY: What is she saying?

ELIZABETH: As far as they are concerned, and as far as we
are concerned, he is not dead. My son is alive.

CICELY: Stop her talking. Get her to be quiet, or go away...

ELIZABETH: He agrees with me. We have had a meeting.

CICELY: The boy is dead, I touched him myself. He is as
dead as a stone.

ELIZABETH: My son is alive. I, his mother, say so.
Who should know better?

CICELY: You intend to make no announcement?

RICHARD: I cannot afford to.

CICELY: You are tampering with God's truth! Alive and
dead are definitions which belong to Him and Him alone.

RICHARD: Mother, no one is disputing the fact of his death,
only the news...

ELIZABETH: There can be no difference. He is not dead.
Not dead. We must believe that. There must be no
slip-ups.

CICELY: Why are you doing this? I can't believe it.

ELIZABETH: There are good reasons for both of us.

RICHARD: It would be disastrous...

CHRYSOSTOM: For his image...

CICELY: But God, Richard, you and this bitch are enemies,
enemies!

RICHARD: We must work together on this one item.
   If Tudor beats me and does not marry the girl, then the
   House of York has no part in the future. Our blood is
   finished.

CICELY: If it uses this logic, it deserves to be.

RICHARD: I have a sound political reason.

CHRYSOSTOM: If I might help, Madam. You do admire
   my art, so may I try to explain? It is a simple process.
   Only we are aware that the boy is dead...

ELIZABETH: Was dead.

CHRYSOSTOM: Was dead. We...seven. Outside this
   chamber everyone who knew of Edward's existence still
   believes him to be alive. So, as far as they are concerned,
   he is alive. That is a fact to them. Go up to any man in the
   street and say, is Edward, the Lord Bastard, alive? And he
   will say, yes. So who is right? If we believe him dead we
   are outnumbered numerically and philosophically.

CICELY: McMasters, throw this charlatan out!

RICHARD: Leave him. It is my mind he is explaining.

CICELY: Richard, stop this now. I do not pretend to
   understand how you have come to this decision, only that
   it is wrong...Do not dispute with God in terms beyond
   his reckoning...

RICHARD: There was no death.

CICELY: But there is damnation. Richard, this is my fault,
   my sin. Let me sort it out. Do not change this much.
   Stay as you are, fight properly...

RICHARD: I am going back to Westminster...

CICELY: I beg you, change your mind...

LOVELL: The King moves!

CHRYSOSTOM: Wait, I haven't got started yet!

McMASTERS: To the side, to the side!

CHRYSOSTOM: This is ridiculous. How can I work
   this way?

LOVELL: Richard of England passes along this road.
   Pull over! Make room!

   (*CICELY, CHRYSOSTOM and ELIZABETH exit.*)

RICHARD: Westminster. If you are a man who conceals
   death, live in Westminster. Leave me.

LOVELL: There is a stack of paper-work…ambassadors,
plenipotentiaries, legates…

RICHARD: I will see no one. Guard the door. Leave
me alone.

(*LOVELL and McMASTERS withdraw.*)

RICHARD: Sit down. Sit down. Keep very still. Try not to
move. I have an itch but by God I will not scratch it, no,
not for days. There, it can stay with me. Strange how it
comes and goes. Good, I can bear it. Stupid bloody man!
What have I done to my child? What have I done to all
children? I have killed innocence and lost my own.

(*TV chimes. Enter CICELY. Lights change.*)

CICELY: Now this is a party political broadcast on behalf
of the Plantagenets. When this boy was born he nearly
died, and several times afterwards. We were all very
surprised that he survived. It was my opinion that this
was because God was unsure of whether to have him
employed in heaven, or here. In those years of
uncertainty I kept Richard prepared for a transfer at any
time, completely acquainted with God's ideas on most
subjects, and saw to it that he was well-taught…

(*McMASTERS and LOVELL come forward.*)

McMASTERS: Boy!

RICHARD: Uncle Warwick?

McMASTERS: What is the nature of God?

RICHARD: The nature of God is good.

McMASTERS: And what is the nature of the Evil One?

RICHARD: He is evil?

McMASTERS: Then what is the nature of Man, lying
in-between?

RICHARD: He is both evil and good but can alter the
quantities by will and God's grace.

McMASTERS: And where stands a King? Between God and
Man or between Man and the Devil?

(*Pause.*)

LOVELL: Come on, Dick, you should know this, mate. We
only did it last week.

RICHARD: Er…in the order of the universe a King stands
as at a station betwixt Man and God, but as a protector
of his people from evil, betwixt Man and the Evil One.

McMASTERS: No lad, a King stands in one place only. Between the Devil and the deep blue sea.

RICHARD: Yes, Uncle.

McMASTERS: Why is it that your friend Frank knows and you don't? Can't you keep up with him? Why should he know more about kings than you?

RICHARD: I don't know, Uncle.

McMASTERS: I'll tell you, because young Frank knows what's what, not what should be. When he grows up he may find peace in an imperfect world. Will you? Supposing that you make it, that is. Feeling well today?

RICHARD: Yes, Uncle.

McMASTERS: Your father, though ill-equipped for the job, very much wanted to be king. That ambition killed him. Your brother Edward now wants to be a king. He will ask for your help. Should you help him suffer?

RICHARD: If that is my duty.

McMASTERS: Tell him, Francis, tell the child.

LOVELL: Honour thy father until thy father is dead. Honour thy brother until thy brother is dead. When the time to be alone has come, honour thyself.

RICHARD: Yes, Frank.

CICELY: As I was saying, I saw to it that he was well-taught and well-fed, brought up to trust his place either in heaven or here on earth. In time it became plain that God had decided to let my son Richard stay with me, yet kept him of an angel's size in readiness for some swift move, upwards. Since those early years God has changed, grown tired, and seems much older, caring less about the things he was wont to be passionate about, such as death. Before this Christmas we never thought of hiding death, no king, no common man. It would have been like trying to hide the edge of the known world, or the shape of our souls. But now God is old, death can go disguised, no longer naked. He agrees with my interpretation. 'Cicely,' he said after my prayers tonight, 'a favour. Let them see me as I was. I will do a deal with you. Richard will have forgiveness for his sin of concealment if, having hidden death, he shows it, gloriously, splendidly, dying on my

behalf in the old way, flags flying.' I could only agree.
So that is fixed, which is a comfort. In conclusion I
would remind the public that Richard bears upon his
shield in battle a white boar. It follows then that if
Richard is an hog, then Richard is a swine, which is only
an edible animal like Christ himself. (*Pause.*) Goodnight.
(*TV chimes out. CICELY exits.*)

LOVELL: Richard, may we come in?

RICHARD: Stay away from me. You are all things to all
men.

LOVELL: Come on Dick, cheer up. We'll crack a bottle
of wine...

RICHARD: Never again with you, Lovell.

LOVELL: Why in God's name?

RICHARD: I will not drink with the Devil.

LOVELL: Dick, I want you popular, I want you safe, I want
you rare and in demand, I want you available to all.
How do you sell such a man to a cynical world? Come
on, don't take it too much to heart. We'll live to fight
another day, find the right face, hit the right note. I'm
optimistic.

McMASTERS: Sire, we have worked hard to make men
love you; suspicious, difficult, tight men with teeth-
marks on their tongues. When they buy you, what thanks
do we get? It's the quality of the goods, they say, never
the sales talk. Would I be fooled by that? But we
introduced them, cultivated them, got them over the
threshold. What is on the counter? Only the man we
believe in.
(*Pause.*)

RICHARD: If you are such merchants of me then I am but
cargo to this country.

McMASTERS: You'll feel better tomorrow. We can sit round
and sort the whole thing out, just as Frank says. It's
nearly midnight. Christ, it's Christmas! The clock is
striking Christmas!

RICHARD: Don't come too close. What a stench you make.
No, don't talk. I want no answers, nor do I want to smell
your stinking breath. Tell me, in confidence, are you the

two men trusted by the King? You are? How does he put
up with it? Who holds his nose? Get down on your knees.
(*They obey.*) Yes, you do make an effort for the King.
Obviously you love the man. Touching. Is it the fashion
to keep sleep in the corners of your eyes and wink
yellow? Can you hear me through the corks of wax in
your ears? Look at me. Who am I? Don't answer or your
teeth will fall out. I am King Richard and I order you to
wash. If I ever find you in such a filthy condition again
I will have you scorched like a pig's carcass. Get out!

McMASTERS: You abuse me for no reason I can
understand.

RICHARD: That is why I abuse you. Get out!

LOVELL: Does the death of one boy matter that much?
(*Pause.*)

RICHARD: Who was it asked me to handle a boy's death
better? Oh, be this way, be that way. Now again. Are you
an expert, Frank? Clot, get out!
(*LOVELL and McMASTERS take off their surcoats.*)

LOVELL: There is a problem with this game.

McMASTERS: Some people take it too seriously.

LOVELL: They get too involved, too worked up. The
manufacturers of Monopoly were blamed by businessmen
for suicides amongst their less gifted children...and
players who landed on Park Lane with three hotels
despaired and died.

McMASTERS: Only last year we had trouble with the Big
Brother game when a trade unionist threw himself from
the top of Transport House after an all-night session in
which he admitted to the Thought Police that although he
loved humanity he could not stand the workers.

LOVELL: As you will see from the top of the box we
disclaim all responsibility for accidents, but see to it that
retailers are warned.

McMASTERS: Do not sell Betrayal to the over-
impressionable.

LOVELL: Our games are based on great movements of
thought, so they do provoke an emotional response.
Just as Monopoly plays with capitalism, and Big Brother

plays with socialism, Betrayal plays with humanism.
And what could be more explosive? But lose the game,
don't lose yourself.

(*RICHARD cries out.*)

RICHARD: No!

McMASTERS: There he goes again.

LOVELL: The kind of child who throws the chess-pieces.

RICHARD: No!

McMASTERS: No cool. No self-control, no objective eye.

LOVELL: The game disappears. It has become too real for
safety. At this point the customers should pack it in, put
it all back in the box and go to bed.

(*Lights dim. Enter CICELY, ELIZABETH and PRINCE
RICHARD. RICHARD sits down, head in hands.*)

CICELY/ELIZABETH/PRINCE RICHARD: (*Sing.*)

LULLY LULLA, THOU LITTLE TINY CHILD,

BYE, BYE, LULLY LULLAY.

O SISTERS TOO, HOW MAY WE DO

FOR TO PRESERVE THIS DAY,

THIS POOR YOUNGLING, FOR WHOM WE DO SING,

BYE, BYE, LULLY LULLAY.

HEROD THE KING IN HIS RAGING,

CHARGED HE HATH THIS DAY,

HIS MEN OF MIGHT IN HIS OWN SIGHT,

ALL YOUNG CHILDREN TO SLAY.

THAT WOE IS ME, POOR CHILD TO THEE,

AND EVERY MORN AND DAY,

FOR THY PARTING, NEITHER SAY NOR SING,

BYE, BYE, LULLY LULLAY.

LULLY LULLA, THOU LITTLE TINY CHILD,

BYE, BYE, LULLY LULLAY.

(*CICELY, ELIZABETH and PRINCE RICHARD exit.
Lights change back. Enter CHRYSOSTOM.*)

CHRYSOSTOM: Sire, I know you are troubled in your
mind and wish to be alone, but I may be able to help.
Will you talk to me? It will help both of us.

RICHARD: I said I was not to be disturbed.

CHRYSOSTOM: They let me through because I can explain your mind. You said so yourself, remember? Your friends are confused, they cannot understand your torment. I can. I have a trained eye for such things. I am an expert.

RICHARD: Then you're welcome, Greek. Sit down.

CHRYSOSTOM: First, relax. Unwind. Close your eyes...

RICHARD: You would not be hurt if I kept them open? Habit.

CHRYSOSTOM: As you wish. Now, King Richard, let me clarify your mood, pull aside the curtains, place your thoughts in a proper perspective. (*Pause.*) Are you feeling less tense now?

RICHARD: Completely at ease.

CHRYSOSTOM: Let us analyse your problem. You are ashamed that you agreed to conceal the death of your nephew. You feel out-manoeuvred, belittled. Dame Elizabeth got the better of you. In your quaint way it seems to you that if you had killed him, that would have been easier. You could have admitted it, asked God for forgiveness, done penance, and come out of it with a clear conscience. Now, you are besmirched. The affair is messy, disgusting. There is no way to get clear of it. The boy is now rotten, and so are you. You have tried blaming others but it doesn't work. It always comes back to you. You have cracked. Now, no self-respect. Why? Because your mind is hide-bound, struggling with a new concept: state control. A king must govern the truth as if it were an unruly and rebellious citizen. Are you following me?

RICHARD: All the way. With great interest. Continue.

CHRYSOSTOM: Your brother Edward, the King before you, would have handled it better. He was in advance of his time. He could step back, get an overall view, and manipulate his resources, and his mistakes. You are far too subjective, and that makes you a very difficult case as you are also chronically old-fashioned. Keeping up with the times imposes an enormous strain on you – your brain bulges, feels as if it will burst. But if you persevere, your nature will change. The human mind has a tremendous capacity for making adjustments under pressure. I think you will come out of this experience a better king, and a better man.

RICHARD: More like Edward.

CHRYSOSTOM: Yes. He is a good model. If you imitate him you will not go far wrong.

RICHARD: As his younger brother I tried to. I only stopped at Amiens.

CHRYSOSTOM: Amiens? His greatest achievement. A textbook example of how the Good Prince operates. Amiens is the best illustration of the new statecraft I can think of. Brilliant. What a splendid way to win a war. Such imagination and flair.

McMASTERS: King Edward went to France in 1475 to reclaim the ancient territories of the English throne…(*Exits.*)

LOVELL: His young brother Richard by his side, champing at the bit. (*Exits.*)

CHRYSOSTOM: Try and remember it, sire. It was a good day for you to be at school and watch the master.

RICHARD: Remember it? Could anyone forget such an illustrious occasion?

(*Enter ELIZABETH and CICELY.*)

RICHARD/CHRYSOSTOM/ELIZABETH/CICELY:

(*Sing.*) AMIENS, QUELLE HONTE,
AMIENS, QUEL CHAGRIN,
QUAND LA PAIX EGALE
THE PAY POUR LE PAYS
LA VICTOIRE SANS L'HONNEUR.

AMIENS, QUELLE HONTE,
AMIENS, QUEL CHAGRIN,
EMPIRE PERDU!

POTAGE IS FRENCH STEW
SEASONED WITH SHAME.
DRUNK IN THE STREET,
FINANCIAL DEFEAT.

PEACE EQUALS VICTORY
MINUS HONOUR.

AMIENS, QUELLE HONTE,

JAMAIS GALANTE,

AMIENS, QUEL CHAGRIN,

LA GLOIRE ENFIN, FIN, FIN.

(*During the song McMASTERS and LOVELL appear as King Edward the Fourth of England and King Louis the Eleventh of France, dressed in crowns, bells, streamers and clogs, dancing. The dance is woven through the scene.*)

LOVELL: King Edward.

McMASTERS: King Louis.

LOVELL: What do you want?

McMASTERS: France.

LOVELL: Naked aggression.

McMASTERS: Legitimate claim.

LOVELL: Pope mediate?

McMASTERS: Your friend, not mine.

LOVELL: Single combat?

McMASTERS: No insurance.

LOVELL: Chivalry?

McMASTERS: Good books, nice pictures.

LOVELL: What is the size of your army?

McMASTERS: Twelve thousand five hundred.

LOVELL: Ah-ha, you have superior numbers. I am in trouble with my traditional allies, have rebellions at home, am not properly equipped. Under pressure I ask, combien, how much?

McMASTERS: How much? How much? What an insult! How dare you! Unthinkable. My reputation – the best general in Europe. Played nine, won nine. How much, indeed. Preposterous. What kind of man are you? You disgrace the whole idea of kingship, honour. You should be thoroughly ashamed of yourself. A hundred thousand pounds.

LOVELL: Execrable.

McMASTERS: Reasonable. And seventy-five thousand a year for life.

LOVELL: Rapacious.

McMASTERS: Inflatious. Been clipping the coinage.

LOVELL: Your problem.

McMASTERS: Now yours.

LOVELL: You are aware, I hope, that after this arrangement no English king can claim an empire in France again with any semblance of credibility? (*Pause.*) I'll give you fifty thousand now and twenty-five thousand a year...

McMASTERS: No. I will not budge from my original price. Nothing will make me accept a lower offer. Eighty-nine point five now and sixty-four point five later.

LOVELL: Sixty-four point five now and thirty-nine point five...

McMASTERS: Seventy-five and fifty?

LOVELL: Done. Friend for life.

(*Exit dancing to song repeat. ELIZABETH and CICELY exit.*)

CHRYSOSTOM: And I hear you sulked in your tent like Achilles at Tray. Tut, tut, such childishness. No bloodshed, maximum profit, satisfaction to all parties. And peace. And you protested. No wonder Dame Elizabeth is so far ahead of you. As King Edward's wife she learnt by watching him at work...

RICHARD: Yes, she picks things up quickly. I am a slowcoach.

CHRYSOSTOM: You will improve. I am sure of it. With a little humility.

RICHARD: Oh, I can manage that.

CHRYSOSTOM: You are not the only king who has to make these mental adjustments. All the rulers of Europe are being forced to do likewise. You are lucky to have me here to give you these hints, I have seen it all before.

RICHARD: I realise that.

CHRYSOSTOM: You see, I am a progressive person, a new man. I have made my own way in the world, not having been born to wealth or greatness. Having come up the hard way I have discovered the colours between the lines. Life is not red and black and blue. It is orange and grey, pink and gold, a blend of blends.

RICHARD: Of course. I have never noticed the way a rainbow is made until now. How you are opening my eyes.

CHRYSOSTOM: One last thing. Don't worry about your guilty feelings. Guilt is good for you, in moderation.

One could say that it is the most intense pleasure of a civilised man, but it must be controlled or you will become dependent upon it. Never be a slave to guilt.

RICHARD: I can see that I have a long way to go. Now I have doubts about whether I will ever make it to the top. You see, my most intense pleasure is that of ancient man.

CHRYSOSTOM: And what is that?

RICHARD: Pricking balloons.

CHRYSOSTOM: Pricking balloons?

RICHARD: Yes, pricking balloons like you, you fatuous trash.

CHRYSOSTOM: I see. You find my analysis inadequate?

RICHARD: No, I agree with everything you say. Why I hold you in contempt, Greek, is because you are on one side, and I am on the other. Mine may be old, but yours is decadent, and not for me! (*Exits.*)
(*Enter ELIZABETH.*)

ELIZABETH: Still here? How are you finding January? Looking forward to March? May is quite mad. August? Interesting.

CHRYSOSTOM: Dame Elizabeth. You remember me?

ELIZABETH: One of the most unforgettable characters I have ever met.

CHRYSOSTOM: You are too kind. Madam, I am at my wit's end, and I am turning to you for help. I am trapped here in England. The Duchess has given orders that I am not allowed to leave the country until I have made this window of the King. He, on the other hand, will not help me. He will not keep still. He will not settle into character. It is an impossible situation for a serious artist to be in.

ELIZABETH: Dear, dear.

CHRYSOSTOM: If I was in Rome working in the Vatican...

ELIZABETH: Which you are not...

CHRYSOSTOM: Which I am not...I would breakfast with the Pope and discuss his dreams. Here I have very little status, Sometimes, in dark moments, I think that the English are barbarians, but I am never entirely convinced.

ELIZABETH: What do you want from me?

CHRYSOSTOM: Advice. Madam, I need the money from this commission. I am in debt back in Genoa, a house, a bad investment...

ELIZABETH: Why don't you do the best job you can with what you have observed so far?

CHRYSOSTOM: That is not in me. I must be useful and true to the purpose. The Duchess wants her son seen in a window, clearly. He must be transparent, all his virtues visible. I cannot do that unless I have the security of an interpretation based on a close study.

ELIZABETH: You will never get close to Richard, no one does, except his henchmen and his mother, and even if you did I doubt whether you would find him attractive.

CHRYSOSTOM: The window the Duchess wants is sheer fantasy as far as I am concerned. I see nothing admirable in the man. He is a left-over, a relic...completely out-dated...

ELIZABETH: So, you have become alienated from your subject. A difficult position for an artist to be in...

CHRYSOSTOM: I am grateful for your understanding.

ELIZABETH: Have you ever sold the same piece of work twice?

CHRYSOSTOM: On the day before an extremely long journey.

ELIZABETH: I will try to get you a second commission from a friend who is abroad at the moment. It will still be for a window of Richard, but he may want you to suggest some ideas for the basic design. Would you object to that?

CHRYSOSTOM: Not as long as I retained my...

ELIZABETH: Integrity? Of course. He would never trespass upon that. And timing will be important. He will, if he agrees to my proposal, want the window delivered at a precise moment, probably some time this summer. Would that be a problem?

CHRYSOSTOM: If I am guided towards a theme I can understand, and be made to believe in, you can have the window when you like.

ELIZABETH: Good. Now, if my idea works out and my
friend puts up the money for a second commission, I think
I deserve a percentage of that, don't you? How much? Ten?

CHRYSOSTOM: Five.

ELIZABETH: Seven-point-five?

CHRYSOSTOM: Done. I feel better already.

ELIZABETH: Come to think of it, I might like another
portrait of myself. I could look very pleasing in glass.
Edward had a painting done of me but it was very stuffy,
very unimaginative. I looked quite bald and rather
distant. The eyes weren't bad. Perhaps he exaggerated the
eyes. We have no great sense of beauty here, I
wonder why?

CHRYSOSTOM: I think it is the weather.

ELIZABETH: It can be a depressing country to live in.

CHRYSOSTOM: Yet your life has been so adventurous.
You have a reputation for style, dignity, pride, beauty.
You are greatly admired abroad, a new woman, the first
English queen with a European mind…(*ELIZABETH
smiles, remains still as if studying herself in a mirror.*)
A splendid subject for a promising painter I know.
The lady with the mystic smile, the I-know-it-all-but-I'm-
saying-nothing smile. Right up his street. Just his kind of
female. We met in Milan when I was doing my window
for the Sforzas, and I said to him, Leonardo, why don't
you concentrate on graphics and put aside – eschew, I
said, eschew – your crackpot schemes for flying
machines and submarines and parachutes? He turned to
me, and with a debonair and good-natured smile replied
– why don't you go and multiply yourself?

ELIZABETH: *Au revoir*, Greek. Keep in touch. Well, look at
that. Catkins already.
(*Enter CICELY and RICHARD with letters.*)

RICHARD: Hello, Elizabeth. We have a surprise for you.

ELIZABETH: A surprise? I love surprises.

CICELY: A letter from abroad. We thought you'd want to
read it straight away. (*Hands ELIZABETH a letter.*)

ELIZABETH: How thoughtful of you. I wonder who it
could be from? (*She exits.*)

RICHARD: (*To CHRYSOSTOM.*) And what are you still doing here?

CHRYSOSTOM: Trying to see you.

CICELY: Oh, speak to him, Richard…

RICHARD: Will you stop hounding me? Go away.

CHRYSOSTOM: What have you got to hide? Do you think that no man can understand you? Listen, I have made men transparent with more tangles in their souls than you will ever have. You know what's the matter with you? You are afraid of the truth. What kind of a king is that?

RICHARD: Once I warned you to watch your tongue. Now watch your head.

CHRYSOSTOM: Madam, I must surrender this commission!

CICELY: You will honour that contract. Now more than ever. Break it and I will have your life. He must be remembered, he must.

CHRYSOSTOM: Why me? Find another.

CICELY: I have tried them all. Malory, here, I said, is a true knight of the Round Table, write a poem, an epic poem…sorry, no time, back to Sir Lancelot, fables, lies…Skelton, Dunbar, anyone, but no – not a wise move to eternalise such an insecure king. Italian sculptors, Flemish painters, the same reply. You are my last chance and I will not release you. When you have finished you can go where you like.

CHRYSOSTOM: Then, if he will not talk to me I will have to ask his friends. They must have some idea of what he is like. Whom should I ask?

RICHARD: (*Sings.*)

I AM A MAN WHO MAKES FEW FRIENDS
AND THAT'S THE PITY OF ME,
THE MEN I'VE LOVED HAVE ALL BEEN SMALL,
PREPARED TO SMILE WITHIN MY SHADOW,
AT GAMES THEY GAVE ME HIDDEN HANDICAPS
AND GRANTED SECRET MERCIES,
NOT KNOWING HOW I WOULD NOT NEED THEM

IN THIS, MY LATER LONELY LIFE.

SO JOIN MY FRIENDS AND BE
MY CLOSE COMPANION, BE ONE
OF THIS SMALL KNOT I'VE TIED
AROUND MY HEART. INTERSECT THIS CIRCLE
AND EXPAND IT TO A LIGHT CROWN'S RIM
SO WHEN YOU SEE ME RIDING FROM AFAR
YOU RISE AND CALL, THAT'S HIM, THAT'S HIM,
IN THIS MY LATER LONELY LIFE.

(*Exit RICHARD, CHRYSOSTOM and CICELY. Enter McMASTERS in his 1984 overalls.*)

McMASTERS: (*In a Welsh accent.*) I, Henry Tudor, while waiting on the coast of France for a fair wind to carry my invasion fleet to Wales, had news of Richard Plantagenet's state of mind from my future mother-in-law...

(*Enter ELIZABETH.*)

ELIZABETH: Well beloved friend, I recommend me and my daughter to you, desiring heartily to hear of your welfare, and, if it please you to hear of our welfare, we are not in good health of body nor of heart, nor shall be till we hear from you. As for intelligence, the Monster is still in disarray but come with all speed I pray you for he ordains new regiments on every chance. On your setting forth, which good report I pray for daily, bring with you such tall men as may repair the fortunes of this kingdom in haste, and, I beseech you, when your worshipful desires shall be accomplished, let the Monster not be exempted from his fate, but suffer it in all severity. Here, I send you this letter, asking that my hand be not seen of none other earthly creature, save only yourself. Yours, Elizabeth Woodville. PS The Monster has taken up hawking and sends envoys all over the land looking for the best hunting birds. It is said that he seeks better health this way, but I trust in God that he may never find it.

McMASTERS: Hawking? Well, it will keep him from my business. And how are your boys? Well I hope. The winters are milder over here...

(Exit McMASTERS and ELIZABETH. Enter RICHARD and
LOVELL with bird-whistlers on strings, swinging them round.
PRINCE RICHARD is with them, a mimed hawk on his wrist.
LOVELL is in 1484 costume.)

RICHARD: Smell that air. Come on boy, enjoy the
    sunshine. The clouds have parted. You can see for miles.

PRINCE RICHARD: I can't, it hurts my eyes to look up.

RICHARD: A Plantagenet who cannot look at the sun?
    Never. Stare it out. Like me. Right in the eye.

LOVELL: There's a pigeon, two! Up with him, boy!

PRINCE RICHARD: I can't, he won't let go.

LOVELL: Now they've gone. You were too slow.

RICHARD: What do you call this clinging hawk, boy?

PRINCE RICHARD: Bacillus, Uncle. Bacillus.

LOVELL: Larks, there, finches, wrens and robins…
    loose him!

RICHARD: Up, Bacillus, up!

PRINCE RICHARD: *(Struggling with the hawk.)* He won't
    leave me…

LOVELL: God's teeth boy, beat him, thrust him from you!

RICHARD: There's a smug, speckled thrush! There's a
    well-fed bird if ever I saw one! Attack! Burst him like a
    bladder!

PRINCE RICHARD: *(Fighting with the hawk.)* He's pecking
    me! He's eating me!
    (RICHARD and LOVELL still watch the sky, turning their
    bird-whistlers as PRINCE RICHARD struggles with the hawk.)

LOVELL: What a day, what a wild spring day. Remember?

RICHARD: The moors and that enormous northern sky…

PRINCE RICHARD: He's eating me, uncle, uncle…

LOVELL: A place to get lost in…

RICHARD: For days you would never see another soul.
    Frank, if I could have the north for my own, I would
    gladly surrender the rest of this nation. There are
    a hundred years of the old ways left up there.

PRINCE RICHARD: Help me! My throat, my throat…*(He*
    falls to the ground, still fighting the hawk. Dies.)

LOVELL: Who will you trust your armies to when the
    time comes?

McMASTERS: (*Still as Henry Tudor.*) I'm listening,
  I'm listening…
RICHARD: Norfolk…
LOVELL: Good…
RICHARD: Northumberland…
LOVELL: No, not him. Not a Percy, they've always been
  Lancastrian. That's asking to be let down.
RICHARD: Isn't it? And Stanley.
  (*Pause.*)
LOVELL: You expect me to ride with you and him in the
  same cause?
RICHARD: If that cause is me.
  (*Pause.*)
LOVELL: And how are we going to pay for this campaign?
  The Treasury is as empty as a scraped plate. We cannot
  offer security for your debts…
RICHARD: God must become a banker. For his own
  anointed he will have low interest rates.
  (*Enter CICELY.*)
CICELY: I hear everything is going very well. You can
  expect massive support from the merchants…
LOVELL: Afterwards.
RICHARD: Don't be so glum, Frank. As if it mattered.
  Where did other kings get their money from?
LOVELL: They had a very effective method of boosting their
  foreign exchange reserves. It was a short-term policy but it
  had distinct advantages as it artificially stimulated cash-
  flow and offset their domestic taxation income deficits.
  It was called…plunder.
RICHARD: It was the only time when running the
  Exchequer was any fun at all. What do you say, mother?
  (*Bitterly.*) Don't we need another Amiens?
CICELY: Don't be flippant, Richard. Those days are over.
CICELY/RICHARD: (*Sing.*)
  THE ENGLAND THAT WAS HERE HAS GONE
  ITS SONG WAS THAT OF LION AND SWAN
  ITS COLOURS GULES NOW CRIMSON,
  (*Enter ELIZABETH.*)

ALL: (*Sing.*)

> ASTUTE MEN HID BENEATH THE LID
> OF HELMET, CASQUE AND BASINET
> TO SEE WHAT PLUNDER THEY COULD GET,
> A SOUND FINANCIAL REASON:
> THE BULL, THE FIERY CRESSET, GOAT,
> PUT ON A STEEL AND LEATHER COAT
> AND SHARPENED LANCE AND SWORD,
> THEN STRUCK THEIR TENT
> AND WENT HELL-BENT
> WITH BLOOD UPON THEIR BLAZON.
> WERE EXETER AND BEDFORD, BEAUFORT,
> SOMERSET AND GLOUCESTER OUT FOR
> ANY MORE THAN HE WHO SMASHES GRAPES
> TO HURRY ON A RAISIN?
> CAN YOU TELL ME THAT TALBOT, PERCY,
> NEVILLE, HOWARD, LOVED THE LORD OF MERCY
> MORE THAN LOOT?
> THEN LET ME TELL YOU ECONOMICS
> WAS OF OLD ENGLAND'S FOREIGN POLICY
> THE BRANCH AND STEM AND ROOT.
> SO NOW THE BOYS ARE DEAD, THE SUMMER GRASS
> GROWS HIGH ABOVE ACCOUNTANTS' HEADS
> IN AQUITAINE AND SWEET CHAMPAGNE,
> ANJOU, BORDEAUX AND AGINCOURT,
> WHILE WE ARE LEFT WITH PENNILESS REGRET AND SPEND
> OUR TIME
> DEVISING SYSTEMS OF RESPECTABLE EXTORTION OF A
> DIFFERENT SORT.

(*Exit CICELY and RICHARD. Enter CHRYSOSTOM.*)

ELIZABETH: Do you find the offer acceptable? Practicable?

CHRYSOSTOM: I will need protection…the Duchess will not be pleased. I appear, in my honesty as an artist, to have compromised myself.

ELIZABETH: The Duchess will be a nobody after this summer. You have nothing to fear from her…

CHRYSOSTOM: You mentioned instructions…

ELIZABETH: Yes…come closer (*Whispers in CHRYSOSTOM's ear.*)

CHRYSOSTOM: Well, at least it is…positive. I'm exhausted with trying to find my own interpretation. I am not happy to accept a client's dictation in these matters, but…beggars must.

ELIZABETH: Do a good job and the Tudor may bring you back to do more…simple people.

(*ELIZABETH and CHRYSOSTOM exit. McMASTERS comes forward. LOVELL has taken off his surcoat and changes to 1984.*)

LOVELL: It's here that the designers of Betrayal have inserted their hook, their special selling feature. Here, just before Bosworth, every player left in the game draws a card from a reserve pack. Imagine, a late night, the bottle almost finished, the fire dying down…then, something truly terrifying…real forfeits, hard-hitting forfeits. It's a lot of fun, a bundle of laughs. The losing players, this being a tightly-controlled, highly-managed game of dynamic relationships, must cough up. You can lose…

McMASTERS: (*Welsh accent.*) Life. Reputation. Respect. Affection. Existence in any real past. Once dead, Dick will be part of my package for the new age. The part that is perforated, ripped along the dotted line, and out of which my genius will pour like freely-flowing salt. I will recreate him.

LOVELL: Tough. But necessary if Henry Tudor as the winner is to consolidate his victory and be seen as the nation's deliverer from a reign of terror. Claim to the throne – nil. Blow that cobweb away. But full marks for opportunism, drive, planning, energy and…here lies his greatest innovation in advertising – selling by the negative.

McMASTERS: Buy this because your old game was dangerous…

LOVELL: Inflammable…

McMASTERS: Got stuck in the kid's windpipe…

LOVELL: An inferior product in every way. Never realised it? Baby, you'd never thought about it. Where's Ludo now? See any Snakes and Ladders?

McMASTERS: He was the granddaddy of us all and, like us, knew himself in the Greek way, and was always aware of what he was doing. In our profession, is anyone unsure of who is father, who is child? Henry Tudor wasn't, and neither are we, are we, boys? To sell, you have to think you are the father and the customer is the child.

LOVELL/McMASTERS: (*Sing.*)

BABY, BABY,

WHO'S CALLING YOU BABY?

BABY, BABY,

WHO'S CALLING YOU CHILD?

MIND IS MENTAL

TRUTH'S ON A RENTAL,

SUCK THIS, SEE THIS

GAME'S DRIVING ME WILD.

(*CHRYSOSTOM and CICELY enter.*)

CHRYSOSTOM: Madam. I have it. The window. May I continue? I would like to deliver the goods, do the work. Please say yes. Sorry for the delay.

CICELY: You may be too late. The Tudor has already set sail from Harfleur. Richard will be going north...gathering his army.

CHRYSOSTOM: Will he come here?

CICELY: I have asked him to, to say goodbye...

CHRYSOSTOM: And good luck?

CICELY: Hear that, God? (*Chuckles.*) Poor man, make your window.

LOVELL/McMASTERS/CICELY: (*Sing.*)

BABY, BABY,

WHO'S CALLING YOU BABY?

BABY, BABY,

YOUR STYLE'S INFANTILE,

CHOICE AND CHUNKY

YOU SWEET LITTLE MONKEY,

GOT YOUR NUMBER

DOWN HERE ON MY FILE.

(*Enter RICHARD with ELIZABETH.*)

ELIZABETH: Resistance is pointless, Richard. You haven't got a chance now. All your generals have been bought and sold.

RICHARD: Is your daughter well?

ELIZABETH: Excellent health. Looking forward to being a bride.

RICHARD: Virgin?

ELIZABETH: I beg your pardon!

RICHARD: It was a thought. Has England ever had a virgin queen?

LOVELL/McMASTERS/CICELY/ELIZABETH: (*Sing.*)

BABY, BABY,

WHO'S CALLING YOU BABY?

BABY, BABY,

YOUR MOUTH IS TOO WIDE.

DOUBLE TISSUE,

OH HOW I MISS YOU,

DEEP, ABSORBENT,

THICK, TENDER PILE.

CICELY: Have you finished yet, Greek? Richard is only hours away.

CHRYSOSTOM: Not long now. Just the final touches, a quick polish and everything will be ready.

CICELY: Is it beautiful?

CHRYSOSTOM: It works superbly. It is strikingly effective.

CICELY: Has it meaning?

CHRYSOSTOM: It is all meaning. It is the significant future.

CICELY: Will it last?

CHRYSOSTOM: For ever, and ever, and ever, Amen. (*Aside.*) And paid for twice. (*Exits.*)

ELIZABETH: And what are you going to leave behind? What testament?

RICHARD: I have left my will blank. Have you learnt to write?

ELIZABETH: What a death you contemplate. So empty.

RICHARD: Not empty, clean. A clean break with the past.

ALL: (*Sing.*)

BABY, BABY,

WHO'S CALLING YOU BABY?

BABY, BABY,

YOUR DADDY HAS DIED.

JOKER JESUS NO LONGER DECEIVES US,

KINGS AND COUNTRIES

ADMIT THEY HAVE LIED.

NO REPLACEMENT

TO YOUR AMAZEMENT,

SUBSTITUTION, NEVER DESIGNED.

LOST AND LONELY,

THE FUTURE IS PHONEY,

SAD AND SIMPLE

TO BATTLE YOU RIDE.

CICELY: Richard, welcome back to Berkhamsted.

RICHARD: Mother, you asked me to call.

CICELY: Richard, God has promised me that I will be the last survivor. I will see it all, the change, the rolling away of my times. Won't that be wonderful? And I will be aware. I won't lose my faculties. No second childhood for Cicely. He is saying, you kept this machine going, and when it stops it can stand in your back garden and rust. Isn't that like him? A sense of what is absolutely right...

RICHARD: I can't stay long.

CICELY: I have a surprise for you. Remember last Christmas?

RICHARD: I have been trying to forget it.

CICELY: Richard, the Greek says that he has found his theme and made something marvellous of it. I have resisted the temptation to look in order to share this moment with you. (*Pause.*) Quiet, please. I have a few words to say. King Richard has given up some of his precious time – the land is in a crisis as you know – to be with us here today...

RICHARD: Mother, shall we get on with it?

CICELY: This window is for my son, and God, the only two men worth talking to as far as I am concerned. It is a gift

to the present, and the future, made from the past.
It comes with love from mother.

RICHARD: Thank you. (*Kisses her.*) It was a nice thought.
Where do I stand? Here? Will this do? Really, I would
have thought it better left aside. However, if it will
please you. Right. Short speech. Usual thing. All set?
What a waste of money. (*Pause.*) We do not know what is
behind this curtain, and we never will. We turn our backs
upon it and go our own way north, to fight. If it helps
you, my people, to look upon another man's image of us,
then that is his profit, not ours. We do not consider him
necessary. Do not look upon us as ungenerous for this
attitude we know who we are, where we are fixed. We do
not have to be interpreted as this king speaks good
English. (*Pause.*) There are things which we have to do,
men we must meet, arrangements we must make.
We have little time left. Let us get it over with.
(*Enter CHRYSOSTOM in a snappy modern suit, carrying a
brief-case. He shakes LOVELL's and McMASTERS's hands
and kisses LOUISE's with an elegant mocking bow.*)

CHRYSOSTOM: You cannot satisfy all of your customers
all of the time. You must choose your market, build up
a good complaints department, and smile.
(*CHRYSOSTOM sits down at the chess-table.*)

RICHARD: We do not accept this picture of us. It was made
by an alien mind from an alien age and it cannot be
right. After you have seen it, remember that we have
remained ourselves and nothing will ever alter that.
This window is a game in glass, played upon our living
years. It is artificial. It is false!

CICELY: Three cheers for God! Hip-hip-hooray! Hip-hip-
hooray! Hip-hip-hooray! Let's see it, let's see it!

RICHARD: Unveil the window. I refuse to look.
(*McMASTERS and LOVELL pull back the Betrayal
board curtains. Blackout. The window flares up in
brilliant primary colours. It is savage political cartoon of
RICHARD killing and eating children. CICELY falls to
the ground. Lights up.*)

CICELY: No, no, that's not him…

CHRYSOSTOM: Like any artist of note, I can accept criticism of my work. I'm interested in how people react to what I put before them. This window? Well, it was done for money and to get me out of England. Justify it? It's useful, oh yes. Here, in this backward village of Berkhamsted there is a positive sigh of relief.
My window pin-points evil for them, provides an answer to the old problem of who to blame for the past and who not to trust for the future. It legislates against confusion and acts as signpost to a better, brighter age.

RICHARD: It is not me. It is not me. It is not me.

(*CHRYSOSTOM takes the bag with the chess-pieces out of his brief-case and empties it on to the chess-table, then sets up the game, giving himself the black. CICELY gets up.*)

ALL: (*Sing.*)

COLLECT ALL THE PIECES
PUT THE GAME IN THE DRAWER,
TONIGHT IS TONIGHT,
THE FACT IS NOT LAW,
GREEN GOES TO AMBER,
AMBER TO RED,
THE CHILD IN HIS DREAM
IS THE CHILD IN HIS BED.

ARE YOU AWARE WHAT YOU'RE DOING TO ME?
WHO ASKED YOU? WHO ASKED YOU?
THE DREAM OF THE CHILD,
THE CHILD UNAWARE,
THE FEAR OF THE FUTURE
WHEN THE GAME ISN'T THERE.

RICHARD: (*Sings.*)

ARE YOU AWARE OF WHAT YOU'RE DOING TO ME?
WHO ASKED YOU? WHO ASKED YOU?
SUBLIMINAL IMAGES OF HISTORY,
WHO ASKED YOU? WHO ASKED YOU?
THERE'S NO CHANCE YOU'RE GOING TO GET ME RIGHT,
I SEE ME, AND YOU SEE SIGHT!
ARE YOU AWARE OF WHAT YOU'RE DOING TO ME?
WHO ASKED YOU? WHO ASKED YOU?

ALL: (*Sing.*)

    ARE YOU AWARE OF WHAT YOU'RE DOING TO ME?

    WHO ASKED YOU? WHO ASKED YOU?

    THE DREAMS OF THE CHILD, GREEN GOES TO AMBER,

    THE CHILD UNAWARE, AMBER TO RED,

    THE CHILD IN HIS DREAMS, THE FEAR OF THE FUTURE

    THE CHILD IN HIS BED, WHEN THE GAME ISN'T THERE.

RICHARD: (*Sings.*)

    ARE YOU AWARE OF WHAT YOU'RE DOING TO ME?

    WHO ASKED YOU? WHO ASKED YOU?

    HAS ANYONE HERE EVER HEARD

    OF A WHORE CALLED HISTORICAL ACCURACY?

    IF YOU BUMP INTO HER GIVE HER A MESSAGE

    FROM DEAD RICHARD THREE,

    SAY I HOPE SHE GETS BETTER PUBLICITY THAN ME.

ALL: (*Sing.*)

    ARE YOU AWARE OF WHAT YOU'RE DOING TO ME?

    WHO ASKED YOU? WHO ASKED YOU?

    ARE YOU AWARE OF WHAT YOU'RE DOING TO ME?

    WHO ASKED YOU? WHO ASKED YOU?

LOVELL: Fade the lights, Louise. The evenings are early in the north.

(RICHARD, ELIZABETH, McMASTERS and LOVELL exit. CICELY is standing in front of the window in a cold pool of light.)

CICELY: This is how my son died. On the battlefield he was deserted by two of his generals and his army melted away. At the head of only a hundred men he charged the enemy and cut his way through to the feet of Henry Tudor himself, killing his standard-bearer. But his momentum had been absorbed by greater numbers and they closed around him and he was slain. His naked body was slung over a horse and taken to Leicester where it was exposed in the market-place so that the people might see he was dead. Friars from a nearby religious house had to beg for his body in order to give it a decent burial. Later, his bones were dug up and thrown into the river. That he would have been grateful for as I cannot see him resting easy in the earth of this new England. The river suited him better. (*Exits.*)

(*Enter ORWELL in his dressing-gown and pyjamas. He goes over to the table and stands by it.*)

CHRYSOSTOM: Another game? Will you be more in control of yourself this time?

(*ORWELL nods, sits down to the white side.*)

CHRYSOSTOM: Oh, I have something for you. (*Brings a book out of his brief-case.*) Your advance copy of 1984. Looks good. (*Puts it on the table by ORWELL'S hand.*) Certainly nothing to be ashamed of. (*Pause.*) Your move I think.

(*Pause. ORWELL knocks over his king.*)

(*Blackout.*)

The End.

Notes on the Music

Where background or incidental music is indicated, the theme from 'Peace is man's richest possesion' (at the end of 'No one knows but the Lord') can be used; e.g. during the Danube Room scene early in Act One and at the beginning of Act Two.

'Sir, Emperor, Lord of all the ground'. The accompaniment can be extended after the song for Chrysostom's dance.

'Lully, lulla'. The music for 'The Coventry Carol' (original version) can be found in the *Oxford Book of Carols*, No. 22

'Amiens'. The verses and instrumental breaks to which the kings dance should be interspersed with the dialogue of the scene.

'Baby, baby'. The guitar accompaniment may be played beneath the scenes linking the verses.

Instruments used in the original production included rebec, crumhorn, Nordic lyre, Appalachian dulcimer and psaltery – as well as guitar and electric piano. However, other instruments of comparable pitch may be substituted. This is only an outline of the score, the full version of which may be obtained by applying in the first instance to: John Johnson (Author's Agent) Ltd, Clerkenwell House, 45/47 Clerkenwell Green, London EC1R 0HT.

Reproductions

Sir, Emperor Lord of all the ground

WORDS TRADITIONAL, ADAPTED BY DAVID POWNALL

Child

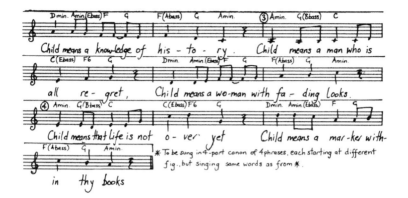

No one knows but de Lord / Peace

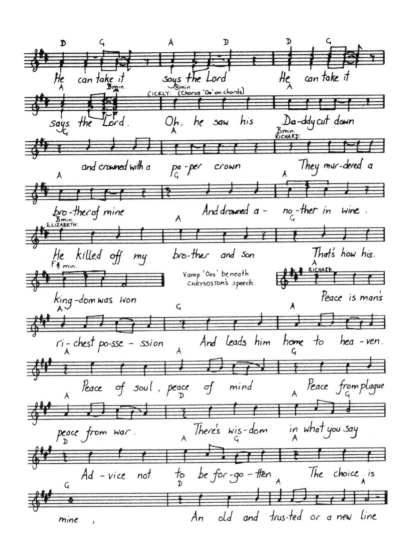

The rules of the game

Take a chance card and then advance to Car- mar- then   Darn it
Barn-et Try a- gain A- mi-ens, You seem to be
hea-din' for a show-down at Edin - burgh Tilt of the board
Sto-ny Strat-ford, Lu- cky man No- tting-ham
In the red Berk- ham- stead What you worth
Bos - worth? Now   these are the rules of the
game   Shake the dice when I call out your name   Throw a
three or a four or a five,   And we'll   see who is
stay- ing   a-   :   Live .

The earth will not be the centre

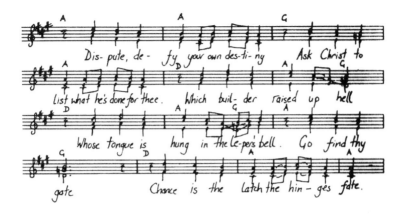

Amiens

Po -tage is French Stew sea-soned with shame

Po-tage is French Stew sea-soned with shame

Peace e-quals vic-tory mi- nus ho- nour, Peace e- quals vic-tory

mi - nus ho- nour

A- mi-ens quelle hon- te ja- mais ga-

Uan- te. A- mi-ens quel cha- grin. La

gloire en- fin , fin , fin.

I am a man who makes few friends

The England that was here has gone

Baby, baby

1. Baby, baby, who's call-ing you ba-by.
Baby, ba-by who's call-ing you child.
Mind is men-tal, truth's on a ren-tal,
Suck this, see this, game's dri-ving me wild.

4. Ba-by, ba-by, who's call-ing you ba-by,
Ba-by, ba-by, your Da-ddy has died.
Jo-ker Je-sus no lon-ger de - ceives us
Kings and count-ries ad- mit that they have lied

5. No re - place-ment to your a - maze - ment.
Sub-sti- tu- tion ne- ver de- signed
Lost and lone-ly, the fu- ture is pho- ney
Sad and sim-ple to bat-tle you ride.

* Verse 2 — tune + lower part.
Verses 3 & 4 — all three parts

Collect all the pieces

fear of the fu-ture when the game is-n't

dream is the child in his bed

there Are you a-ware of what you're do-ing to me, Who asked you, who asked you, Has

a-ny one here e-ver heard of the whore called his-to-ri-cal a-ccu-ra-cy If you bump

in-to her, give her a me-ssage from dead Ri-chard

three, Say I hope she gets be-tter pub-li-ci-ty than

Are you a-ware of what you're do-ing to me, Who asked you, who asked you.

me Are you a-ware of what you're do-ing to me, Who asked you, who asked you.

MOTOCAR

For John Edward Adams
and the company

Characters

MOTOCAR

PICKERILL

DONAHUE

SYMONDS

LEWIS

NOTE

The play benefits from being played without an interval, though provision for a break is made in the text. Running time is 100 minutes.

Seating-plan for Motocar's meeting is seen as below:

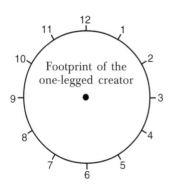

1. Kissinger
2. Price
3. Silveira
4. Lobengula
5. Moshesh
6. Sophocles
7. Mzilikasi
8. Moffat
9. Mauch
10. Tshaka
11. Victoria
12. Monomotapa

Motocar was first performed by Paines Plough at the Traverse Theatre Club, Edinburgh on 1 February 1977, with the following cast:

MOTOCAR, Joe Marcell

PICKERILL, Eric Richard

DONAHUE, Fiona Victory

SYMONDS, Diana Kyle

LEWIS, Stephen Boxer

Director, Edward Adams

ACT ONE

The linen-room of a mental hospital for Africans near Salisbury, Rhodesia. Shelves of clean, folded sheets. Six big wickerwork laundry baskets, some of them open, with dirty sheets, pyjamas, overalls, underwear, spilling out into jumbled piles on the floor. Graffiti on the walls and shelves – VOULEZ-VOUS VORSTER? BISHOP, BLESS US ALL. ZZZZZZZZIMBABWE. VAKOMANA WELKOM HOME. GO MUGABE GO. BLACKSMITH. GENEVA. ZANU. ZAPU. STEVE BIKO WILL SELF-DESTRUCT IN FIVE SECONDS.
Telephone rings, then stops.

MOTOCAR: (*Off.*) Dlhodlhodlho.

PICKERILL: (*Off.*) Tulake, tulake…Quiet, man, keep the noise down for Christ's sake, this is a hospital…you've got to keep quiet in here.

MOTOCAR: (*Entering with PICKERILL.*) Dlhodlhodlho.

PICKERILL: Now that's enough, man…Stop it…(*Sees the room.*) What's this? This can't be the right room. That bloody fool on the switchboard has sent us to the wrong place…it would be nice for them to get something right, just once in a while, eh? Just once in a while…Come on, back we go.
(*PICKERILL turns MOTOCAR round to leave. Enter SISTER DONAHUE.*)

DONAHUE: What's going on here?

MOTOCAR: Head-ring.

PICKERILL: We've been sent to the wrong place…

DONAHUE: Did he do this? (*To MOTOCAR.*) Did you make this mess? I've been after you for a long time my lad…

PICKERILL: No, he's with me…We were sent here by mistake…

DONAHUE: Three times this week this has happened. I've had enough of it. D'you hear? Stupid kids playing games! Why are you holding hands with him?
(*PICKERILL holds up their handcuffed hands.*)

219

PICKERILL: He's a prisoner. I've brought him here for a psychiatric examination.

DONAHUE: Is he dangerous?

PICKERILL: They're all dangerous at the moment, aren't they?

DONAHUE: Don't ask me. All I know is they're making my life impossible. This country's had it. Politics, you see, politics. Everything has to be politics. Even my houseboy, politics in the morning, politics at night. If he breaks a plate, it's politics.

MOTOCAR: Dlhodlhodlho...

DONAHUE: Ach, and the same to you. You tire me out. They haven't got half a brain between the whole lot of them, have you? Have you got a brain in there?

MOTOCAR: Head-ring. Head-ring. Head-ring.

PICKERILL: Tulake! Well, I'd better find out where the right room is for this examination. It's not here, that's for sure.

DONAHUE: Who told you it was here?

PICKERILL: The boys on the switchboard...

DONAHUE: Don't believe a word they say. That whole gang out there in reception are loafers. They think they're very amusing. I'd fire the lot of them tomorrow. Politics again, you see, very cocky, very uppity.

PICKERILL: He said room twelve. Do you think they can count that far?

DONAHUE: Well, this is room twelve.

PICKERILL: They've just cocked it up. Well, you can't expect them to get a simple thing like that right, can you? That's a real intellectual problem, getting a room number right. I'll go back and sort it out. Come on, chamware.

DONAHUE: Hold on, I'll find out for you. I'll ring through and ask. (*Looks for phone.*) Very funny, very grown-up sense of humour the boys have here. Do you feel confident about being governed by a bunch of clowns and bullies? They're trying my patience. And I came here for a quiet life. You can laugh if you like.

(*Finds phone under a laundry basket.*) See what I mean?
Children. Tiny-tots.

PICKERILL: You have got some right jokers here.

DONAHUE: (*Dialling 0.*) Sister Donahue here...Yes, it's
me...That's right...Will you be quiet and let me talk?...
I have a person here...

PICKERILL: Inspector Pickerill to see Doctor Grobbler.

DONAHUE: Yes...Inspector Pickerill...yes, he's a
bwana...yes...you remember him, do you?...Now that's
remarkable in itself...Which room did you send him
to?...Twelve? Now why twelve? It's the linen-
room...Doesn't that strike you as odd? Very funny, what
a gentleman you are...Why did you send him to the
linen-room, you bloody fool?!...Oh...Doctor
Lewis...er...alright...(*Replaces receiver.*) This is the right
room. We're very short of space. Beds everywhere.

PICKERILL: Oh...I'd better wait then. I think I'll take
these cuffs off. They're playing hell with my
wrist...Stand still...

(*PICKERILL unlocks the handcuffs.*)

DONAHUE: Are you sure that's wise?

PICKERILL: I've been with him all day. He's not violent...

DONAHUE: Yet. I don't trust any of them. I've been
burgled five times in the last three months, insulted
every day at work, jostled in the street...They're out of
control. I used to like this place, I did, after Belfast it was
Paradise...

PICKERILL: Things change.

MOTOCAR: Things change. Things change.

PICKERILL: Alright, man. I don't need you chipping in.
Go and sit down. Like I do. Go on, sit, squat.

MOTOCAR: Half a brain. Which half?

DONAHUE: What's that you said?

MOTOCAR: Catch a train. Witchcraft.

DONAHUE: You think you're so clever, don't you? I'll
leave you to it, Inspector. I'd like you to imagine trying
to work with fifteen hundred comedians like this, real
thickheads. I'll tell Doctor Lewis you're here. He's the
Deputy Chief Psychiatrist. He's running the place, now,
trying to...

221

PICKERILL: Actually, my appointment is with Doctor Grobbler.

DONAHUE: Doctor Grobbler's in Johannesburg. He flew down last night. He's gone for good, run, run, just left us to it. That's what I feel like doing. I don't really want to go back up there on the wards. Isn't that terrible? I'm doing no good you see, they hate me. I can feel it coming out of them, real hate. I thought I could take everything they handed out but I can't. Not an atom of gratitude. (*Pause.*) Well, no good putting off the evil day. Where else would have me, eh? I liked it here. I liked everything about it. You could live with some self-respect, until now.

PICKERILL: I know what you mean.

DONAHUE: They're children. It's going to be Peter Pan land. A fantastic country like this given to a gang of kids. We'll be governed by thugs and murderers...Christ, it makes me so mad...Ah, to hell with it. Have you got a cigarette? Let them break the place up for a while...

MOTOCAR: I want my head-ring. I have worked hard for it, quietly in small rooms, with books. No man has worked harder. Do not deny me my head-ring.

DONAHUE: (*Taking a cigarette and light off PICKERILL.*) See, here you have a future Prime Minister. We got so tired, you know. This place is on its last legs. They don't care. Let the grass grow over the roof. That's what one of the orderlies said, let the grass grow over the roof. They don't care. They don't care about their own people. Death, madness, they've always been very close to the African. He has no respect for human life. That's why they live like they do.

PICKERILL: Yes...I see what you mean...er, my instructions were to have the prisoner examined by Doctor Grobbler specifically. If he's not here any more I'd better check with headquarters in Salisbury to find out what I should do...

DONAHUE: (*Giving cigarette to PICKERILL.*) Here, you finish this. I'd better push on. Would you like some tea?

PICKERILL: That would be great. I take sugar. He doesn't.

DONAHUE: Oh, If you see Doctor Lewis would you ask him to ring the Sister's desk on ward seven. Tell him it's urgent. There's a couple of jokers up there who reckon they're conspiring to commit suicide together, a pact, you know what I mean? Just say amytal...amytal – we need amytal. It's the Mpesu brothers. Twins. Now isn't that sweet?

PICKERILL: Is it alright if I make a call on that phone?

DONAHUE: Sure. Just dial zero for the operator and ask for a line.

PICKERILL: Thanks.

DONAHUE: You're welcome. Well, back into the breach, dear friends.

(*DONAHUE exits.*)

MOTOCAR: What a charming woman.

PICKERILL: Don't you be insolent. Keep quiet now while I make this call. (*Dials 0.*) Operator? A line to Salisbury, please. No...not Salisbury England...Don't try and be funny, boy, it doesn't wash with me...(*Pause. Then he dials.*) Hello. Stan...hello, Stan? Yes, Ray here...Look, there's been a mix-up here...Who is that? You again... man, have you been listening in on my call?...Man, I'll be out there chop chop and sort you out...Why can't you give me a line?...What meeting?...Alright, alright...But just cut the fun and games, eh? This is government business...Give me a line as soon as you can. (*Replaces receiver.*) This really is a madhouse you know. They're all bloody mad. You see what you've achieved here? Complete confusion.

MOTOCAR: You mentioned a meeting.

PICKERILL: Yes, he says all the lines are being used for this meeting, for the delegates.

MOTOCAR: What were their names?

PICKERILL: I can't remember. This is a real cock-up. I drive all the way from Marandellas and find the psychiatrist has buggered off to Johannesburg. Typical.

MOTOCAR: Was one of them called Mzilikasi?

PICKERILL: I don't know. They were probably talking bullshit, anyway.

MOTOCAR: Do you know if they perform the split-brain operation in this hospital?

PICKERILL: I shouldn't think so. To split a brain you've got to have a brain to split.

MOTOCAR: May I have another cigarette?

PICKERILL: Man, you're costing me money. This is the last. (*PICKERILL gives MOTOCAR a cigarette, lights it. As soon as MOTOCAR takes the first draw, DOCTOR LEWIS enters.*) (*PICKERILL snatches the cigarette out of MOTOCAR's mouth and puts it under his shoe, with his own.*)

PICKERILL: Hello, are you the deputy?

LEWIS: Yes, my name is Lewis. (*Shakes hands with PICKERILL.*) Inspector Pickerill? (*Bends down and picks up the flattened cigarettes, dropping them in a waste bin.*)

PICKERILL: Right…er…this is the prisoner… (*Telephone rings. LEWIS is nearest, he answers it.*)

PICKERILL: I think you'll find that call is for me.

LEWIS: Hold on, operator. (*To PICKERILL.*) Are you Mr Mzilikasi?

PICKERILL: No. Isn't the call for me?

LEWIS: (*To MOTOCAR.*) Is that your name?

MOTOCAR: Yes.

LEWIS: Then you'd better take the call.

PICKERILL: His name is not Mr Mzilikasi.

LEWIS: Well, the call is for someone of that name. Perhaps there are two of you? Try elsewhere, operator. (*LEWIS replaces the receiver. Enter NURSE SYMONDS with two cups and a sugar-bowl on a tray and some folded sheets under her arm.*)

SYMONDS: Excuse me. Is this your tea? Did you ask for it?

MOTOCAR: Ah, the first-year essays. Good. Put them in my in-tray.

PICKERILL: Yes. The sister said she'd arrange for it. Is that alright, Doctor?

LEWIS: Certainly. (*SYMONDS gives MOTOCAR his tea.*)

MOTOCAR: No sugar, thank you. He does, three. (*SYMONDS gives PICKERILL his tea. He puts in three sugars, self-consciously.*)

LEWIS: You know Doctor Grobbler is in Johannesburg?

PICKERILL: Yes, it's a nuisance. I've got to get this okey looked at.

LEWIS: Why are you bothering?

PICKERILL: Those are my instructions.

LEWIS: I'm afraid that I am not prepared to do it. Don't leave, Martha.

SYMONDS: I have to get back. Did Grace see you about the amytal for the Mpesu brothers? They've been terrible today. You've no idea the things they get up to...

LEWIS: I don't think we have any amytal left.

PICKERILL: I'm not sure that I was going to ask you anyway. (*Telephone rings. He answers it as he speaks.*) Headquarters said Doctor Grobbler – extension 68 – Stan? Ray here...I've run into a problem...The proper doctor is away and this place is – very busy, they can't fit me in...Yes...I realise that...I can only ask...No, I saw nothing on the way here...Where've they been sighted? Christ, that many?...Right, I'll wrap it up as soon as I can and get out of here...Yes, don't worry. I'll be back before dark...I'll keep a look out for terrorists...No, man, they can't shoot straight, you know that, not at a moving target...See you, Stan...(*PICKERILL replaces the receiver, takes an envelope from his pocket and draws out a paper.*) Right, Doctor, we haven't got much time.

LEWIS: May I ask what is that?

PICKERILL: The request from the Ministry for the examination. His name is Motocar, as far as we can tell...

SYMONDS: Motocar. The names they get given, Motocar.

PICKERILL: Please be as quick as you can. I've got other work to do.

(*PICKERILL offers the paper to LEWIS, who does not take it.*)

LEWIS: And we haven't of course. How long has he been in custody?

PICKERILL: About six hours.

LEWIS: (*Angrily.*) After eleven, twelve years of bungling, stupidity and arrogance, we can streamline a case like this in six hours, yet I am kept waiting for decisions, supplies, staff...all of them urgent. Have you any idea how impossible life has been made for us here? This hospital is falling apart. I'm trying to run it single-handed. I simply haven't got time for this kind of thing.

SYMONDS: All the nurses are getting out as fast as they can. We can't keep track of what's going on. Half the patients are moving their families in. Right, I'm going back to Grace...Don't forget the amytal. Doctor, we must have it...

MOTOCAR: At a place called Lôwê, twelve miles north of Machudi, is a hole in the dry river-bed. On the rocks there are hundreds of footprints made by the first creatures ever to appear in the world. (*Hands the cup and saucer to SYMONDS.*) The hole itself is the footprint of the one-legged creator who retired into the mark of his own life when he was disappointed with what he had made.

PICKERILL: Will you examine him?

LEWIS: No. Martha, I want you to witness my refusal.

SYMONDS: Alright Doctor, but make it snappy. Grace is expecting me back. I only popped out for a minute. She can't manage by herself up there.

LEWIS: You can go as soon as we've sorted this out...

PICKERILL: This is a government order, an order. We have to have him examined.

LEWIS: Not by me. It is quite pointless. We are two weeks away from Independence.

PICKERILL: How do you know he's political?

LEWIS: Because you are here, and it is obviously urgent. Under normal circumstances we do our examination at the prison hospital. I'm not interested in the details. The answer is no. Nor will I allow any other member of my staff to examine him.

SYMONDS: Let me go now, Doctor. Grace will kill me!

LEWIS: She'll just have to wait!

PICKERILL: Doctor, this is a serious business. This man is accused of a crime, an offence against the law. We reckon he killed a man. But he doesn't act normal. We can't follow him. He could be acting...

(*Enter DONAHUE with a bundle of dirty sheets, shouting.*)

DONAHUE: Christ Almighty, Martha, can't you leave him alone for a minute? I thought I told you to get back straight away? Did you get any amytal? Did you give her any amytal for the Mpesu brothers, Doctor? They're tearing the recreation room apart. Ping-pong, I said, play ping-pong. They're using the bats as hatchets...

LEWIS: Grace, please...we have a problem here. I'll be with you shortly...

DONAHUE: (*Moving to go.*) Then we'll leave you to it. Come on, Martha.

LEWIS: Don't go.

DONAHUE: What are you talking about? I've got to go...and Martha as well.

LEWIS: Grace, the Inspector here is trying to force me to give a psychiatric examination to a political prisoner. I am refusing. I want your support, please.

PICKERILL: You want her as a witness as well?

LEWIS: Isn't that the way you work?

PICKERILL: Isn't it your job to stand in for your chief?

LEWIS: That is correct.

PICKERILL: Then you've got to examine him. It's your responsibility.

DONAHUE: (*To MOTOCAR.*) Don't smile like that. Sorry, Doctor. Alright, we'll stay. Okay, Martha, we'll take our break now. I declare this our break-time. You two lads do your stuff now. Let chaos reign.

LEWIS: (*To PICKERILL.*) I am rejecting that particular responsibility. Whether this man is sane or mad is not something we can judge within the present situation. It is not a psychiatric opinion you are seeking, it is a political attitude.

PICKERILL: Doctor, all I want is a scientific opinion...

DONAHUE: You can have my opinion if you want.

LEWIS: Grace!

DONAHUE: We're still in our break-time. Do you mind if my junior and me have a smoke while we witness this confrontation? It's impolite, I know, but we do need it. The whole place is falling to pieces you see. Nothing is

227

worth it. The orderlies don't take a blind bit of notice of what I say to them. Have you got your little tin of equipment there, Martha my love? Roll us a couple while we're waiting. Carry on now Doctor. Stick up for yourself. Don't let him walk all over you now, the great bully. You've let us down you know, you soldiers and all. I never want to see another soldier as long as I live. You're useless, useless.

(*SYMONDS rolls two cigarettes.*)

LEWIS: Grace, I'm sorry that I have to ask you to do this but I must protect myself. Do you think I should examine him?

DONAHUE: (*Throwing the bundle of sheets on the floor.*) I don't care! Why should I care?

(*Pause. DONAHUE sits on a basket next to SYMONDS and they light their cigarettes.*)

MOTOCAR: Dodadodadodadoda. I'd better get down to it. Yawn.

PICKERILL: Shut up, man. Give me time to think. I don't know what the hell to do.

LEWIS: I suggest you simply take him back and tell your superiors of my decision.

PICKERILL: I can't do that. He goes on trial in two days.

LEWIS: You're actually going to put him on trial ten days before Independence?

PICKERILL: Of course. He committed a crime, we think.

DONAHUE: Why don't you just shoot him?

PICKERILL: (*Angrily.*) I don't like that kind of talk from a woman! It's not right.

DONAHUE: He's a terrorist, isn't he? You don't bother to keep them when you catch them. What's so special about him?

PICKERILL: I didn't say he was a terrorist. He might be. And what the army does out there in the bush is their affair. You've no right to assume that I agree with it...

MOTOCAR: Dodadodadoda...

PICKERILL: Shut up, damn you! Three hours in that bloody jeep I had of you, now keep quiet!

MOTOCAR: I will get married within the next year and join the ranks of the ama-Doda. The ama-Tjaha is for boys, not men.

LEWIS: (*To PICKERILL.*) Will you go now?

PICKERILL: No. I'll have to ring through and ask headquarters what steps to take. Will you give me your reasons?

DONAHUE: He's given you his reasons. He thinks it's a waste of time.

PICKERILL: I asked him, not you.

SYMONDS: That's what he said. It's a waste of time.

LEWIS: Don't get involved, Martha. I'll do the explaining thank you.

SYMONDS: And I just sit here? Okay, I'll do that. My ward is going to be in chaos but I'm needed here. He's smiling again, Sister.

DONAHUE: What are you smiling at? Have you wet yourself, you bad boy?

MOTOCAR: (*Sniffing up the smoke of their cigarettes.*) Waaah! Waaah!

DONAHUE/SYMONDS: (*Laughing.*) Waaah! Waaah!

PICKERILL: (*Picking up the telephone and dialling O.*) Hello...operator...get me a line will you?...Twenty minutes? Why so long?...Alright...(*Replaces receiver.*) Twenty bloody minutes. This is ridiculous!

(*MOTOCAR explores the shelves, picks up a clean, folded sheet.*)

LEWIS: In that case we shall just have to leave you to it, Inspector...

(*Goes to leave.*)

PICKERILL: No way. You stay right where you are!

LEWIS: I have a hospital to run...

PICKERILL: (*Barring his exit.*) I said stay where you are. You'll have to wait.

LEWIS: (*Flaring up.*) I'm sick to death of this stupid behaviour and I am leaving to get on with my work. You have no right to stop me.

PICKERILL: (*Standing aside.*) Okay, go on, leave. (*Pause.*) As long as you realise you'll be committing an offence.

DONAHUE: Oh, he's a hard man this one. I bet the hairs on his chest would put a scrubbing-brush to shame. You're a great lad, one of the best.

LEWIS: Grace, it would be helpful if you would let me deal with this. (*To PICKERILL.*) Get out. Get out of this hospital. Go on, get out.

PICKERILL: You are obstructing the law. You are obstructing a policeman in the execution of his duty. You are defying a government instruction.

DONAHUE: Sounds like a hanging job to me, Doctor.

LEWIS: You can't make any of that stick. It's completely fatuous and I shan't let it pass. I will report you for this. (*Pause.*) What a sense of priorities you people have. But you must have your own way, oh yes, to hell with all the rest. I am appalled by your behaviour…atrocious stupidity…this place won't survive and who will wonder?

MOTOCAR: (*Over SYMONDS's shoulder, looking at the folded sheet in his hands.*) What did I give you for your last essay? C-minus? I hope this will be better. Before we even leave the first paragraph, I don't remember saying that I thought Ernest Hemingway was the best African writer of his generation. Whom did I say it was? Wilbur Smith surely? Robert Ruark perhaps? Maybe Doris Lessing?

PICKERILL: Not now, eh?

MOTOCAR: Yours was no better. If you get any more than D-plus for this garbage you'll be doing well. When did I say in any tutorial of mine that *The Imprisonment of Obatala* had anything to do with Samuel Beckett? Samuel Beckett is alive and doing well. Why should I usher him through the portals of the University of Pittsburg?

PICKERILL: Knock it off, will you?

MOTOCAR: (*Throwing the sheet on the floor.*) I give out the titles here!

PICKERILL: Pick those up!

MOTOCAR: What easier task for you than to write an essay when there are no texts to study? All Africans are illiterate. What is the point of writing for them?

PICKERILL: I said, pick those up. You put them there now pick them up.

LEWIS: (*Picking up the sheets.*) Don't worry. Relax. The answer is still no. No. No. No.

PICKERILL: Are you saying there are practical difficulties?

LEWIS: No. I am just refusing to go through the motions.

PICKERILL: Then you're breaking your contract.

LEWIS: My notice of resignation went in a week ago.

PICKERILL: That doesn't make any difference. You're still bound by your contract.

MOTOCAR: (*Inhaling the smoke again.*) Waaah!

DONAHUE/SYMONDS: Waaah!

MOTOCAR: Eater of men. Stabber of heaven. Calf of a black cow. Thunderer. Black pig. May I marry? (*DONAHUE and SYMONDS laugh.*)

PICKERILL: What are you girls smoking?

DONAHUE: We're witnesses.

PICKERILL: You run a pretty shambolic hospital here.

LEWIS: Put it out.

DONAHUE: We're still in our break.

LEWIS: I said, put it out!

DONAHUE: (*Pause.*) What did this African do then?

PICKERILL: You heard what he said, put it out! You talk to me about witnesses. That's illegal, you know. And in a hospital, a bloody mental hospital. Christ, no wonder we're in the mess we're in. You've got chaos here, d'you know that? (*Telephone rings. PICKERILL answers it.*) No! There's no one called Mr Moffat here! Stop putting wrong calls through to this number man...Now get me that line...Never mind about the cost centre...tsetsha! (*Pause.*) Hello? (*Rattles the cradle.*) Hello...Bastard, he's cut me off. (*Replaces receiver.*) Absolute chaos you've got here. What an organisation.

SYMONDS: Do you want to hear my latest, Grace?

DONAHUE: She writes songs, beautiful songs. I've told her to send them to a publisher or a group but she never does.

SYMONDS: I've only got the words, no music.

DONAHUE: Sometimes I think your words are better than your music and then I think, no, the music is better than the words.

LEWIS: Not now if you don't mind.

SYMONDS: I haven't even got a title for it yet...

PICKERILL: Christ Almighty.

DONAHUE: I feel ten times better. This morning I felt as though my heart was going to crack right open but that's gone away now. Come on, Martha, let's hear it.

SYMONDS: They're not interested.

MOTOCAR: I am, I am. Creative writing is my speciality. I trained up a whole generation of American novelists and taught them the ways of Zen, Captain Marvel and moose-hunting.

SYMONDS: Of what a perfect length is the African day.

How strange is sleep.

How odd is darkness.

Here on the high plateau the air is cool

And my plants grow to eight feet and more

Outside the dispensary door.

MOTOCAR: Excellent. I particularly liked the juxtaposition of a spatial mystery, e.g. 'how odd is darkness' with a vegetable conundrum, 'my plants', i.e. plants which are an extension of my own being becoming eight feet and more viz. outstripping my physical height while extending my consciousness through genial hallucinations affecting Time. I like, yeah, I like it.

SYMONDS: Thanks.

(*Telephone rings. PICKERILL snatches it up.*)

PICKERILL: No...there's no meeting, no palaver here...

MOTOCAR: (*Rushing for the telephone.*) Ngi Nzula mine!

(*PICKERILL stops MOTOCAR in his tracks with a punch. MOTOCAR doubles up and kneels on the floor, groaning. PICKERILL carefully replaces the telephone.*)

PICKERILL: That's quite a switchboard you've got there. Same as everything else in this bloody place. Help me with him.

LEWIS: Don't sit him up, he's better off where he is. I think I'll go now. The Mpesu brothers will have massacred each other...

PICKERILL: (*Loudly.*) He was found on the Inyanga mountain two hours after old chief Senzangakona was shot in his own chicken-run. He had this case in his hand. He was wearing a suit and a hat. He only got as far as me because it was a couple of journalists picked him up. No gun. No alibi. He told me in the jeep on the way here that he had just graduated from Bible college in Glasgow.

DONAHUE: Now you mention the Bible. We've got thousands of men who know about the Bible in here. Do you know that there are seven hundred sects of the Christian church in Africa alone? If he went to Bible college you can assume he's mad.

MOTOCAR: No, no, he got it all wrong. I only did a short course...(*Sits up.*) What a punch. Did you see that punch? It only travelled six inches.

(*PICKERILL helps MOTOCAR to his feet.*)

PICKERILL: Go on then, I'll take him back. (*Pause.*) Have you applied for your exit visa yet, Doctor?

MOTOCAR: May I have that cigarette now? You hurt me.

LEWIS: Would you care to amplify that question?

PICKERILL: (*Giving MOTOCAR a cigarette and lighting it for him.*) You are leaving I think. You are one of those who are leaving. You've got to be. There's a look about you. Yes, you're on your bicycle alright.

DONAHUE: Don't start, Martha.

(*SYMONDS cries quietly.*)

LEWIS: Did you hear that? He threatened me. I will report you for that.

PICKERILL: Why should the government help you if you won't do the job you're paid for? Yes, it's a threat. Think about it.

LEWIS: You heard what he said, Grace? Martha? He threatened me.

DONAHUE: Did I? Grobbler's gone. He won't be back.

You're going. What's going to happen to us? Who's going to run this place? And look at poor Martha, a picture of misery. You know, she believed all that crap you talked, Doctor. Doctor Lewis is a great bleeding heart you know. Famous throughout the wards.

LEWIS: Come on, Martha, snap out of it.

SYMONDS: I renewed my contract because of you. I'm stuck here for three years.

LEWIS: You can always break your contract.

PICKERILL: That's your prescription for everything, isn't it?

SYMONDS: You did say we might go away together at one time.

DONAHUE: Oh, he's moved on from there. It's all over, Martha my love. Don't say he didn't warn you. Impossible he said. You were an aberration. He must marry a woman of his own faith. Isn't that right, Doctor? A big, juicy Jewess. And he can't abide people who change their religion for emotional reasons.

LEWIS: You don't seriously expect me to bow to this kind of pressure do you? The Ministry of Health will cancel any attempt to interfere with the granting of my visa.

PICKERILL: The Ministry of Health is run by Africans, Doctor, which is why you are leaving.

LEWIS: That is not so.

DONAHUE: Don't lie. Of course it is.

LEWIS: I'm leaving for personal reasons. I have always supported the idea of independence and majority rule.

PICKERILL: Ideas are ideas. He's an idea. I'm an idea. These two women are ideas. Why don't you support us?

LEWIS: Don't be deliberately naive, Inspector. You and your short-sighted colleagues have seen to it that there can be no rapport between the races here. It will take at least ten years before any kind of trust can be re-established. I cannot wait that long before I have the right conditions in which to do my work. You, and prejudiced bureaucrats like you, have forced me to abandon this country. And when it does collapse, and when there is wholesale butchery as we had in the Congo and Uganda and Nigeria, I would like you to remember who created the situation. You have brought ten years of profiteering and unwritten apartheid in this country at the expense of the entire future, and for that you can have my utter contempt. You are blind, ignorant bigots.

PICKERILL: Have you quite finished?

LEWIS: I could go on, but, I think, to little effect. You don't listen. People like you never do.

PICKERILL: I can't choose, Doctor. I have to listen. That's what I'm paid for. But don't expect me to like you for it. Now, listen to me, let me put it quite straight to you. Either you give this prisoner a psychiatric examination, or you don't leave Rhodesia, or Zimbabwe.

LEWIS: You can control the former, but not the latter.

PICKERILL: You'd be surprised Doctor. I'm actually staying on. Now isn't that a turn-up for the books? And you know, they will probably promote me as well. That couldn't be because I know my job and do what I'm paid for – it must be because they're all crazy these black people. Don't you think so?
(*Pause.*)

LEWIS: I give up. Don't tell me any more. That's it. (*Pause.*) Do they want him certified insane?

PICKERILL: Who's they?

LEWIS: Your superiors.

PICKERILL: Any particular colour you fancy?

LEWIS: I don't care who they are. Just tell me exactly what they want. I want to satisfy their needs to the letter. There's no problem, none whatsoever. They shall have what they want. I will give you a certificate to say he is mad, and another certificate to say he is sane. You can then use which one you like.

PICKERILL: Don't be so bloody stupid!

LEWIS: Not at all. I am in no position to behave with any honesty. You need a certificate to get him either on or off the hook, I'll give you one, two! Integrity has nothing to do with this situation. I will be corrupted, gladly. Use me.

PICKERILL: I want a proper test.

DONAHUE: (*Waking SYMONDS.*) You're sleeping with your mouth open. Aaron here finds that off-putting. Do you ever wake up and find her sleeping with her mouth open?

LEWIS: You may go now.

SYMONDS: I had a dream.

DONAHUE: Martha had a dream, Doctor. I don't think we'll bother to go back on the wards. Half an hour without us and there is absolute confusion. They'll be eating each other.

SYMONDS: In my dream I was allowed to break my contract and keep my termination benefit, and my pension accrual. I was allowed currency clearance and I drove to Johannesburg but you'd gone to Australia. So I drove to Australia. Sod!

(*Telephone rings. LEWIS picks it up, beating PICKERILL to it.*)

MOTOCAR: That will be for Moshesh.

LEWIS: (*Pause.*) Are you Moshesh as well?

MOTOCAR: Am I Moshesh? Have I got the face of the BaMokotedi?

LEWIS: (*Into phone.*) No, he's not here…(*Replaces phone.*)

MOTOCAR: Ah, he is, he is. (*Stands up.*)

PICKERILL: Sit down, man! Who keeps making these calls?

MOTOCAR: North of the Black Umfolosi River lived the Ndwande under Zwide; south of it the Mthethwa under their chief Dingiswayo; in between was a small clan ruled by Senzangakona. They called themselves the Zulu and many had loud voices.

PICKERILL: Who is Moshesh?

MOTOCAR: He is at the meeting.

PICKERILL: What meeting?

MOTOCAR: He is at this meeting.

PICKERILL: There's no meeting here.

MOTOCAR: Oh yes, there is. First a prayer-meeting. This is the prayer-meeting. We are all praying for a miracle. Then we will have a meeting to discuss my marriage in terms of the miracle. What is the greatest miracle in the Bible? Ah, not too good on religious knowledge. You will get Z minus for that.

LEWIS: Shall we get on with it? The examination will only take fifteen minutes.

MOTOCAR: Certainly Doctor.

(*MOTOCAR bustles about, shifting SYMONDS and DONAHUE and making a throne to sit on. PICKERILL follows him.*)

PICKERILL: Hey, hold on. Have you got any friends in this hospital?

MOTOCAR: Only you.

LEWIS: What's the matter?

PICKERILL: He's tied in with that joker on the switchboard somehow. Bloody mind-readers or something.

DONAHUE: Inspector, those men are monkeys. Don't take any notice. Come on. Let's get this over with…

PICKERILL: Nurse, would you go and check that switchboard for me? All I want to know is whether it's the regular operator. Just have a look, you don't have to say anything.

LEWIS: Inspector, the switchboard here is notorious…

PICKERILL: It's more than that at the moment. It's psychic. Will you do that for me, Nurse?

SYMONDS: If it will get me out of here, with pleasure. Shall I get some tea?

MOTOCAR: Please, no sugar. (*SYMONDS exits.*) Now, check the list…Mzilikasi…Moshesh. Lobengula. Should I have asked Lewanika and Khama? A quick rehearsal of my opening address before the doors of the conference chamber are opened…(*Clears his throat.*) There will be delegates here who will recall in their opening speeches the Festival of the First Fruits when, as young men, they slew a pitch-black bull with their bare hands. As we speak a common language, or common enough, there will be no need for simultaneous translation though old pictures may be circulated in brochure form. Before it is too late, I ask to be married. I ask permission from this great assembly to wed; not the woman of my choice but

the woman whom you give to me, from any land,
anywhere. I think that hangs quite well together. Yes.
(*Pause.*) You're not the brightest group to have in a
tutorial, not by a long stretch. At times you irritate me
most profoundly. Try this. Compare the affirmative
cynicism of Chinua Achebe, James Joyce and the bare
bones of Sophoclean drama. Criticise, discuss and
explode all myths connected with Oedipus and the
Easter Rising of 1916. What was Doctor Johnson's
dictionary definition of the equator? That which goes
round the earth once and twice round the neck of Africa.
You have all failed and I will recommend your removal
from this place of learning, by force if need be, children,
dogs and cattle! Out! Out of my sight, you halfwits,
morons!

PICKERILL: (*Whispering.*) Any the wiser? He was like this
all the way here. Complete rubbish. I don't understand a
word of it.

LEWIS: Inspector, please don't interfere. It might be better
if you left…

MOTOCAR: No! That man is my friend. My bodyguard.
Would you leave your Emperor unprotected? Think of
the risk of assassination, a *coup d'etat.* He stays, he stays…

LEWIS: Very well, very well.

DONAHUE: See, somebody loves you. Does that make
you feel good?

MOTOCAR: Niga mina lo wetu!

LEWIS: What is he saying?

PICKERILL: He wants the brief-case. He says it's his
friend.

LEWIS: Give it to him then.

PICKERILL: I'll have to remove a few things first.
(*PICKERILL opens the brief-case and takes out a big stone.*)

DONAHUE: Is that a stone? What does he lug a great
stone around for?

MOTOCAR: I want everything.

PICKERILL: Not the stone, chamware, not the stone.

MOTOCAR: Tell this masepa hela to give me my goods!
And those papers. I must have those papers.

PICKERILL: You keep a civil tongue in your head. What do you want the papers for?

MOTOCAR: Every meeting must have papers. Haven't you found that out for yourself? Agendas, minutes, essays, notes.

DONAHUE: Well, a real smart alec. Do you have to have stones in your meeting, boy? African confetti for your wedding?

LEWIS: Grace, I'd be obliged if you wouldn't interfere. Give him what he wants.

(*PICKERILL hands MOTOCAR the papers and the stone. MOTOCAR takes out twelve books and puts them in a neat pile, checking their titles.*)

LEWIS: Are you prepared to give me any background to his offence?

PICKERILL: Alleged offence. I told you before, we think he shot a chief. Well, the old man used to be a chief, poor bastard. I knew him from when I was on bush patrol.

LEWIS: Any idea why...

(*Telephone rings. PICKERILL runs across, grabs it.*)

PICKERILL: Voetsak man! (*Slams the receiver back.*) Bloody bastards!

DONAHUE: Temper, temper.

LEWIS: And who was that one for?

PICKERILL: For Mr Sophocles, a Greek gentleman. Was he at the meeting? I'm going to sort these bastards out.

(*PICKERILL strides off. MOTOCAR carries the stone above his head. Lays it down reverently. Shouts, crashing, confusion from off.*)

PICKERILL: (*Off.*) What do you want? Hey...Christ man...get off...

LEWIS: (*Coming across.*) What's going on out there? Inspector, are you alright?

(*PICKERILL is catapulted back on stage, blood on his mouth, his jacket half-off, his shoulder-holster empty.*)

PICKERILL: Bastards...They took my gun...they jumped me...

LEWIS: Grace, this is an emergency…Alert the security…
  (*Explosions, gunfire, ululations off.*)
DONAHUE: It's a bomb! It's a bomb! Clear the building!
  (*DONAHUE runs for the door. PICKERILL pulls her down.*)
PICKERILL: Get down!
  (*LEWIS throws himself flat, DONAHUE continues
  screaming, struggling. Pop-soul music off.*)
MOTOCAR: (*Holding a book aloft.*) Opposite me, at six
  o'clock, a chief and apostle of words, James, son of
  Apheus, Sophocles. Welcome, welcome. Will you sit
  down? (*Places the book.*) Good of you to have come so far…
  (*Enter SYMONDS wearing a grotesque African mask, a
  transistor radio under one arm, a cardboard-box in the other.
  She charges into MOTOCAR's arms. He grabs her, spins
  her round.*)
  Do you think you can love me? Do you think you can
  settle down with me?
  (*MOTOCAR takes the radio and cardboard-box away from
  her and she collapses into DONAHUE'S arms.*)
DONAHUE: Martha…is that you Martha…Oh, your poor
  face, your poor pretty face…(*Heaves at the mask.*) Keep
  still and I'll get this off you…
SYMONDS: (*Pushing DONAHUE away.*) No, no! Don't
  touch it!
MOTOCAR: Oh, it suits her. Beautiful. The masks my
  people make are prized the world over.
PICKERILL: Shut up! Just stay put, keep down…
  (*SYMONDS and DONAHUE whisper, whimper, argue.*)
MOTOCAR: (*Holding another book aloft.*) Here is an old
  comrade, Father Goncalo de Silveira, a creeping Jesuit.
  Is the black produced by burning blacker than the black
  produced by an absence of white Christ in the washing?
  (*Places the book.*) At three. (*Stands by SYMONDS.*)
  Hm…isn't she beautiful? Would you like to have her,
  Inspector?
PICKERILL: Get down, man. Stop that shit!
MOTOCAR: (*Returning to his throne, switching off the radio on
  the way.*) They must sit in the correct order of
  precedence. At a round table this poses its problems…

PICKERILL: Get down off there!

MOTOCAR: When Monomotapa sits, all sit.

PICKERILL: Motocar, do as you're told...

MOTOCAR: Monomotapa. Monomotapa. You don't listen when a man gives his name.

PICKERILL: Do you want to get yourself killed, you stupid bastard?

MOTOCAR: I will not be killed, but you will unless you behave yourselves and try harder with your homework. (*Telephone rings MOTOCAR gets off his throne and crosses to it.*)

PICKERILL: Leave it! Don't touch that phone...

MOTOCAR: (*Picking up telephone.*) Hold on. (*To PICKERILL.*) Don't be anxious, Inspector. It will only be the news that Lobengula's indunas are back from London. I have asked them to address the meeting and give their report. (*Into phone.*) Sorry about that. There is some confusion in here...yes...oh yes, they will help me, I'm sure they will...(*To PICKERILL.*) You will help me with my meeting, won't you? (*Into phone.*) Yes, very readily. They are most kind, most sympathetic...They should keep away from the door which is now being locked until the meeting is over...

(*To PICKERILL.*) Do you understand that? You must not go near that door. Alright? (*Into phone.*) Yes, give us a few minutes to sort ourselves out and we'll get started in here...(*Replaces receiver.*)

(*Lights fade to blackout.*)

End of Act One.

ACT TWO

Lights snap up on the characters in the exact positions they were in at the end of Act One.

MOTOCAR: Know much about the brain, Inspector?

PICKERILL: So you are a bloody terrorist. That's nice. And you've brought your mates along for the ride. Perfect. All I need. Christ, I know you bastards like a soft target but I thought you might have more dignity than to attack an undefended mental hospital for your own people!

MOTOCAR: Do you know anything at all about the human brain, Inspector?

LEWIS: Please...Inspector. Don't react. (*To MOTOCAR.*) Now I think you want us to help you with your meeting. Is that right?

MOTOCAR: What shape is the human brain, Inspector?

LEWIS: Am I correct? You seem most anxious we should help you.

MOTOCAR: Yes, yes, in a moment. First things first. Inspector, seen from the left, what shape is the human brain?
(*Pause.*)

DONAHUE: Either you men do something, or I'm just getting up and going out that door with Martha...

PICKERILL: Stay put! You're not going anywhere. (*Pause.*) Shit.

LEWIS: Answer him, Inspector.

PICKERILL: I don't know. I really don't. You tell me.

DONAHUE: This child is terrified out of her wits, she can hardly breathe. She won't let me take this mask off...

LEWIS: Grace, sit still, give me a moment! Be sensible!

MOTOCAR: Look closely at the Doctor, Inspector. He is a long-headed Caucasian type. He has a truly European skull. Yours is similar. Mine, rounder, like a football. The human brain, seen from the left side, is in the shape of Africa. It is in that continent that my meeting must take place. Here. Inside this bucket of old bone. Hard outside, soft in.

PICKERILL: Man, that's very interesting, but…to more practical matters. All I want is this – those hooligans called off. You're not going to achieve anything here…

MOTOCAR: See, Ethiopia is swallowing and mastication. The Congo is hearing. Nigeria is conscious thought. The Sahara, salivation. Egypt, sensory elaboration. Tunisia, tongue. Namibia, perceptual judgement. South Africa, contralateral vision. Rhodesia, visual and auditory recollection.

DONAHUE: (*Furiously.*) Will you do something with him, you hopeless pair of dummies? Get him out of here at least…

LEWIS: That is extremely perceptive of you. Yes, I enjoy that…er…that analogy.

MOTOCAR: Now, my problem is this. How do I get inside that brain to have my meeting? Obviously I must operate. This is the right kind of place. You do lobotomies here I believe. So, there must be tools. I will have to shave the scalp, incise the skin, drill several holes, then out will come the bone-saw, a little square lifts out. Trepanning, I love that word, reminds me of looking for gold. Trepanning.

PICKERILL: Man, just drop all that. You can't touch anyone in this room. That is out of the question. Now, these girls are very frightened. The Doctor has work to do. You and I must get back. (*Pause.*) I accept that you are sick. If that's enough, call off your friends, eh? Ring the switchboard.

MOTOCAR: Well, if you're not going to let me do an operation, I'll just improvise. (*Picks up the cardboard-box which SYMONDS brought in.*) A poor substitute. I could do brain surgery. My hand is steady enough. So, trepanning, trepanning, trepanning. (*Takes off the lid.*) Hmmm. Just as I thought. Phew. This one has gone off.

DONAHUE: (*Screaming.*) Will you stop this fucking nonsense before I go mad? You, Motocar, whatever your bloody name is, you're crazy. Do you understand? You're not right in the head. Now…let us help you, properly… like we're trained to do…I'm sorry, but give us a chance…

MOTOCAR: Maggots.

DONAHUE: Let my girl take that thing off her face.

MOTOCAR: No, she has to keep it on for the meeting. This brain needs cleaning out. If we're going to have a meeting in it we need the right atmosphere. Jesus, the maggots have laid eggs. Look. (*Takes out a plastic container of capsules.*)

LEWIS: Where did you get those?

MOTOCAR: Who is short of amytal in this hospital?

DONAHUE: Thieving bastards. We needed those!

MOTOCAR: And you may have them. (*Brings out three more containers and places them at the four compass points around the stone.*) Doctor, how many pills have you made my people swallow? How many sedatives? How many bromides? One for you. One for you. One for you. And one for you.

PICKERILL: For the love of God, stop this now.

MOTOCAR: Inspector, you were silent on the subject of the brain. I suggest you extend that curfew to God as well. My people opened their mouths for you, Doctor. Have you got the courage to do the same for them? Who is curing whom in this house of strange medicines? Now, the meeting. I could do with some help in ushering the delegates to their places. (*Picks up books.*) Here is our Chief Lobengula whom I usher to four. Now, Inspector, I want you to take Carl Mauch, gold prospector, to nine.

PICKERILL: Here?

MOTOCAR: Exactly. Now, Doctor – a doctor for a doctor. Will you take Doctor Matthew Price of London to two o'clock? (*Gives him one book, then another.*) And next to him our Lobengula at four.

(*LEWIS quickly places the books on the clock.*)

I think I'd better do the next one myself. Protocol demands it. Here, on my right, at eleven o'clock, Simon Peter Victoria, Queen of Great Britain and Ireland, Empress of India. No mention of Africa…(*Places the book.*) How good of you to come all the way to my barren and miserable land. (*Picks up the sheaf of papers.*) Sister, see these papers? Would you be so good as to place them for

us? This delegate, our man at one o'clock, is still in
flight. He will need them as reference documents as soon
as he joins us. When he touches down at the airport I
will have to pop out to meet him. He will expect it.

DONAHUE: Why should I be interested in your
bloody papers?

MOTOCAR: (*Sternly.*) These are the minutes of the
meetings which Doctor Henry Kissinger, the American
Secretary of State, has had with Mr Vorster, Mr Smith,
Mr Kaunda, Mr Nyerere, Mr Callaghan, Mr Everybody,
about the settlement of the Rhodesian question. (*Thrusts
the papers under DONAHUE's nose.*)

LEWIS: Do as he asks, Grace. Do as the Emperor asks.

DONAHUE: Where do you want him? (*Takes the papers.*)

MOTOCAR: Can you not tell the time? Here!
(*DONAHUE takes the papers and returns to SYMONDS.*)

MOTOCAR: (*Taking a pile of books.*) Simon Zelotes Mzilikasi
here, at seven, next to his friend Bartholomew Robert
Moffat of Kuruman at eight. Old chamwares, mates.
They work well together. Here at five, Thomas Moshesh,
wise Chief of the BaMokotedi of the Sutho nation,
already sitting at ease, resting, thoughtful of great
questions. (*Pause.*) Are we all here? No, here is an empty
seat, at ten o'clock. What does the name read, Doctor?

LEWIS: I cannot see from here.

MOTOCAR: It is a difficult spelling. Hm. We are missing
one delegate. He may still be outside. We will have to
wait for him. (*Pause. Phone rings.*) That will be him. He is
here. (*Answers the phone.*) Yes, we are ready, all set. Has
he arrived? Oh...I see. (*Replaces the receiver then places two
books at ten o'clock.*)

PICKERILL: Who's the double-helping?

MOTOCAR: Eater of men. Stabber of heaven. Calf of a
black cow. The great elephant is late. We have had a
ship-to-shore cable from Tshaka the Terrible. There have
been contrary winds all the way from the West Indies.
He is having a difficult passage. (*MOTOCAR stands in
front of each book on the clock in turn. Bows, greets the
delegate. Dialogue continues over.*)

245

PICKERILL: (*To DONAHUE.*) What is the amytal stuff?

DONAHUE: It's one of the strongest tranquillisers we use here. Twenty-five will kill you.

PICKERILL: Jesus Christ. They're ruthless these bastards. Half of them are schoolchildren, schoolchildren with bloody machine-guns.

DONAHUE: You couldn't beat them though, could you?

PICKERILL: In this terrain? No chance. They're back in the bush in five minutes...

MOTOCAR: May we have silence please? I am about to give my opening address. (*Beckons SYMONDS over.*) Come on.

PICKERILL: Yeah, yeah, sorry. You carry on. What a balls-up.

LEWIS: We have no choice but to co-operate. Come on. Make the best of it.

(*Pause. MOTOCAR mounts his throne, sits down. SYMONDS below.*)

MOTOCAR: You see before you a simple bachelor who has much to share. My empire stretches from the Gwai River in the east, all the way west to the Indian Ocean: from the Zambesi River in the north to the Limpopo in the south. It is a great, wide, rich land, the heart of Africa. Now I wish to take a wife. It is customary to consult all interested parties as to whom should be my partner.

PICKERILL: Somebody as mad as yourself! I've gone as far as I'm going...

SYMONDS: You can't get out of it. They're serious. (*To MOTOCAR.*) We are ready. Which one of the delegates would you like to speak first?

MOTOCAR: The Jesuit, the Portuguese Jesuit. Will he rise?

SYMONDS: Will you do it, Doctor?

LEWIS: Oh, I see...you want me here? (*Moves to three o'clock.*) Three o'clock.
(*Pause.*)

MOTOCAR: Well? What are you apostle of? Olive oil? Cork? Port-wine?

LEWIS: Exactly what do you wish to know?

MOTOCAR: What does your God say about marriage?

LEWIS: He says it is a good thing.

MOTOCAR: That's not what you told me last week.

LEWIS: Didn't I?

MOTOCAR: Saint Paul. You said Saint Paul said that a man should only marry if he has to. So, the question is, do I have to?

LEWIS: Yes, I suppose it is.

MOTOCAR: Not much use then, are you?

LEWIS: It appears not.

MOTOCAR: Time for my favourite story of yours, out of your thousands and thousands.

LEWIS: Which one is that?

MOTOCAR: The matje mhope story. (*Picks up the stone, weighs it in his hand.*)

LEWIS: I do not know that story.

MOTOCAR: You do not know the white stone story?

LEWIS: That is one I do not know.

MOTOCAR: The Whitsun story? No? (*Turns to DONAHUE.*) Queen Victoria will know it. Tell him the Whitsun story. What is Whitsun all about?

DONAHUE: I have forgotten.

MOTOCAR: The Queen of Ireland has forgotten Pentecost?

DONAHUE: I have heard of it.

MOTOCAR: (*Putting the stone down.*) You have heard of what you celebrate? That is sound practice. (*Pause.*) My favourite story, told me by this Jesuit gentleman here, concerns the descent of a holy bird from heaven, bringing the gift of tongues to twelve Apostles that they might speak to men of all nations. Strange that you should have forgotten the best story in the Bible. (*Pause.*) So, my Portugoose, you have nothing sensible to say about my marriage? Nothing at all?

LEWIS: I am sorry that I am not able to help.

MOTOCAR: I have killed men for less.

LEWIS: Yes.

MOTOCAR: You want to die? Are you as tired of life as I am?

LEWIS: No, I do not want to die. I wish to live.

MOTOCAR: Then you can fold the sheets.

(Pause.)

LEWIS: The sheets?

PICKERILL: Do as he says.

(LEWIS picks up some dirty sheets.)

MOTOCAR: No, not those. Those. *(Points at a pile of clean sheets.)*

DONAHUE: They're folded already.

MOTOCAR: Do you want to die? I have absolute power. I ask you again. Do you want to die?

DONAHUE: No!

MOTOCAR: A sheet that has been folded may, under certain circumstances, usefully be folded again. Take one end…*(Helps LEWIS with the sheet, taking an end across to DONAHUE, then involving PICKERILL.)*…break it out. Three ends, not four. Fold it, fold it. *(To PICKERILL.)* Sophocles, a delta, delta! *(He organises them so they form a triangle with the sheet.)* Now, lift it. Raise it! *(To SYMONDS.)* Babiyane! Whistle, whistle. *(SYMONDS tries to whistle through the mask, fails.)* No, no, a long whistle, like this. All of you whistle. Come on, whistle. *(Whistles.)* I can't do it for you. I am in the reception lounge contemplating the fact that a one-legged creator is nothing but a God who limps. Whistle, more, more. A long, sustained blast. That's it. *(Holding the sheet aloft, they whistle one long high note.)* Henry is coming, Henry, Henry, Henry, the Kiss-in-the-ringer who will save those who cannot save themselves. He will establish the first Feast of the Handover amongst his Chosen People. The great bird descends. The earth shakes. The Holy Spirit flies down on his wide American wings, landing on runway twelve! *(They lower the sheet slowly, stretching it taut so it vibrates.)* Here at the airport a large crowd has gathered. As the dove alights, tongues of flame streaming from its throat, the people burst into spontaneous song, holy, holy, holy! The whole of this land dwells in the shadow of his swept-back wings. His jet-engines go into reverse-thrust to assist it with the braking process. On the tarmac the twelve Apostles suddenly speak their minds in all the languages of Man. (*Pause.*) Speak...please...speak up for me. Help me. Speak, I beg you, speak.

(*Pause. They let go of the sheet. MOTOCAR paces over it, beseeching, tense, expectant. Then they all speak together.*)

SYMONDS: Spiritus Domini replevit orbem terrarum alleluja: et hoc quod continet omnia, scientiam habet vocis.

DONAHUE: M'anam go raibh sé millteanach fuar ar an loch.

LEWIS: Kai ten potheinen patrida paraschou autois, Paradeisou palin poion politas autous.

PICKERILL: Basopa zimvwana yena hayi lahlega; noko wena lahiegile yena mina zo tshaya wena.

MOTOCAR: (*Delighted.*) That's it. Now don't lose it, stay with it, hold on...(*Sweeps the sheet up and puts it round PICKERILL's shoulders, steering him to four o'clock.*) Lobengula, the indunas have arrived back from London. Will you see them now?

PICKERILL: Me? You want me to do him?

MOTOCAR: You are him. You are my friend. Squat. (PICKERILL obeys.) Assume your seat. (Going to SYMONDS and taking her hand, bringing her across to PICKERILL.) My wife here is suddenly very old, very frightened...an old, old man who has been a long way across the sea. Lobengula is tired after his heavy lunch in the luxury dining-suite of the conference centre. (Rattles a container of amytat capsules under PICKERILL's nose.) Wakey-wakey! We have a report from Babiyane. Queen Victoria...(Turns to DONAHUE, puts a container of capsules at her feet.) ...you won't mind if this is given in your presence? I'm sure you won't be embarrassed. (Pause. MOTOCAR puts another container at LEWIS's feet and the final one at SYMONDS's.) Now, speak, Babiyane, induna of Lobengula. And keep it short. The delegates are likely to nod off at this hour of the day. (Pause.) Well, cat got your tongue? We are waiting. Very nervous. Let me help you. Let me help you all.

(*MOTOCAR picks up the container of capsules at LEWIS's feet and puts them in LEWIS's hands, then pushes the container to the edge of LEWIS's lip. Pause. Then he tilts the container to one side so it rattles, then back, smiling at LEWIS, nodding his head in rhythm. LEWIS cottons on, relief flooding his face. He shakes the container in the right rhythm. MOTOCAR moves on to PICKERILL, DONAHUE. They have already understood and are shaking their containers. MOTOCAR laughs, urges them on, bounding around the clock. Rhythm rises. Light changes. SYMONDS starts to tremble, breathes very deeply, then screams. PICKERILL, LEWIS and DONAHUE buckle, groaning, breathing very deeply.*) First Babiyane, tell us how you were received by Queen Victoria. What is she like? (*LEWIS starts to crawl from three to nine, DONAHUE stumbles to eleven.*)

SYMONDS: (*In a clear, altered voice.*) When she entered the room where we were waiting, I was stricken with fear and I crouched on the floor with my hands on my stomach and the Queen laughed and said, 'Rise, rise O Babiyane!' And I stood up and saw, ha! She was very small, very, very small, no higher than a calabash of beer, but terrible to look at – a great ruler.

MOTOCAR: You have a letter, Lobengula, sent from this terrible Queen. What advice does she give?

PICKERILL: (*As Lobengula.*) I have no letter.

MOTOCAR: We know. The letter that the Queen sent you was intercepted by Cecil Rhodes. It will be too late. It made him very angry. He wanted to drop it in the sea. It was a good letter.

DONAHUE: (*As Victoria.*) Dear Friend, as you are now being asked by many for permission to seek gold and dig it up in your country, we would have you be wary and firm in resisting proposals that will not bring good to you and your people.

MOTOCAR: And why do these men seek gold in my empire, Mr Carl Mauch?

LEWIS: (*As Mauch, German accent.*) When I saw the white reefs of auriferous quartz glistening in the sun I was startled by the conception of the wealth before me.

The vast extent and beauty of these goldfields is such
that I stood transfixed, struck with wonder and amazement
at the sight. These goldfields are greater than those of
California and Australia put together.

MOTOCAR: And Babiyane, what did you see in London?

SYMONDS: We saw many things. We saw a display of the
new British machine-gun. We saw the vaults of the great
bank where all their gold is kept. We wondered why they
must come to Matabeleland to gather more when they
had so much already – and we were given none as gifts,
a thing we thought miserly. What Matabele would take a
distinguished guest to his kraal to show him a herd of
cattle and not offer the guest one beast? Also we saw the
men of the Aborigines Protection Society.

MOTOCAR: Were they men of God, these men of the
Aborigines Protection Society?

SYMONDS: Some were, some were not.

MOTOCAR: Was one of them our delegate here, Doctor
Price, also of London...(*PICKERILL takes off the sheet,
goes to two o'clock.*) Did you meet Babiyane Doctor?

PICKERILL: (*As Price.*) I did not. It was after my time.

MOTOCAR: You are a political divine, so I am told.

PICKERILL: A fighting parson, sir. A man of the people.
On the fourth of November 1789, I preached a goodish
sermon in which I asserted that by the principles of the
Glorious Revolution of 1688, the English people had
acquired three fundamental rights: one, to choose their
own governors; two, to cashier them for misconduct;
three, to frame a government for themselves.

MOTOCAR: Are the people of England aborigines Doctor?

PICKERILL: They are aboriginal in England.

MOTOCAR: Are these the rights of an aborigine or
an Englishman?

PICKERILL: They are the rights of those who have fought
for them.

MOTOCAR: Do those who have fought for them have any
spare rights for others, especially aborigines who are
not English?

PICKERILL: What rights they have are all spoken for.
    Other men in other lands must find their own rights.
MOTOCAR: So the export of English rights is prohibited?
PICKERILL: Impractical. They do not travel well, like
    some wines.
MOTOCAR: Oh some do, some do…They keep their
    flavour as well as any claret.
PICKERILL: Which may I ask?
MOTOCAR: Prospecting rights. (*Pause.*) And now I am
    pleased to announce that two old comrades, men who
    can see into each other's minds, Moffat, the missionary
    and Mzilikasi, the Chief of the Matabele –
    (*DONAHUE joins PICKERILL. Arm in arm they go to seven
    and eight.*)
    – have got their heads together.
    (*They sit down on the floor. PICKERILL slumps forward.*)
    Mzilikasi, I know that you are sick, I know that you are
    old and find it difficult to speak, but can you remember
    what you said to Mr Moffat here on that first day when
    he entered your kraal with his Bible in his hand?
    (*PICKERILL beckons MOTOCAR to come close. He whispers
    into his ear.*)
    What? Yes…yes…this is what you said…Mzilikasi, say
    this to my friend in the presence of all my indunas. Mr
    Moffat, sir, I do not want to hear the cry of a white man's
    child. I do not want to hear the bark of a white man's
    dog. I do not want to hear the lowing of a white man's
    calf in Matabeleland. (*Pause.*) And then Mzilikasi, after
    Mr Moffat had cured you of a great sickness and saved
    you from death? What did you say then? Ah yes…
    (*PICKERILL whispers again.*)
    My heart is all white as milk. I am still wondering at the
    love of a stranger who never saw me. You have loved
    me. You have fed me. You have protected me. You have
    carried me in your arms. I live today by the stranger of
    another nation. (*Pause.*) Mr Moffat, that love, the love
    you showed the dying chief, was not your own, was it?
    Time and again you said it – Christ it is who loves you
    through me. Moshesh –

(*LEWIS moves to five.*)

– on this point you have made a minority report. You suggest that I marry a white woman but make her accept my ways. Persuade us. Make the meeting accept your proposal. The floor is yours.

(*LEWIS stands in the centre of the clock by the stone.*)

What have you got against Christ?

LEWIS: (*As Moshesh.*) Moffati ka e re Morimo ki khosi ka ena...

MOTOCAR: Mosheshi, these others have used the gift of tongues to speak up for me. Return their favour. Use the Apostles' international language. Show you are prepared to bend that far.

LEWIS: Moffat said that God is a chief like any other chief. I treated this with disdain. I am a king and I will not put myself under the authority of another, especially this ambitious man Christ. I have my kingdom and he has his. Let him stick to his and I will stick to mine. And if he, or any of his people, wish to live with us then they must accept our ways. I am also suspicious of this man Christ as I hear that he orders the brains of men to be drunk from cups and I will have none of that impurity near me, nor the eating of human flesh.

(*PICKERILL, DONAHUE, SYMONDS and MOTOCAR cheer, applaud.*)

MOTOCAR: The delegates are rising in their seats...a standing ovation for Moshesh, well done, well done, well said! Splendid speech!

(*The cheering subsides, then the clapping. Suddenly PICKERILL pitches forward. Then LEWIS. DONAHUE gropes her way to a basket, sits down. Pause.*)

LEWIS: (*As LEWIS, very tired.*) Have you finished with us now?

MOTOCAR: No.

LEWIS: How else can we help you?

MOTOCAR: I would like to provide some entertainment for my guests.

LEWIS: Entertainment?

MOTOCAR: You know...singing and dancing.

DONAHUE: Well, get on with it...

MOTOCAR: No, I mean these chaps here. I want them to do it.

PICKERILL: Oh piss off...no...

LEWIS: (*Struggling to his feet.*) What exactly would you like us to do?

MOTOCAR: 'Izigizumba'.

LEWIS: 'Izigizumba'.

MOTOCAR: Come on, you both know it. You've sung and danced it round a thousand camp-fires as Boy Scouts and on countless buses coming home from rugby games. Izigizumba, when you are ready.

PICKERILL: That's it...this is as far as I go...

LEWIS: (*Half-crawling.*) Izigizumba zumba zumba...(*Pulling at PICKERILL's arm.*) Come on, Inspector...izigizumba zumba ze...

PICKERILL: Man, have you got no pride left?

MOTOCAR: Dance! Dance!

(*PICKERILL and LEWIS, hanging on to each other, circle, stamp and sing.*)

PICKERILL: Izigizumba zumba zumba...

LEWIS: Izigizumba zumba ze...

Hold him down you Zulu warrior

Hold him down you Zulu chief chief chief

(*Repeat.*)

MOTOCAR: Enough! (*LEWIS and PICKERILL collapse.*) Magnificent. The delegates are delighted. A wonderful performance. Thank you, thank you. Now all that remains is the closing hymn and the meeting will be over. You all know it. I could ask for no better choir. Sing for me, sing for us all, 'Nkosi Sikalele Afrika', 'God Save Africa'. (*Pause. LEWIS starts to sing, very shakily. The song comes out of their exhaustion, one by one until they are singing together. MOTOCAR joins them.*)

ALL:

NKOSI SIKALELE AFRIKA,

ASIPHAKHAMISE IGAMA LAYO,

YAMUKHELE INKULEKO ZETHU,

NKOSI SIKALELA,

THINA BANTWANA BAYO.

(*Repeat.*)

HOZA MOYA, HOZA MOYA, SIKALELA,

HOZA MOYA, HOZA MOYA, SIKALELA,

HOZA MOYA, HOZA MOYA, UNQWELE,

HE-USI SIKALELE

HE-THINA BANTWANA BAYO.

(*Repeat.*)

(*From outside the final lines of the chorus are heard, sung by hundreds of voices. Pause. Telephone rings. MOTOCAR crosses and picks it up.*)

MOTOCAR: (*Covering the mouthpiece.*) Excuse me a moment. And thank you, thank you. (*Uncovers mouthpiece.*) Yes, a great success. They have advised me to marry a white woman, the African White Butterfly, if I can catch her. Yes, I am very happy, very happy indeed. Thank you all. Thank all my friends. Now, I am sending one of my helpers out for the file. Give it to her without question. (*Replaces receiver, returns to throne.*) Queen Victoria, will you go and get the file for me? (*Pause. Sits on the throne.*) You have all done wonderfully well. I thank you from the bottom of my heart.

DONAHUE: Me? Go out there? You're joking!

MOTOCAR: Do as you are told, woman.

DONAHUE: They'll make me wear a mask. They'll touch me!

(*MOTOCAR descends from the throne, puts a hand on SYMONDS's head. She stiffens.*)

MOTOCAR: And how do you like your new face?

SYMONDS: It hurts. It's cutting into me.

DONAHUE: You brutal sod! Keeping her in that ugly rotten thing with wire cutting into her head...

MOTOCAR: I thought I told you to go and get the file.

(*DONAHUE exits.*)

The land goes to those who want it most. There are no friendly spirits. We are grazing animals, we wander where we like. Empty! Empty!

(*He flings open a basket and tears the contents out, hurling them all over the stage.*)

We were hollow men for a hundred years. (*Pause. He grins at PICKERILL.*) Do you remember the bit in the Merry Wives of Windsor when Falstaff hides in the laundry-basket? I like that bit. You, get in.

PICKERILL: What for?

MOTOCAR: I like to be reminded of Shakespeare. His greatest comic character was, of course, Othello, or Shylock, but I still have a soft spot for old Falstaff. Hop in.

PICKERILL: No.

MOTOCAR: You don't feel in character?
(*Pause.*)

PICKERILL: I'll do you a deal. I'll get in if you let her take that thing off her face.

MOTOCAR: Oho, then I'll do you a deal. She can take that thing off her face if you'll get in and let me sit on top.

PICKERILL: Christ, you're a cockeyed person. Why do you want to do that?

MOTOCAR: You are luggage. You look like luggage. You are luggage. Get in! The sister is out there...do you wish to jeopardise her life? Get in!
(*PICKERILL climbs into the basket. MOTOCAR sits on top.*)
Here I am, at the railway station, sitting on my luggage. Here I am at Kennedy Airport, Heathrow, Charles de Gaulle, Moscow...sitting on my luggage. Alright in there?

PICKERILL: Hurry up man, there's not much room in here. These sheets stink.

LEWIS: May I take the mask off now?

MOTOCAR: I never break my word.
(*LEWIS takes the mask off SYMONDS.*)

MOTOCAR: Listen, my luggage is talking. Tired of movement. Tired having no home. It creaks with despair. The sound of the exhausted swallow forever in flight across all the oceans of the world. Just how I felt in my migrations. In and out of those rooms, rooms, libraries, libraries, welcomes, scholarships and fellowships, universities and societies, pamphlets and magazines, causes and demonstrations, sympathies and arguments. Me and my luggage, oh, a brilliant student! A special case, send him abroad, fly him away. I said goodbye to my father and his empty hundred years, goodbye to the Matabele, goodbye to the Mashona, goodbye to Africa, and went away to write the truth about this country. One day I would return and set the record straight, in peace like Noah's dove after the flood, bringing hope. I failed. I wrote no book. I could not start, I could not finish. I was too bitter to stay on the page and burned through the paper, brown vinegar. (*Furiously attacks the basket, kicking and punching it, spinning it round. Muffled shouts from inside.*) So how much have we got in there? How many pairs? How many animals two by two? Or is it Pandora's Box, full of infectious diseases and misery? I should have left my luggage behind! Thrown it overboard!

LEWIS: Don't you think you've had enough fun out of him now?

MOTOCAR: Man is a detestable animal!

(*Enter DONAHUE, knocked about, dishevelled, her hair down, panting, with file.*)

DONAHUE: So he is!

MOTOCAR: It is an act of wisdom to see Man as a detestable animal. (*Grabs a heap of dirty sheets and clothing.*) Look at this, blood, snot, piss, shit, vomit, yagh! (*Throws them away.*) I ask, who is it detests Man with such passion? What other creature bothers to hate him? God? Never, one-legged or two. From my studies I deduce that only Man has the gift of self-disgust. Push those baskets together.

LEWIS: How do you mean?

PICKERILL: (*From in the basket.*) What's going on? Have you finished?

MOTOCAR: (*Assembling the baskets in an upstage-downstage line.*) Put them end to end, come on, quickly, Tshaka is returning. (*They obey, pushing the baskets into a line.*)

PICKERILL: Don't you get me going now...Let me out of here...

DONAHUE: What's the game now?

MOTOCAR: Come on, build, build...

PICKERILL: Have you finished now…We had a deal man…It's not much bloody fun in here…

MOTOCAR: (*Opening the lids of the other baskets.*) Now all get in, all of you. Doctor, you in the forward compartment, the women aft. You will be fed once a day and let out for a short promenade in the early evening…

LEWIS: I refuse…I won't do it…

MOTOCAR: Get in the hold!

LEWIS: I flatly refuse. You must stop tormenting us.

MOTOCAR: (*Grabbing LEWIS.*) Get down in the hold!

LEWIS: (*Struggling.*) No! Don't force me. Let me get in by myself.

PICKERILL: Bloody mad filthy bastard!

MOTOCAR: Hurry, hurry! (*Slams the lid down, fixes the fastener.*) Now you girls…

DONAHUE: I'm not getting in there. You can do what you like to me but I'll look you in the face while you're doing it. I don't think there's an ounce of madness in you, not an ounce. You want to see us all dead…
(*SYMONDS makes a bolt for the door. MOTOCAR catches her and carries her to the baskets, puts her in. DONAHUE gets in of her own accord. MOTOCAR closes the lid.*)

MOTOCAR: The wind is getting up, a strong east wind veering to south-east. All aboard! Cast off!

PICKERILL: Let me out of here or there'll be trouble! You'll get me going! I'm getting cramp…
(*SYMONDS and DONAHUE can be heard crying. LEWIS muttering. PICKERILL groaning throughout the next sequence.*)

MOTOCAR: (*Taking off his shoes and tee-shirt.*) Tshaka the Terrible, Tshaka the Zulu, never got to my meeting. His ship was slow, weighed down by a pale, shining cargo. He has crossed the Atlantic back to Africa. The West Indian experience fades in the following wind. The long shame is over.

PICKERILL: Damn you, you mad bastard, I'm choking in here…

MOTOCAR: Check the bills of lading. Forward hold, man-slaves of thought, thinkers, justifiers, watch them closely.

Centre hold, man-slaves of action, chain them tight. Aft
hold, sisters of mercy, mothers, women-slaves, all as
white as ebony. (*Gets on top of the central basket –
PICKERILL's – now he is Tshaka.*) An impi salutes us from
the fortress, We return to the mouth of the Black
Umfulosi River. Home! Home! Africa! I see the coast.
After a hundred years I am coming home, a rich man.
Do you hear me? This is Tshaka speaking. Through the
roar of the breakers, the threads of the sea-mist, do you
hear me? (*Drums reply from outside.*) Open the estuary,
Reverse your spears. Lower your shields. I, Tshaka, the
son of Senzangakona, am coming home. (*Drums reply.*)
Oh, the smell, the smell of the land. After so long at sea
with this cargo of stars. Who was it wanted a white wife?
Who wanted a skilful servant? (*Drums reply.*) I have wives
and women here in the hold. I have doctors and witch-
doctors, I have priests and policemen. I have
administrators, governors, bishops, generals, judges,
chairmen, do you want them? (*Drums reply.*) I have
technologists, sociologists, anthropologists, economists,
ecologists, nuclear physicists, dieticians, paediatricians,
engineers...Do you want them? (*Drums reply.*) How will
you treat them? Like men? Like the animals we are?
And where will they live? (*Pause.*) Becalmed again, I am
waiting at the harbour mouth, There is still sea between
us. We are drifting. The anchor will not hold. My ship
drifts in the current. No rope is long enough. Stop me.
I am losing sight of Africa. I am being carried round the
Cape of Good Hope by contrary winds. I will never see
Africa again.
(*MOTOCAR gets off the baskets, exhausted, heart-broken.
Silently he opens the baskets one by one, PICKERILL's being
last. LEWIS, SYMONDS and DONAHUE get out quickly
and quietly, but PICKERILL bursts out in a tremendous
rage, faces MOTOCAR.*)

PICKERILL: Don't you get me going! Don't mess me
around! Cut it out...Just watch it, eh...Leave me
alone...bastard...Don't you get me going again...Don't
you wind me up, you stupid munt!

(*Pause. MOTOCAR glares back fiercely.*) Forgive me.

LEWIS: Forgive him.

PICKERILL: Forgive me. Forgive me. Forgive me.

MOTOCAR: I do, I do.

PICKERILL: I'm very sorry. I apologise. Forgive me. Forgive me.

MOTOCAR: Give Doctor Lewis the file.

(*DONAHUE hands LEWIS the file. PICKERILL crumples, leaning back against the baskets.*)

PICKERILL: You got me going...Don't get me going like that again, please...Don't wind me up...

MOTOCAR: Fold the sheets.

SYMONDS: Us?

MOTOCAR: Yes.

(*SYMONDS picks up a clean sheet.*)

PICKERILL: Not those sheets, the other sheets.

SYMONDS: But they're dirty sheets...

PICKERILL: Don't you understand? He wants dirty sheets.

DONAHUE: Is that right?

MOTOCAR: Yes, I'm only interested in dirty sheets. Come on, girls, tidy up, fold...

(*DONAHUE takes a dirty sheet from a basket and gives it the other end to SYMONDS. They start to fold it.*)

MOTOCAR: Will you read the cards for Senzangakona, Albert, please Doctor? Begin at the beginning. Fold girls, fold, keep going...

LEWIS: These are all for Senzangakona...

MOTOCAR: A busy man, my father. His case history is in your hands.

PICKERILL: Senzangakona? The old man was your father?

MOTOCAR: Come on, girls, tidy up. Fold these sheets for me.

(*SYMONDS and DONAHUE work through the basket of dirty sheets as the file is being read out by LEWIS. The sheets get progressively greyer.*)

LEWIS: Senzangakona, Albert. Tribe, Matabele. Born Bulawayo 1900 approx. Religion, blank...

MOTOCAR: A Christian at Christmas, a Mohammedan at Ramadan.

PICKERILL: You killed your own father. Bloody hell.

LEWIS: First date of admission: nineteenth June 1922, suffering from depression and acute paranoia. Incipient schizophrenia.

MOTOCAR: A self-governing colony, that's what they asked to be in that year, those farmers, those miners, a self-governing colony. Father did not understand the western concept of self. There is a white self and a black self.

LEWIS: The resident psychiatrist suspected alcoholism as a contributory factor to his condition. Traces of adolescent bookworm.

MOTOCAR: More distinguished than acne.

LEWIS: Malarial. Claimed army service in Flanders but could not prove it. Lost pay-book and discharge papers. Sapper with native troops was his description of the rank he attained.

MOTOCAR: Sapper with native troops. Sapper with native troops.

LEWIS: Discharged third September 1928. Re-admitted seventh August 1934. Discharged. Re-admitted.

MOTOCAR: Discharged. Re-admitted.

LEWIS: Discharged. Re-admitted. Discharged. Re-admitted. After most of these entries it says voluntary. You understand that? He asked to come in, he asked to go out.

MOTOCAR: It was this man, my father, Senzangakona, who advised me to accept the offer to study abroad. Go, he said, learn to think, then write the true history of your people. I would rather die. I would rather die and be thrown into one of those ditches he dug.

LEWIS: 1953 was a bad year for him.

MOTOCAR: The Federation.

LEWIS: Fragmentation. Disorientation. Crisis of identity. Re-admitted. Discharged. Re-admitted. Discharged.

MOTOCAR: Ten years of it, ten years.

LEWIS: There appears to have been an alleviation of symptoms in 1964. He seemed far more optimistic.

MOTOCAR: The Federation collapsed. These was freedom all around him.

LEWIS: 1965 saw his worst breakdown yet. Paralysis. Loss of speech and motor power in one leg. Perpetual state of anxiety. Psycho-surgery, November fifteenth.

MOTOCAR: UDI.

LEWIS: The operation was not a success. Schizophrenia advanced. Sense of inferiority. Acute depression. After several abortive courses of treatment he was sent to work at a farm near Inyanga, doing a job that was commensurate with his disability. He became a chicken-guard. (*Pause.*) That is the last entry.

MOTOCAR: Will you give the file to Inspector Pickerill now? Put it in my bag with my stone, my books, my friends. He should have them all. Give him all the evidence he needs. I am guilty.

(*LEWIS gives PICKERILL the file. PICKERILL looks at it, then gets the briefcase and puts the file inside, then collects the books and stone.*)

MOTOCAR: I killed. We are always killing. I have heard it said that it is necessary, if so, then it is necessary to be mad. I found my limping, split-brain father and put him out of his misery. That is in the power of emperors. It is in the power of Jesuits. It is in the power of those who understand the truth of murder and the truth of emptiness, the truth of madness and the truth of necessity. Four truths, four Gospels, twelve Apostles, one hundred years, many numbers. Have you all your evidence, Inspector?

PICKERILL: I have.

MOTOCAR: And all your numbers? And all your words?

PICKERILL: I am trying.

MOTOCAR: I killed my father, Mr Sophocles. I put him down like an old dog who cannot see. Now I am going blind. He wanted to die as I do now, and take it all with him. We have no future in our family. That belongs to my friends on the switchboard. Hm, what names my father gave his children, what names we get given. Lobengula. Victoria. Mauch. Moffat. Moshesh. Mzilikazi.

Monomotapa, Motocar. Who has heard of us? And who will ever listen but ourselves?

(*DONAHUE and SYMONDS have worked through all the shades of grey and are now holding a pitch-black sheet.*)

Now, don't fold that one away. That's my father's. I would like to have it for the journey.

(*DONAHUE puts the sheet over MOTOCAR's shoulders. He wraps it round, squats.*)

The door is being opened. We can all go through. Goodbye, Mr Sophocles. Goodbye.

(*Slow fade to blackout.*)

The End.

Nkosi sikalele Afrika

BY ENOCH SONTONGA, ARRANGED BY STEPHEN BOXER

Unaccompanied